DESPERATE VICTORIES

DESPERATE VICTORIES

From Dunkirk to the Battle of Britain:

Military Despatches on Operations against German forces in Western Europe 1940

G. H. BENNETT
In association with the National Archives

AMBERLEY

First published 2018

Amberley Publishing
The Hill, Stroud
Gloucestershire, GL5 4EP

www.amberley-books.com

Copyright © G. H. Bennett, 2018

The right of G. H. Bennett to be identified as
the Author of this work has been asserted in
accordance with the Copyrights, Designs and
Patents Act 1988.

ISBN 978 1 4456 6816 1 (hardback)
ISBN 978 1 4456 6817 8 (ebook)

British Library Cataloguing in Publication Data.
A catalogue record for this book is available
from the British Library.

Typesetting and Origination by Amberley Publishing
Printed in the UK.

CONTENTS

ACKNOWLEDGEMENTS

In writing this book there are many people and institutions that have assisted my research. While a book may have just one author listed on the cover, in reality it is a team effort in which many may be involved. Some are aware of their role, others not so.

The staff at Amberley publishing have been a joy to work with, facilitating a smooth process of production.

My colleagues at Plymouth University (those still active, those who are retired, and those who are no longer with us) have invariably been a great help.

The history students at Plymouth University have similarly been of great help including Tom Meaden, Chris Arnold, Tyler Colton, Maddison Roberts, Laura Gilmour and Callum Obee. They gave constructive and insightful advice and criticism on the manuscript. Ladies and gentlemen, you were, indeed, a hard audience to please, but thank you for your hard work. I am sure that this book is immeasurably improved thanks to your cogent advice and trenchant criticism.

The staff at libraries and archives great and small have never been less than outstandingly helpful including those at The National Archives UK; US National Archives; The National Maritime Museum, Britannia Royal Naval College Library; Plymouth, Exeter and Bristol University Libraries.

At the level of individuals on the academic side I am indebted to Professor Gibson (for reading and critiquing the book), Professor Black, Professor Lambert, Dr Cummings, Dr Harrold, Dr Clarke, James Smith, Mike Pearce and Richard Porter.

Lastly, thank you to Mr Jason King – truly the 'best a man can be'.

INTRODUCTION

What General Weygand called the 'Battle of France' is over. I expect that the battle of Britain is about to begin. Upon this battle depends the survival of Christian civilisation. Upon it depends our own British life and the long continuity of our institutions and our Empire. The whole fury and might of the enemy must very soon be turned on us. Hitler knows that he will have to break us in this island or lose the war. If we can stand up to him all Europe may be free, and the life of the world may move forward into broad, sunlit uplands; but if we fail then the whole world, including the United States, and all that we have known and cared for, will sink into the abyss of a new dark age made more sinister, and perhaps more prolonged, by the lights of a perverted science. Let us therefore brace ourselves to our duty and so bear ourselves that, if the British Commonwealth and Empire lasts for a thousand years men will still say, "This was their finest hour."[1]

In 1940 Britain faced a series of battles that would define the early years of the Second World War and with it British identity for the next 70 years. On those battles turned the survival of a nation, and the hopes of others that had been overthrown by the military forces of Nazi Germany. This

---

1   Winston Churchill, *Parliamentary Debates [Commons]*, 18 June 1940, vol.362 cc.60-61.

book contains the Official Despatches of some of the military leaders who took part in those battles. They originally appeared in the 1940s in the journal *The London Gazette*: a publication established in 1665 as the official public record. The despatches are reproduced here in association with The National Archives. They go into unusual levels of detail and are written in a straightforward style. They give unvarnished insights into what the commanders at the time felt was important for the public and politicians to know about the military operations they concern. They have an immediacy and an authenticity which modern popular history can never approach. The writers of these despatches did not seek to be controversial, but their subject matter was at the time (and in some cases still is today) a matter of heated debate. As the wartime generation passes on, these debates will once again be revisited in a Britain much changed since the dark days of 1940. Despite the passing of the decades "The Dunkirk Spirit" and "Keep Calm and Carry On" remain powerful evocations of national spirit, resilience and innovation in the face of crisis. Likewise, the victory of "The Few" of the Battle of Britain encapsulates a range of positive national images ranging from the heroism of the pilots of the RAF, the stoicism of the British public faced with aerial bombing, through to the genius of British engineers whose contribution to victory in 1940 included radar, the beauty of the Supermarine Spitfire and the utter dependability of the Hawker Hurricane. First framed by Churchill in 1940, in the years of national decline after 1945, the mercurial deliverance of national survival in 1940 has become an iconic testament to the strength of British character.

Perhaps, though, we should look a little deeper at the events of 1940 and be prepared to question the iconic truths held dear by popular history. The intricacies and outcomes of the military campaigns, the political and public responses to changing military fortunes in the critical months of that year, were infinitely more complex and difficult to interpret than the public recognised at the time. Victory was anything but certain, or even likely, despite the assurances of the leading politicians of the day. The events of that year had been romanticised into a national myth even before its end, and that process of myth-making continues to this day. Those myths served a variety of purposes, from convincing opinion in the United States that aid to Britain should be dramatically increased, through to obscuring deep national divisions behind exhortations to unity and national effort.

Churchill's "Finest Hour" speech of 18 June serves as a useful starting point. Perhaps the most famous piece of oratory in British history it is just as much a vital element in the story of 1940 as the "Dunkirk little ships" and RAF squadron scrambles from Biggin Hill airfield. All too often, though, popular histories reduce the speech down to soundbites. The speech was not constructed as a series of soundbites for the modern media age, but as a carefully crafted and nuanced narrative for Parliamentary and public consumption. It could be read at face value, and those in the know could read between the lines to deeper meanings. The speech contained a beginning, middle and an end, giving information, shaping opinion and providing reassurances for a range of audiences ranging from the domestic to the international: from the working class family living in a dockyard terrace in Plymouth through to Franklin Delano Roosevelt at the White House in Washington DC. It was at once a call to arms, a declaration of British determination to continue the fight, and a calm analysis of a beleaguered nation's strategic position.

The man who delivered the speech, widely regarded today as one of Britain's finest Prime Ministers, headed a coalition government rocked by political intrigues, concerns at national failures and confronted with the looming possibility of defeat. This was not a nation united behind a powerful leader – but a divided country pondering the possibility of foreign invasion and annihilation. Some elements within the upper ranks of British society considered better a peace deal with Hitler rather than another ruinous world war leading, perhaps, to the triumph of world communism.[2] Within Nazi Germany there was a very strong sense that it was a matter of time, and a question of the right approach, before a negotiated peace could be secured with the British.[3] The "Finest Hour" speech on 18 June was intended to send a very clear message to Germany that a negotiated peace was not an option under Churchill's leadership, and that Britain would fight the war through to a conclusion. Churchill himself recognised that his political position in the summer of 1940 was less than secure.

Despite later perceptions, Churchill in 1940 was an anachronism. He was the great Conservative leader who had spent much of his political life with the Liberals, the man who became Prime Minister years after his career appeared to be over, and the strong war leader who couldn't necessarily trust the loyalties of some members of the establishment to which he belonged. Elected in 1900 as the Conservative Member of Parliament for Oldham, he had joined the Liberals in 1904, making Cabinet rank in the great Liberal reforming ministries before the First

---

2   See, for example, James Leuze [ed.], *The London Journal of Raymond E. Lee, 1940-41* (Boston: Little Brown, 1971), entry for 8 December 1940, pp. 165-66.

3   Scott Newton, *Profits of Peace: The Political Economy of Anglo-German Appeasement* (Oxford: Oxford University Press, 1996), p. 189ff.

World War. As First Lord of the Admiralty from 1911 he had played a major role in preparing the Royal Navy for the coming conflict. However, following the failure of the Dardanelles landings in 1915 Churchill had resigned. After service in the trenches he had rebuilt his political career and had once again risen to Cabinet rank. Under Lloyd George's premiership he had played a key role as Secretary of State for War, then Air, and finally as Colonial Secretary in reshaping Britain's military and imperial policies. Churchill lost his seat with the fall of the Lloyd George government in 1922, but got back into Parliament in 1924 as a Constitutionalist candidate for the Epping constituency with the assistance of local Conservatives (he would formally re-join the Conservative Party the following year). Remarkably, in forming his new government in 1924, Stanley Baldwin offered Churchill the post of Chancellor of the Exchequer. An amazed Churchill had very gratefully accepted. As Chancellor of the Exchequer he controversially brought Britain back to the Gold Standard in 1925.[4] Following the 1929 general election, and the advent of the second Labour government, he had spent much of the 1930s in the political wilderness, partly because of his opposition to greater political independence for India and, from 1935 onwards, his concerns about the government's policy of appeasing Germany, Italy and Japan. During the late 1930s he had repeatedly warned the National Government of Neville Chamberlain about the growing threat of Nazi Germany. Widely seen as a "has been" Churchill's warnings were dismissed as the nation backed Chamberlain in the appeasement of Hitler and the false hopes of "Peace for our Time". With the outbreak of war in 1939, there was a clamour to bring back Churchill, whose warnings had

---

4   Keith Robbins, *Churchill* (London: Routledge, 2014), p.95.

been borne out by the German territorial expansionism that now threatened Poland. He returned to the post of First Lord of the Admiralty: the post he had held at the outbreak of war in 1914.[5] It was a remarkable comeback: "Winston is back"!

During the early months of the war Chamberlain was unable to demonstrate the kind of effective and dynamic leadership that might have assuaged doubts about his character stemming from the days of appeasement. He remained the Prime Minister who had in September 1938 delivered Czechoslovakia up to Hitler as the price of maintaining European peace.[6] He was also the man who twelve months later had made the radio broadcast to the nation declaring war on Nazi Germany: his voice burdened with emotion and pain at the defeat of his diplomatic efforts for peace. With the last months of 1939, after the defeat of Poland, and the early months of 1940 constituting a phoney war, as little action took place along the Franco-Belgian-German border, Chamberlain's critics were convinced that he lacked the necessary vigour to prosecute the war to an effective resolution. When in April 1940, as British forces readied to seize control of the strategically important Norwegian state, Chamberlain's initiative was pre-empted by the Germans who staged landings on and after 9 April.

The Norwegian campaign was to play a pivotal role in the rise of Churchill.[7] Although the fighting dragged on until 10 June, on 24 May the Cabinet approved plans

---

5   Chris Wrigley, *Winston Churchill: A Biographical Companion* (Santa Barbara [CA]: ABC Clio, 2002), pp.9–11.

6   Robert C. Self, *Neville Chamberlain: A Biography* (Aldershot: Ashgate, 2006), p.325.

7   Anthony Dix, *The Norway Campaign and the Rise of Churchill, 1940* (Barnsley: Pen & Sword, 2014).

for an Allied withdrawal from Norway as the Germans successfully extended their hold on the country. The withdrawal was skilfully handled and successful, but it could not disguise an Allied defeat, and the fact that Norway was now firmly under German control. After months of phoney war the Allied attempt to take the strategic initiative had been anticipated by the Germans and decisively thwarted. Losses of personnel, killed, wounded and missing, on both sides were comparatively light (around 5,300 for the Germans, 7,100 for the Allies, and 1,700 for the Norwegians). The material damage was far more significant, especially for the German *Kriegsmarine*, which had committed most of its surface fleet to the operation. While the Royal Navy had lost an aircraft carrier, two cruisers, seven destroyers and a submarine, the German Navy had lost three cruisers, 10 destroyers, six U-boats and 17 other light naval vessels. With damage and wear and tear to the heavy units of the *Kriegsmarine* the Norwegian campaign impacted very severely on German forces. At least for the short term, the *Kriegsmarine* was not in a position to play a decisive role at the strategic level. The Norwegian campaign amounted to a gambler's roll of the dice for the German Armed Forces, and while they were successful, the price of victory was considerable.

If the implications of the Norwegian campaign at the strategic level were important, the political repercussions were perhaps even more significant. The Norwegian campaign could have damaged Churchill considerably, especially given his reputation as a firebrand and "hatcher of schemes" such as the disastrous Gallipoli landings in 1915. As First Lord of the Admiralty in 1940 he had played a leading role in organising the strategy and detail of naval operations in Norway. In the Palace of Westminster

Conservative Party whips did their best to pin the blame for the Norwegian withdrawal on Churchill. Instead, it was Chamberlain who found his position hopelessly damaged.[8] On 7 and 8 May 1940 Members of Parliament debated what amounted to a motion of no confidence in the handling of the Norwegian campaign. The debate quickly focussed on the issue of the Government's competence, and especially Chamberlain's position as war leader. Even though Chamberlain won the vote, he did so without the support of around a quarter of Conservative Members of Parliament, some of whom had made particularly effective attacks on Chamberlain and those who shared the same stigma of appeasement. Remarkable speeches by Conservative MP, Admiral of the Fleet Sir Roger Keyes, and by former Conservative Minister Leo Amery, inflicted further damage on Chamberlain's standing with the Conservative Party. Sensing that his premiership had been fatally damaged by the Norwegian campaign and the Norway vote, Chamberlain resigned on 10 May just as German troops launched an offensive in the West directed at France, the Netherlands and Belgium. The phoney war in the West had ended.

Chamberlain's successor was Winston Churchill who faced a difficult job in trying to restore confidence in the Government's handling of the war effort, just as German forces began to push into the Netherlands and Belgium. Within days, British, French and Belgian troops were forced to retreat as German armoured columns, supported by tactical airpower, punched huge holes in the defensive line. While German forces practised the fast-moving art of

---

8 John Kelly, *Never Surrender: Winston Churchill and Britain's Decision to Fight Nazi Germany in the Fateful Summer of 1940* (New York: Scribner, 2015), p.111ff.

lightning war (Blitzkrieg) Anglo-French forces appeared to be fighting the Second World War with the mindset, equipment and tactics of the Great War. By 21 May the bulk of the British Expeditionary Force was trapped against the coast near the Franco-Belgian border, together with the remains of three French Armies, and what was left of the Belgian Army. Remarkably, on 23 May the German tank columns were ordered to halt with seemingly little to stop the armoured forces from fighting through to the coast and sealing the fate of the Allied units trapped with their backs against the sea. The reasons for the "halt" order, endorsed by Hitler the following day, have been a matter of speculation ever since.[9] The unsuitability of the marshy ground along the coast, the impact of weeks of fighting on German armoured forces, and Hitler's desire not to humiliate the British with whom he wanted to make peace, have all been suggested as reasons why the halt order was given. Whatever the reason, the significance was considerable. It was not until 26 May that orders were given for the advance to resume and most units took more than half a day to come back into action. By this time the perimeter of the pocket had been reinforced, and an evacuation by sea (planning for which had begun on 20 May) was underway. From small beginnings (less than 8,000 men were brought home on 27 May) Operation Dynamo grew in extent to become a major operation. By

---

9   Charles More, *The British Expeditionary Force and the Battle of the Ypres-Comines Canal, 1940* (London: Frontline Books, 2013), p.33. John Lukacs, *The Duel: The Eighty Day Struggle between Churchill and Hitler* (Newhaven [CT], Yale University Press, 1990), p.87. William McKinley Runyan [ed.], *Psychology and Historical Interpretation* (Oxford: Oxford University Press, 1988), p.138.

4 June the bulk of the British Expeditionary Force had been evacuated from the ports and beaches on the Franco-Belgian border. Over just eight days more than 338,000 troops had been rescued from death or captivity by a mixed force of 800 vessels ranging from the smaller warships of the Royal Navy through to cross-Channel steamers, fishing and sailing vessels and civilian crewed small boats. Behind public images of the "Miracle of Dunkirk" (the rescue of an Army and the heroism of the "Dunkirk" little ships), lay the grim realities that over 60,000 British troops hadn't been brought home and the Royal Navy had lost six destroyers with 19 others damaged. In the months ahead, as the U-boat campaign in the Atlantic intensified, those destroyers would be badly missed. While the troops waiting to be evacuated had shown amazing stoicism and discipline, and those manning the ships and little boats had displayed steadfast professionalism and courage, there were exceptions to the rule. While the newspapers and newsreels turned defeat into victory, those coming back from France recalled scenes of near panic and a sense of bitter betrayal towards the politicians entrusted with national defence and the generals charged with the development and execution of strategy.[10] For the Germans the halt order had squandered a monumental opportunity to inflict a war-ending catastrophic defeat on the British. The so-called "Miracle of Dunkirk" owed just as much to the mysteries of the halt order as it did to British pluck and organisational genius.

Even as troops were being withdrawn from Dunkirk fresh forces were being sent to Western France in the hopes that they could reconstitute an effective front line against the Germans. Without a fresh British commitment of troops

---

10 Lucy Noakes and Juliette Pattinson, *British Cultural Memory and the Second World War* (London: Bloomsbury, 2014) pp.59-60.

there was every chance that the French would sue for peace. Hopes that the front could be stabilised were very quickly dashed. On 14 June Paris was occupied and on 18 June French and German officials met with each other to negotiate an armistice.[11] As final complete collapse threatened, a second Dunkirk-style rescue had to be rapidly organised for the troops trapped in Western France.

This second evacuation (Operation Ariel) has been all but lost from public understanding of the Second World War but it was an enormous undertaking nevertheless. While the majority of the 51st Highland Division (around 6,000 soldiers) were trapped and forced to surrender on 12 June, around 192,000 Allied personnel (144,000 British) were withdrawn before the armistice via the ports along the French Atlantic coast. Losses in this second evacuation were, in some ways, just as shocking as those off the coast of Belgium and Northern France in May and early June. In particular, in the sinking of the liner HMT *Lancastria* on 17 June around 3,500 people lost their lives.[12] British newspapers were immediately instructed not to publish details of the sinking out of concern about the likely impact on public morale. It was against this background that Churchill rose to speak in the House of Commons on 18 June. The Battle for France was over. A nation which had held out against the Germans from 1914 to 1918 had succumbed in just six weeks. While the British Expeditionary Force had been saved, much of its equipment could not be brought home. Millions of pounds of stores,

---

11 Allan Mitchell, *Nazi Paris: The History of an Occupation, 1940-1944*, (Oxford: Berghahn Books, 2008). p.3ff.

12 See Jonathan Fenby, *The Sinking of the Lancastria: Britain's Greatest Maritime Disaster and Churchill's Cover Up* (London: Simon and Schuster, 2005).

vehicles, guns and equipment had been abandoned, sabotaged or destroyed. The future did, indeed, appear to be bleak and without credible prospect of victory for the British. Churchill knew that his speech had to be a judicious mix of determination and hope, tempered by realism.

Preventing a wave of defeatist sentiment sweeping the country was one of his primary concerns in making the speech on 18 June. The recriminations had already begun for the defeat of the Allied armies in the West. Amongst the public the defeat of the French Army was blamed on the existence of a fifth column of pro-Nazi sympathisers, rather than the nature of French strategy, military leadership and morale. In making his "finest hour" speech on 18 June he once again called for political unity between the anti-appeasers and those who had been close to Chamberlain in the late 1930s. In the midst of national crisis divisions could not be afforded:

> We have to think of the future and not of the past. This also applies in a small way to our own affairs at home. There are many who would hold an inquest in the House of Commons on the conduct of the Governments – and of Parliaments, for they are in it, too – during the years which led up to this catastrophe. They seek to indict those who were responsible for the guidance of our affairs. This also would be a foolish and pernicious process. There are too many in it. Let each man search his conscience and search his speeches.[13]

With the battle of France effectively lost, Churchill was only too well aware of the dangers of another Norway-style debate,

---

13 Winston Churchill, *Parliamentary Debates [Commons]*, 18 June 1940, vol.362 cc.51–52.

and another motion of no-confidence in the government's handling of the war effort. In the event Parliament was willing to put the failure in France down to the French. Whatever mistakes had been made in the conduct of the British military campaign in France and Belgium (detailed in the despatches which follow this introduction) could be set at the door of the previous prime minister who, after all, had resigned just as the German offensive in the West had broken.

On 18 June Churchill prepared his audience, and the nation, for an even more desperate struggle, on which the fate of Britain would depend. It is important to note that what we understand as 'The Battle of Britain', was very different to the struggle which Churchill envisaged in his 'Finest Hour' speech on 18 June 1940. Churchill was at pains to highlight that the battle, likely to involve an invasion attempt, would involve all arms and be fought across land, sea and air. The Prime Minister sought to prepare the nation for the struggle while reassuring his listeners that Britain was well prepared for anything that the Germans might do. On the land he argued that, with the arrival of reinforcements from the Empire, and the formation of the Local Defence Volunteers (Home Guard), a substantial force was ready to repulse any German troops that landed in the United Kingdom.[14] Before that battle took place the Germans would first have to cross the English Channel, and Churchill was highly sceptical that, in the face of the powerful Royal Navy, the *Kriegsmarine* would be able to carry out a successful landing:

It would not be easy to collect such an armada, marshal it and conduct it across the sea without any powerful

---

14 Winston Churchill, *Parliamentary Debates [Commons]*, 18 June 1940, vol.362 c.53.

naval forces to escort it, and with the very great possibility that it would be intercepted long before it reached the coast, and the men all drowned in the sea or, at the worst, blown to pieces with their equipment while they were trying to land.[15]

Before even this stage was reached, Churchill considered that the initial stage in the Battle of Britain would involve a contest in the air between RAF Fighter Command and the German Luftwaffe. The destruction of the former was necessary to allow the Germans to land paratroop forces which would act as the spearhead of the invasion.

This brings me, naturally, to the great question of invasion from the air and of the impending struggle between the British and German air forces. It seems quite clear that no invasion on a scale beyond the capacity of our land forces to crush speedily is likely to take place from the air until our Air Force has been definitely overpowered. In the meantime, there may be raids by parachute troops and attempted descents of airborne soldiers.[16]

It is this contest in the air that took place during the summer and late autumn of 1940 that we now understand as the Battle of Britain, even though Churchill in his 18 June speech envisaged that the aerial battle was just one element, and first phase, in a wider battle. In making the speech Churchill was painfully aware that he was trying to sway four audiences:

15 Winston Churchill, *Parliamentary Debates [Commons]*, 18 June 1940, vol.362 c.55.
16 Winston Churchill, *Parliamentary Debates [Commons]*, 18 June 1940, vol.362 c.56.

The House of Commons; the population of the United Kingdom; opinion across the British Empire; and opinion in neutral countries (especially the United States). Churchill's memoir of the Second World War also emphasises how public speeches were coupled with private telegrams designed to reassure dominion leaders and reach out to Franklin Roosevelt, the President of the United States.[17] The speech was reproduced in newspapers around the world, and on propaganda material in the United Kingdom and beyond.[18]

The "finest hour speech" was referenced repeatedly in popular culture during the summer and autumn of 1940 as the Battle of Britain raged in the skies about southern England. Since 1945 that battle has been the subject of works by historians, novelists and film makers. Most controversially among the historians there has been an active debate over whether Britain's salvation in the late summer of 1940 should be ascribed to "The Few" of RAF Fighter Command or whether, included in our understanding of the Battle of Britain, should be "the many" of the Royal Navy and the Army, and the deterrent effect on German thinking which those forces exercised.[19] This

---

17 Winston S. Churchill, *The Second World War*, vol.II, (New York: Houghton Mifflin, 1949) p.197ff.

18 Mark Connelly, *We Can Take It: Britain and the Memory of the Second World War* (London: Routledge, 2014), p.3.

19 For this wider view of the Battle of Britain see Duncan Grinnell-Milne, *The Silent Victory: September 1940* (London: Bodley Head, 1958). Telford Taylor, *The Breaking Wave: The German Defeat in the Summer of 1940* (London: Weidenfeld & Nicolson, 1967). H.R. Allen, *Who Won the Battle of Britain* (London: Granada Publishing, 1976). Anthony J. Cumming, *The Royal Navy and the Battle of Britain*, (Annapolis [MD]: United States Naval Academy, 2010).

debate has been acrimonious. Although at no point has any historian sought to question the bravery of the pilots who flew against the Luftwaffe, the Battle of Britain has assumed such mythic and iconic significance that any attempt to question it meets a hostile popular reaction.

Despite this, the popular perception of the Battle of Britain maintained by an unceasing stream of books, documentaries and films has been challenged in a number other ways.[20] The mythic image of the pilots of RAF Fighter Command in 1940 has been broadened out by the work of historians who have emphasised the multinational nature of the squadrons taking on the Luftwaffe in the skies over southern England. The acknowledgement of Czech, Polish, Canadian, New Zealand, French, Irish and other non-British pilots from another nine nationalities now vies with an older stereotype of the RAF fighter pilot as a good-looking, silk scarf-wearing English former public schoolboy. Meanwhile, questions have been raised about the strength and capabilities of a Luftwaffe that in 1940 appeared all-conquering. James Holland in *The Battle of Britain* (London: Bantam, 2010) depicted a German Air Force that was both under-manned and, after success in Poland, Belgium and France, over-confident in its abilities. The few of RAF Fighter Command were, in fact, fighting the few of the Luftwaffe. More recently, Swedish historian Christer Bergström in *The Battle of Britain: An Epic Conflict Revisited* (Oxford: Casemate UK, 2015) has extended the process of revisionism to cover such things as the effectiveness of the leadership of the Luftwaffe and the much-maligned performance of the ME.110 twin-engined

---

20 See for example, S.P. Mackenzie, *The Battle of Britain on Screen: 'The Few' in British Film and Television Drama* (London: Bloomsbury, 2016).

fighter. The bitterly contested aerial battles of 1940 have evolved in the years following the war into a hotly contested multinational debate over the nature, fine detail and outcomes of the Battle of Britain.

That battle drew towards a close in September 1940 as the Luftwaffe turned its attention to night-time attacks on London, and away from the goal of destroying the RAF on the ground. With winter approaching, and Hitler increasingly turning his thoughts towards an invasion of the Soviet Union in 1941, German forces stopped preparing for amphibious landings on the south coast of England. Indeed, given the state of the German Navy after the Norwegian campaign and the continued strength of the Royal Navy, which made any landing potentially a very costly affair, it may be that Hitler hoped that the threat of invasion alone would be sufficient to bring Churchill to the negotiating table. It was not to be, and in September the Battle of Britain slowly evolved into the London Blitz of 1940–41, with daylight bombing giving way to night-time attacks, which the Royal Air Force found harder to respond to. While over 40,000 civilians would lose their lives, and thousands more become injured and lose their homes, the German invasion threatened in the summer of 1940 would never come: a truly remarkable deliverance from those days in May and June when the British Army stood trapped with their backs against the sea, and those long weeks in July and August when the pilots of RAF Fighter Command checked the seemingly invincible Luftwaffe.

The Battle of Britain, and before that the evacuations from Belgium and France, had been remarkable defensive 'victories' for the British – victories snatched from the jaws of looming defeat. The bulk of the British Army had been saved from the continent to defend the beaches of the United Kingdom. The Luftwaffe had been unable to win control of the skies over the English Channel, and the Royal Navy retained control over Britain's coastal waters and the convoy routes to North America and the British Empire. Despite the odds, despite the difficulties and despite the predictions of many, Britain remained secure. The Second World War had reached a turning point. By the end of 1940 Hitler felt that Britain had been neutralised and could be discounted as a threat to Nazi Germany's domination of the European continent. Crucially, German forces had not achieved the threshold of success defined by Churchill in his speech of 18 June: 'Hitler knows that he will have to break us in this island or lose the war.'[21] Britain had weathered the immediate storm. Churchill not only recognised, in the circumstances of Dunkirk, that "Survival is victory" but also that to survive the initial onslaught was to win the war. The resources of the British Empire would slowly be brought to bear against a Nazi-dominated continent and an alliance could be forged with the United States. Russia and Germany would inevitably be drawn into conflict with each other. In giving his speech on 18 June Churchill had a prophetic sense of just how the war might be won.

More than seventy-five years after 1940, and as we say farewell to the generation that successfully defended us in one of the darkest passages of our nation's history, the debate around the Battle of Britain seems to be building rather than reducing. As the United Kingdom wrestles with issues such as "What are British values?" and "What unites us?" the dark days of 1940 continue to serve as significant reference points in on-going national debates. Likewise, the release of Christopher Nolan's film *Dunkirk* in the summer of 2017 will no doubt begin a fresh reappraisal of

---

21 Winston Churchill, *Parliamentary Debates [Commons]*, 18 June 1940, vol.362 cc.60–61.

the Battle for France and the desperate retreats to the coast which followed as a result. In the midst of this reappraisal, publication of the original despatches in this volume offers us a way to access key primary material unaffected by the layers of historical writing which have been added since 1940. They give us a level of detail which is often lacking in later accounts.

The Britain of the twenty-first century is very different to that of 1940, and the fact that we continue to debate the events of that year perhaps tells us much about national insecurities and decline after the Second World War. Curiously, though, that decline and the continued cultural relevance of Dunkirk and the Battle of Britain are testament to the veracity of Churchill's speech of 18 June. Although the British Empire began to dissolve immediately after the end of the Second World War, the low points of 1940 remain Britain's "Finest Hour". Against the odds, Britain was able to stem the tide of the German forces that had enslaved the rest of the European continent. While Britain's security did not rest solely on RAF Fighter Command the images of fresh-faced fighter pilots running to their Spitfires to climb into the sky to engage streams of enemy aircraft retain their potency. They represent the perfect combination of idealism, patriotism, bravery and professionalism with the aesthetic and engineering perfection of airframe and British industrial design. In today's Britain, beset by the uncertainties of the future, there is a continuing resonance to phrases such as "Dunkirk spirit", exhortations to "Keep Calm and Carry On" and the iconic imagery of the Battle of Britain.

While Churchillian rhetoric continues to frame public memory of the events of 1940, the despatches in this volume take us to the heart of the fighting – to the sharp end of the battlefield and the commanders trying to grasp victory in the face of desperate odds. Outnumbered, in some cases outclassed, and fighting a battle for national survival, each commander faced desperate choices. On the outcome of the Battles for France and the Battle of Britain hinged the fate of the United Kingdom and of the European continent. The realities of battle contained in the despatches can be contrasted with the lofty, visionary rhetoric of Churchill's speeches of 1940. While the despatches contain the details of battles won and lost, Churchill strove for the mythic, the immortal, the spirit rather than the matter of fact and public record. Churchill shaped the history, evoked the images, and provided the phrases, that would not only provide comfort and inspiration to a nation on the edge of defeat, but which would define the British identity for the next seventy years. The despatches contained in this volume need to be read against the sense of myth and invincibility carefully crafted in Churchill's speeches, and echoed through posters, newspapers and newsreels throughout the war. Both the despatches and Churchill's speeches constitute "the official view" – what the authorities/politicians/military commanders/British state wanted to present to the British public, and what they hoped they would believe.

To offer a useful counterbalance, then – if only in a small way – included in this volume is an introduction by someone who lived through the dark days of 1940 (in this case the author's father who by the end of the war would find himself orphaned and at sea in the British merchant navy): an ordinary person rather than a politician, a general or one of the leading lights of the day. This first-person account gives an insight into how the ordinary public reacted to Churchill's speeches, to the rapid and unexpected turn of events in 1940, and to the battles detailed in the official despatches that form the heart of this book. It is the interaction between these three levels (the Churchillian mythic, the cool professionalism of the military commanders, and the public response and resilience in the face of bad news from the battlefield and blitzed cities) that meant that 1940 saw both Britain's darkest and finest hours. To stand against the tide of battle in 1940 took remarkable faith in the past, present and future of a Britain that had to find a way to be more united than any time in its history. To this day, 1940 remains the defining moment of modern British history.

G.H. Bennett
Plymouth

1940: A YEAR TO REMEMBER

History presents us with an ever-changing picture of the past as we continually re-interpret events in the light of new information and fresh perspectives. While the generations after 1940 continue to argue about aspects of some of the key battles, those who lived through Britain's finest hour tend to have rather more settled views. Here, then, is the view of one young man who was a schoolboy in 1940.

Like so many of his generation he had a keen understanding of the price of war. His uncle had won a Military Medal at Passchendaele in 1917, been killed in the German Spring offensive of 1918 and whose medals and photo portrait hung on the wall of his mother's house; she continued to grieve for her loss. She would lose a second son, the young man's father, in the 1930s.

His father's early death owed much to the effects of being gassed during the First World War, and looking after a chronically sick war veteran took its toll on the boy's mother, who would die in 1944. For the young man's generation, the names on the war memorials conjured up images of lost fathers and brothers. During the twenties and thirties they had watched the war veterans parade on Armistice Sunday, and had got to know the war disabled on the streets of their home towns.

When war came again in 1939, his generation had the keenest sense of the horrors of war and a deep awareness that the price of war could only be paid in blood. When the phoney war of September 1939 to May 1940 gave way to the German onslaught against the low countries, most feared that the Butcher's Bill would be considerable.

A friend recently presented me with a framed picture and asked, 'When do you think this would have been taken?' The long, panoramic photograph was instantly recognisable. It showed the headmaster, teaching staff and all 300 pupils of Queen Elizabeth's Grammar School, Ashbourne – and the uniform check dresses worn by the girls enabled me to say confidently, 'Summer Term', while a quick identification of the head boy and his fellow prefects fixed the date as '1940'.

Inconspicuously tucked away in the middle ranks was a group of boys I knew as Form 3A. They would have been completing their sixth term at the school – and I was one of them, standing there rather awkwardly with my head tilted to one side. I recalled how my eyes watered with the struggle to look directly at the camera while facing into bright sunlight. Although more than 75 eventful years have passed since the photograph was taken, I had good reason to remember the eventful summer term of 1940 very well indeed.

Our country had been at war with Germany since the previous September. My friends and I had mixed feelings about the war. At a personal level, we were irked by the inconveniences of rationing, blackout and having to carry a gas mask. We had seen enough cinema newsreels of the Sino-Japanese War and the Spanish Civil War to understand the dangers of bombed cities, sinking ships and exploding shells. We certainly did not want anyone we knew to face dangers like that; but we also found that war created interest, excitement, and uncertainty. Even in a small Derbyshire market town, wartime life would no longer be boring and predictable, and in our immature way we welcomed this new feature in our lives.

We all took steps to set ourselves up as military experts. We pored anxiously over any map that we could get hold of;

we gathered information from old cigarette cards, newspaper reports, radio news bulletins, and cinema newsreels; we knew the responsibilities of Lord Gort, General Gamelin, Air Chief Marshal Newall or Leslie Hore-Belisha; we could argue about strategic places with strange names – Saarbrucken, Danzig, Brunsbuttel, Sylt, Scapa Flow – and we knew all about differences in uniforms, rank insignia and regimental badges. We prided ourselves on our ability to recognize Hawker Hurricanes, Bristol Blenheims, Vickers Wellingtons, Junkers 87 dive-bombers and other types of aircraft. Boys with artistic ability could draw them with great accuracy (a skill which eluded me). Somehow, we seemed to soak up all this information like blotting paper, while our teachers grumbled that we showed no comparable appetite for quadratic equations, photosynthesis, adverbial clauses, exports of Malaya, irregular French verbs or variations in Latin declensions.

In fact, the opening stages of the war proved to be something of a disappointment for the budding strategists of Form 3A. Poland had collapsed in a few weeks; Germany seemed fully occupied in digesting her conquests in the east; Russia was disappointingly eager to co-operate with Germany; the French army was content to sit in their Maginot Line fortifications and wait; and the small British Expeditionary Force in France had spent a bitterly cold winter practising digging trenches facing Belgium, then determinedly neutral. Apart from some action at sea and in the air, the war had almost 'slipped into hibernation.' All through that hard winter we were hungry for news of great battles and national heroes, gallant defensive actions, clever offensive ploys, enemy plans thwarted, enemy territory overrun. We longed in vain for news of that kind – so we hurried through our homework to seek different thrills in skating and sledging.

The summer term at school began on April 8th, and German forces invaded Denmark and Norway on the following day. The war suddenly burst into flames at last. My friends and I struggled to keep up with events, while our morale fluctuated wildly. Had the Germans embarked on this Scandinavian venture because they feared the Anglo-French armies were now too formidable? Or had they taken us completely by surprise and snatched a great strategic victory?

Our optimism led us to hope that the widely scattered enemy forces had recklessly placed themselves in a trap. The Royal Navy would cut them off from Germany, and our landing parties would join the Norwegians in rounding them up. Within ten days, we could see on a map the clever way in which our own troops, which had landed at Namsos and Andalsnes, could mount a brilliant pincer movement to recover Trondheim. Then northern Norway would be held, and Narvik would fall into our hands like a ripe plum.

Within a fortnight, we were in despair again. There seemed little progress at Narvik, while the optimistic arrows we had drawn on our maps of the Trondheim area looked ridiculous. Our landing parties, attacked from the air, had to be unceremoniously evacuated. There was little about the Norwegian campaign to satisfy patriotic 12- or 13-year-old boys in Derbyshire. Obviously, there was much for us to digest and evaluate. Did air power now mean that our navy would no longer be able to dominate important parts of the sea? In a time of crisis, could we be certain that English traitors would not be found to match the despicable treachery of Vidkun Quisling? Was it possible that German parachute troops might be dropped in England? What if they seized the Royal Family or destroyed the Rolls-Royce aero engine works in Derby?

Of course, concern about these weighty matters and dismay about our reverse in Norway were not restricted to bellicose little schoolboys. Blame came to be fixed on the prime minister, Neville Chamberlain. Somehow his voice, his mannerisms, his rolled umbrella, his wing collar and formal striped trousers did not project the aura of a military leader. His pre-war record of appeasement and the humiliation of the Munich Agreement were remembered against him. Failure in Norway caused him to lose the support of a significant group of MPs from his own Conservative party. On 10th May Chamberlain resigned, making way for Winston Churchill to form a government of national unity.

Once more, my boyish faith in our eventual victory was rekindled. Here was a man who looked pugnacious and uncompromising. One only had to compare the way cartoonists depicted him and his predecessor to see which was the more likely to inspire the nation to great deeds. His greatest asset, however, was his gift for oratory. His speeches may seem old-fashioned to modern readers. They may even seem little better than an audacious bluff, skilfully crafted to hide the parlous state of Britain's armed forces behind a smoke screen of archaic phrases, hot air and cigar smoke. But at the time I thought them magnificent. Here was a man we could follow. If he told us that he had 'nothing to offer but blood, toil, tears and sweat', that is what we would willingly supply. If his policy was 'to wage war against a monstrous tyranny, never surpassed in the dark, lamentable catalogue of human crime', we ought to support that policy wholeheartedly. If he said his 'aim was victory, however hard and long the road may be', we would march with him along that road.

We needed something to restore our spirits. On the day Churchill became prime minister (and only a month into our school summer term) the German army had marched into Holland, Belgium and Luxembourg. This time the British and French forces were poised for action. They rushed forward into the Low Countries, determined to block the enemy's advance as far to the east as possible. From the map, I could see that they were quickly establishing a defensive line to protect western and northern Belgium. Unlike 1914, we would not just cling on to a small area of Belgium near Ypres. This time Brussels, Antwerp, Louvain and Namur would be kept out of enemy hands, and our Air Force would acquire bases from which to attack targets deep in Germany.

Then everything seemed to disintegrate. In just five days, Dutch resistance had been overwhelmed by the ruthless bombing of Rotterdam and the daring deployment of German parachute troops. The next week saw the main Belgian cities passing into enemy hands, while British, French and Belgian troops retreated. Newspapers and radio news bulletins assured us that they were retreating 'in good order' to 'better positions' – but it did not look like that.

Further south, the German main thrust broke through the French front in the Ardennes, and their armoured and motorised divisions raced through the gap. Of course, amateur strategists – schoolboys and journalists – knew perfectly well how to deal with such a breakthrough. All you had to do was hold firm on the flanks, counter attack to seal the gap, then, mop up the enemy as his tanks and lorries ran out of petrol. Draw two bold red arrows on your map, and a brilliant victory was within your grasp.

It did not work out like that, however. The German spearheads found enough free petrol for their needs in the abandoned filling stations of northern France. Seemingly unstoppable, they raced on to reach the English Channel at Abbeville. The French were left trying to re-establish a defensive front to protect Paris. Meanwhile, in Belgium the British, French and Belgian armies were cut off, hemmed into a restricted pocket which shrank further every day, while heavy fighting drained their dwindling reserves of food and ammunition. Even from strictly censored news reports, it was obvious that they were in a desperate plight.

Ought they, perhaps, to mount a 'do or die' attack in a south-westerly direction, in the hope of breaking through to link up with the already shaky French defensive line along the River Somme (an ominous name in British memories)? Should they, instead, retreat northwards towards the port of Dunkirk in the hope of getting some, at least, away by sea? The boys of Form 3A discussed these alternatives. Neither course of action offered much hope. We began to fear that nothing could save most of the British Expeditionary Force from capitulation or annihilation.

The commander-in-chief of the British Expeditionary Force, Lord Gort, opted to retreat on Dunkirk, and the Royal Navy hastily set about organising another evacuation. It all seemed a pretty forlorn hope. What could they hope to achieve in the face of German air power and the triumphant German army? Even if the Royal Navy could find enough ships, how many men could be embarked from a port already seriously damaged or across open beaches? Was there any hope of establishing a secure defensive perimeter after a yawning gap was opened by the Belgian King's decision to order his army to stop opposing the Germans?

Britain needed a miracle: and something close to a miracle was eventually achieved. In the last five days of May and the first couple of days in June over 330,000 British and French servicemen were brought away and safely landed in British ports. Their deliverance was made possible by a strange armada conjured up by the Royal Navy. Destroyers and cross-Channel ferries provided high speed and high capacity; minesweepers, coasters, deep sea fishing vessels and overcrowded pleasure steamers found that they could cram in more men than expected; tugs, Thames barges, motor launches, naval small craft, a boat from the London Fire Brigade and many private motor cruisers ventured into the fray to ferry men from the beaches out to bigger craft in deeper water. Over 850 British and allied vessels were involved; a quarter of them were sunk; but Operation Dynamo (as it was called) achieved its purpose. The army was not abandoned.

Everyone who lived through those anxious days built up, in their memory, a personal gallery of vivid images from the photographs and newsreels they saw – the great cloud of smoke hanging over Dunkirk, the queues of troops snaking across the beach and into the sea, a man with no trousers clambering over the rail of a rescue ship, exhausted troops giving the thumbs-up sign as they were offered tea and sandwiches on English soil, battered ships leaving harbour for a further trip across the Channel. For many pupils of our school there was a further memory. One morning, as the caretaker and his wife handed out our free bottles of milk, their eyes were filled with tears, for they had just learned that their son had been among those killed at Dunkirk.

The staunchly patriotic boys of Form 3A found what comfort they could in the 'Miracle of Dunkirk'. Perhaps it was the result of Divine Intervention. At the last-minute, things had turned out better than we had dared hope, but further misfortunes quickly followed. German armies raced through northern France, and attempts to re-establish a British Expeditionary Force there ended with further evacuations from ports in Brittany and down the Bay of Biscay. On 10 June, the French government fled from Paris and Italy declared war on France and Britain. Since 10th June was my twelfth birthday, from that day I harboured a personal grudge against Mussolini.

One week later, a new French government under Marshal Pétain announced that France could not continue: she would negotiate a separate armistice with the Axis Powers. I heard this dreadful news from the radio while I was eating lunch at home. I am ashamed to admit that I, a 12-year-old grammar school boy, immediately burst into tears. I was convinced that, without the French, all hope of victory had disappeared. We were beaten: German forces would soon occupy the British Isles, Mussolini would grab the Suez Canal and General Franco would grab Gibraltar for Spain. What would become of our country? What would become of my Mum and me? My father, a veteran of the First World War, might have known what could be done, but he had died two years before.

In my misery, I turned to my granny, who always cooked lunch for me on school days. She listened patiently as I poured out all my fear and despair. Without hesitation, she rejected the whole idea. She assured me that the French were no great loss. They had not been much use in the First World War either – and we would be 'better off without them'. The Germans would never get past the Royal Navy. Britannia ruled the waves, and it was a well-known fact of history that Britain always won wars in the end. In any case, God himself would not allow our country to be conquered by people like the Nazis. The old lady could never have claimed any deep knowledge of international affairs. Elementary schooling in the 1870s had provided her with only a vague, distorted grounding in history. She was no Churchillian orator. Nevertheless, her serenity and confidence were sufficient to dry my tears and send me back to school for the afternoon session.

After the Dunkirk evacuation Churchill, had roared defiance: 'We shall prove ourselves able ... to ride out the storm of war ... if necessary for years, if necessary alone. We shall go on to the end ... we shall defend our island, whatever the cost may be. ... We shall never surrender.' As that summer term moved into its final weeks, I wondered whether Britain could survive for those few weeks, let alone Churchill's 'thousand years'. When the invasion came, how could we manage without all the tanks, Bren-gun carriers, lorries, artillery pieces, machine guns and other heavy equipment abandoned at Dunkirk and elsewhere on the Continent? Could military units that had counted themselves fortunate to get away from Dunkirk be re-equipped and retrained in time? Could their confidence and fighting spirit be restored? Enemy aliens and Oswald Mosley's British fascists had been interned, but were there other potential traitors? Was some 'British Pétain' already waiting to crawl to Hitler once German troops were established on British soil?

What did Churchill's 'brace ourselves to our duties' actually amount to for boys like us in Ashbourne? We still had the inter-house cricket matches, the athletics sports and the summer exams, but the prime minister must have meant more than that. So, we dutifully bought National Savings stamps to help pay for the war. At home, we dug for victory in our gardens. We volunteered to act as mock casualties for the training exercises of the ARP rescue and ambulance services. In the school cadet corps, we polished our buttons, perfected our drill and rehearsed the band ready for inspection by a First World War brigadier general. We meant well – but it all seemed a pretty feeble response to the anticipated threat from panzers, paratroopers and Luftwaffe.

What if Churchill's rather imprecise exhortation to fight them on the beaches, in the fields and streets and in the hills soon turned into the urgent reality of fighting them in Ashbourne market place, on Compton bridge and outside Ashbourne railway station? The local units of the Territorial Army – Sherwood Foresters and Derbyshire Yeomanry – had long since been moved 'somewhere in England'. Of course, there were real military units close at hand on the Osmaston manor estate. They consisted of a Royal Army Veterinary Corps depot training horses and a rather forlorn group of Punjabis from the Royal Indian Army Service Corps recently evacuated from France. They looked the part, but no one could pretend that these were the equivalent of a crack infantry regiment.

There was one further armed formation in existence locally. As soon as Churchill had become prime minister, the War Office had appealed on the radio for volunteers who would be prepared to hunt down small enemy groups who might be landed anywhere in Britain. They would be known as Local Defence Volunteers (LDV), they would be given an arm band;

and they would be armed with whatever they could lay their hands on. In an emergency, they would be summoned to action by the ringing of church bells. Placed in command of the Ashbourne LDV was our headmaster, Major C. F. Ball, while our mathematics master, H. J. Mears took the role of adjutant. They were supported by veteran NCOs from the previous war, by middle aged men who had also learned their soldiering then and by young men still waiting to be called up into the armed forces.

Drilling in civilian clothes and brandishing shotguns and pikes made from old bayonets welded to lengths of metal piping they sometimes looked rather comical. Nevertheless, the motley assortment of volunteers was gradually taking shape as a disciplined force. The name was changed to Home Guard, and in a surprisingly short space of time they began to receive proper uniforms, rifles and a few Lewis light machine guns. Weapon pits were dug to cover key road junctions and bridges. Major Ball also recruited a group of schoolboys who knew the area well enough to act as messengers and lookouts. I was proud to be one of that select band. I had no doubt that the Home Guard would offer determined armed resistance if the invaders came. (They were certainly not the sort of pantomime troupe of well-meaning geriatric blunderers depicted in the post-war television series *Dad's Army*.)

Our headmaster seemed particularly worried by the possibility that the enemy might arrive in gliders. The school playing field – seen as a possible landing ground – was obstructed by several redundant, horse-drawn refuse carts and wagons, which he had borrowed from the local council. We had to admire his ingenuity. We could push the carts off pitches when they were required, and push the obstacles back into place when games were finished. We were less impressed by his decision to create a further obstacle of deep trenches and mounds of earth in a little-used corner of the playing field. We were set to work with picks and shovels – an exhausting task in blistering sunshine with the ground baked hard. It was all very well making the school playing field impregnable, but there were plenty of other big, flat fields still open for glider landings. We would much sooner have been learning about how to disable cars, make Molotov cocktails, construct booby traps and extinguish incendiary bombs.

Britain's prospects looked no brighter. In July, we learned that the enemy had occupied the Channel Islands and the Luftwaffe was trying to gain air supremacy over the Straits of Dover and southern England. Newspapers published aerial reconnaissance photographs of German-occupied ports crammed with huge barges collected from the waterways of northern Europe in readiness for carrying German troops across the narrow seas to invade Britain.

Sometime in the middle of July we arrived at the pre-ordained date for the end of the summer term. Three months and a few days had passed since we had gathered in the school hall on the first day of term to sing *Lord behold us with thy blessing, once again, assembled here*. In that one short term, we had seen our armed forces routed, six different countries overwhelmed by the seemingly invincible Germans, and our homeland awaiting invasion.

As school broke up for the summer holidays many of us wondered what was to become of us. The future seemed to consist of one huge question mark. Yet, when our parents opened the large envelopes containing our school report books, the contents looked the same as in previous terms. There, week by week, was the damning record of our performance in the weekly orders of merit painstakingly compiled by our form teachers. There, subject by subject, was the traditional mixture of 'Good', 'Satisfactory', 'Moderate' interspersed with perceptive judgments like 'improving' and 'might be better'. In my own case, I blessed Miss Becket for her 'intelligent and interested' and I forgave her the additional 'sometimes careless'. My age was

12.1, my weight was 81 pounds and my height was 5 foot and half an inch. In the bottom left hand corner of the report were the words, 'Next Term begins on Sept. 2nd, 2 p.m.' 'Would it really?' I asked myself. Perhaps, by 2 September, decisions on such matters would no longer rest with the school governors and the Derbyshire Education Authority.

Roy Bennett
Ashbourne

THE BRITISH EXPEDITIONARY FORCE IN FRANCE AND BELGIUM
1939–40

Introduction and Summary

The British Expeditionary Force (BEF), established in 1938 as war clouds began to gather, moved to France in September 1939 to take up positions along the Franco-Belgian border. With Belgium neutral, and much of the French Army in support of the Maginot line in the East, the British commitment was significant and potentially vital. With the launch of the German offensive in the West on 10 May 1940 Belgium and the Netherlands were invaded. The 10 divisions of the British Expeditionary Force, under the command of Viscount Gort, moved into Belgium to take up positions along the Dyle River and to close the open flank of the Maginot line. Within four days, on 14 May, British Forces had been ordered to fall back on the Escaut River as Franco-Belgian units on the flanks of the BEF were forced to withdraw. Over the next five days it became clear that the French Army had no reserves to commit to try to stabilise the front in the North and that the BEF was being forced back towards the Franco-Belgian coast.

On 20 May the British began planning for Operation Dynamo: the seaborne evacuation of the BEF from the ports of Calais and Dunkirk and the surrounding beaches. Dover Castle became the headquarters for the operation under Vice Admiral Bertram Ramsay of the Royal Navy. Unnecessary personnel were evacuated as Gort's forces tried to break through the German lines to establish a common front with the French Army. When this failed Gort was left with no choice but to try to evacuate the BEF from a pocket seemingly in imminent danger of collapse.

On 23 May German spearhead units advancing on Calais and Dunkirk were ordered to halt as German commanders were concerned about problems of supply after a rapid advance. They were also worried at rates of attrition in Panzer units and the difficulties of operating in marshy ground as they neared the coast. Hitler supported the order on 24 May. The order to resume the advance was not given until 26 May and it was not until the following day that many units could return to action. The order to commence Dynamo was given on 26 May by which time 28,000 troops judged not immediately useful had already got away.

The numbers of vessels evacuating troops on the first day of the operation was pitifully small (one cruiser, eight destroyers and twenty-six other vessels). Hopes to get away 45,000 men in the first two days of the operation were not fulfilled as only 25,000 escaped. Although the scale of the defeat facing the BEF was kept from the public, news of the returning troops spread widely. As the Admiralty requisitioned boats, fishing trawlers and other craft to supplement the evacuation force, many civilians volunteered to take their boats across the Channel. The first of the little ships arrived off the beaches on 28 May as every available vessel was pressed into service. In total 861 vessels were used in the evacuation with 243 being sunk during it. By the time the operation finally ceased on 4 June 338,226 had been evacuated from Calais, Dunkirk and the beaches (239,555 from the ports – 98,671 from the beaches). The BEF had lost 68,000 troops (killed, wounded and captured) and the material losses were staggering (85,000 vehicles, 2,472 artillery pieces together with hundreds of thousands of tons of stores and ammunition). Three French and six

British destroyers had been sunk and 19 British destroyers damaged: losses that would be keenly felt as the country faced the dangers of possible invasion and submarine blockade. The RAF meanwhile had lost 145 aircraft during Operation Dynamo. The losses were staggering, but the fact that the BEF had brought home was more telling still. Through brilliant and desperate improvisation, and the grace period afforded by the halt order, Ramsay's planners had achieved the near impossible: salvaging the majority of the BEF from the beaches of France and Belgium.[22]

Received by the Secretary of State for War from General the Viscount Gort (10 July 1886 – 31 March 1946 – VC, GCB, CBE,

---

22 For further reading on the Dunkirk evacuation see Ronald Atkin, *Pillar of Fire: Dunkirk 1940*, (London: Sidgwick & Jackson, 1990); Gregory Blaxland, *Destination Dunkirk: The Story of Gort's Army*, (London: William Kimber, 1973); John Costello, *Ten Days That Saved the West*, (London: New York: Bantam, 1991); Douglas C. Dildy, *Dunkirk 1940: Operation Dynamo* (Oxford: Osprey, 2010); W. J. R. Gardner, *The Evacuation from Dunkirk: 'Operation Dynamo' 26 May – 4 June 1940*, (London: Routledge, 1949); Norman Gelb, *Dunkirk: The Incredible Escape*, (London: Michael Joseph, 1990); Nicholas Harman, *Dunkirk; The Necessary Myth*, (London: Hodder and Stoughton, 1980); Julian Jackson, *The Fall of France: The Nazi Invasion of 1940*, (Oxford: Oxford University Press, 2003); Sean Longden, *Dunkirk: The Men They Left Behind*, (London: Constable and Robinson, 2009); Walter Lord, *The Miracle of Dunkirk*, (London: Allen Lane, 1983); Geoffrey Stewart, *Dunkirk and the Fall of France*, (Barnsley: Pen & Sword Military, 2008); Julian Thompson, *Dunkirk: Retreat to Victory*, (New York: Arcade, 2008); John de D. Winser, *B.E.F. Ships before, at and after Dunkirk*, (Gravesend: World Ship Society, 1999).

DSO & two bars, MVO, MC), Commander-in-Chief, British Expeditionary Force (France and Belgium 1939–40).
TNA: CAB 106/246. Published as supplement 35305 to *The London Gazette*, 17 October 1941, pp.5899–5934.

FIRST DESPATCH:
(Covering the period from 3rd September, 1939, to 31st January, 1940).
General Headquarters,
British Expeditionary Force,
25th April, 1940.
Sir,
1. I have the honour to submit a report on the employment of the British Expeditionary Force in France from 3rd September, 1939, the date I assumed command, until 31st January, 1940.
2. The move of the Force to France began as a whole on 10th September, although small advanced parties and technical personnel had been arriving since 4th September. The success of the initial operation was due primarily to the many detailed and complex plans carefully prepared under conditions of absolute secrecy in peace time. The perfection of these plans, the ready co-operation of the Board of Trade, the complete arrangements made by the Admiralty for the safety of ships while at sea, and the willing help of the French Naval, Military, and Civil authorities all combined to ensure the successful landing of the British Troops in France.
3. The plans for the despatch of the Force differed in two important respects from those of August, 1914.

The possibility of attack by sea and air made it necessary to use the Western ports of France instead of the Channel ports, while the total replacement of animals by mechanical vehicles, which had been completed by 1939, presented a new problem in transportation.

The troops were landed at Cherbourg and their stores and vehicles were despatched to Nantes, St. Nazaire, and Brest.

This plan entailed the early despatch of staff with the proper complement of units of the Docks and other Transportation Services. The personnel of these Services were in the main recruited from the Port Authorities in Great Britain at the outbreak of war.

These units were operating to full capacity the berths allotted to the Force, within forty-eight hours of landing, and the programme was carried out according to the time table throughout the whole period of the disembarkation of 1st and 2nd Corps. This I regard as a feat deserving of the highest praise.

4. On landing the fighting troops were passed rapidly through transit camps and their vehicles were cleared at once to Vehicle Marshalling Parks, whence they were despatched in convoys, while troops left by rail on the same day as they landed.

Since the troops and their vehicles were landed at different ports they had to be collected in an assembly area which had been chosen in the vicinity of Le Mans and Laval. The assembling of troops by rail and vehicles by road took about six days. The resource of individual drivers was tested by changes of programme, inevitable in an operation of this kind, by the damage which some vehicles had sustained during the sea passage and by mechanical failures. Drivers and vehicles were on the road for long periods, but their duty was lightened by the hospitality of the French inhabitants, which all ranks will recall with gratitude.

5. On 13th September I moved my headquarters from the War Office to Camberley, where General Headquarters was forming. On the following day, accompanied by Lieutenant-General (now General) Sir John Dill, Commander of 1st Corps, and by my personal staff, I embarked in H.M.S. "Skate," and,

landing at Cherbourg, left by motor car for the Chateau de la Blanchardiere, Le Mans, which the French Government had kindly placed at my disposal.

6. On 21st September the concentration of the General Headquarters Staff and of the essential Lines of Communication units was complete. The next day the advanced elements of 1st Corps and of General Headquarters Troops arrived, the former moving to an area around Laval and the latter to an area around Le Mans. Units were given a minimum of one week in which to assemble and reorganise and although some of the units of 1st Corps were still incomplete, the limited accommodation available in the assembly area made it essential to begin the move forward before 26th September when the leading units of 2nd Corps were due to arrive.

7. During these early weeks the maintenance of the Force presented a problem which called for the greatest resource and initiative on the part of my Quarter-Master-General, Lieutenant-General W. G. Lindsell, his Staff and Services.

In the units of the Royal Army Service Corps were many officers and men fresh from civil life who were constantly called upon to surmount unforeseen difficulties. By their unflagging energy and the assistance of the French authorities the Force was maintained without any failure of supplies. It should be added that with the exception of eleven regular officers, the personnel of the Movement Control organisation was built up from Supplementary Reserve officers and men.

The administrative staff were obliged to deal with the day-to-day work of landing troops, their vehicles and current supplies, and to undertake the equally important task of building up reserves of ammunition, supplies, and ordnance stores. Covered accommodation was difficult to obtain and temporary dumps of non-perishable stores had to be established wherever the necessary space could be found in the vicinity of the ports of entry.

8. In these early days the Staff met for the first time the problem arising from the wide dispersion imposed by the necessity to guard air attack.

The towns of Le Mans and Laval were fifty miles apart, and the base ports were on an average one hundred and fifty miles from the assembly area. Helpful though the French authorities were, the unfamiliar conditions made telephone communication difficult, apart from the danger of breach of security which it entailed. Since many despatch riders spoke no French it was often found that control could only be properly maintained by personal visits; Commanders and their staffs were therefore forced to spend many hours on the road.

The dispersion dictated by the possibility of aerial bombardment greatly increases demands upon signal communications and transport and thus lengthens the time which must elapse between the issue of orders and their execution.

The Move to the Belgian Frontier.

9. On 22nd September, I left Le Mans for Amiens. Arriving at Mantes-sur-Saine, I was handed a telegram from General Georges, Commander of the French Front of the North-East, which read as follows:-

"Pour Général Commandant, B.E.F.

"Limite envisagee prévoit front de B.E.F. droite a MAULDE gauche à MENIN ou gauche à AUTRYCHE-SUR-ESCAUT. Général GEORGES désirerait avoir accord 22 Septembre."

In the meantime, however, General Gamelin had proceeded to London to discuss with His Majesty's Government the frontage which was to be held by the British Expeditionary Force. After I had made a reconnaissance on 24th and 25th September of the sector which it was proposed to allot to the British Expeditionary Force I visited General Georges at Grand Quartier General on 26th September, in the company of my Chief of the General Staff, Lieutenant-General H. R. Pownall.

I then agreed to accept the sector offered by General Georges to the British Expeditionary Force. This sector was from Maulde exclusive to Halluin inclusive, and thence a defensive flank along river Lys/Armentières. General Georges placed 51st French Division (Général de Brigade Gillard) under my command, and I decided to employ it in my left sector, covering the towns of Roubaix and Tourcoing.

10. It had been originally intended that formations, as soon as they had completed their reorganisation in the assembly area, should move to a concentration area in the North of France, and remain there in readiness to occupy the line not earlier than 5th October. General Georges decided, however, that it was inadvisable to await the arrival of the whole British Expeditionary Force in the concentration area and expressed a wish that 1st Corps should move without delay into the sector north of Maulde. I accordingly informed General Georges that 1st Corps would take over its sector on 3rd October and that 2nd Corps would be able to go into the line about 12th October.

1st Corps began the two hundred and fifty-mile move from the assembly area on 26th September.

Tanks, tracked vehicles, and slow moving artillery proceeded by train and the remainder of the force advanced on three parallel routes. Three days were allotted for the move of each formation. Two staging areas were arranged on each road, south of the rivers Seine and Somme respectively, and anti-aircraft defence was provided at these river crossings. The weather was fine throughout the whole period of the move.

The first stage was one hundred and twenty miles. An average of five hundred vehicles moved daily over each stage of the route, maintaining a distance of one hundred yards between each vehicle as a precaution against air attack. A halt of one day for maintenance purposes was made after the first day's move.

In the initial stages of the move, the Provost service were responsible for the regulation of traffic, but on entering the French Zone des Armees, columns came under the direction of the French road control (Regulatrice Routiere) organisation, which gave valuable help in marking detours and in directing traffic through towns. A French-speaking British officer was established in Amiens to ensure liaison between my headquarters and the French authorities.

Breakdowns and accidents were few, which reflects great credit on the drivers, who were unaccustomed to long hours at the wheel and to driving on the right-hand side of the road. Among the many important lessons which were learnt during the largest road movement ever undertaken with motor transport by any British Army were the need for early reconnaissance of staging areas, for control at the dispersal points, and for allowance for unforeseen delays.

11. The move forward continued without incident or interruption, and on the agreed date, 3rd October, 1st Corps took over from the French the sector Maulde-Gruson on the Belgian frontier. This sector lay between that of the 1st French Army and of the 16th French Corps, with 2nd Division (Major-General H. C. Loyd) on the right and 1st Division (Major-General Hon. H. R. L. G. Alexander) on the left.

General Headquarters opened in and around Habarcq (8 miles west of Arras) on 2nd October.

On 12th October, 3rd Division of 2nd Corps (Major-General B. L. Montgomery) moved into the line between Bouvines and Lannoy, relieving the left brigade of 1st Corps and the right regiment of the French 51st Division. 4th Division of the same Corps (Major-General D. G. Johnson, V.C.) was located in General Headquarters reserve.

The initial occupation of the line by the British Expeditionary Force was thus completed arid the organisation of the position was undertaken at once.

The Organisation of the British Positions.

12. In allotting sectors the geographical features of the pronounced salient occupied by the British Expeditionary Force had to be considered. East of the Tournai-Orchies road the country is flat, much wooded and intersected by small streams. Further to the north lies open and undulating agricultural land which lends itself to artillery observation and to the movement of armoured fighting vehicles. Further north again the sector is for the most part on the fringe of a highly industrial and mining district.

When 1st Corps arrived in the sector assigned to the British Expeditionary Force in the first week in October, an almost continuous antitank obstacle already existed in the form of a ditch covered by concrete blockhouses built to mount anti-tank guns and machine guns. In accordance with plans prepared in peace time certain French technical troops continued to work in the sector under the command of the French Commander of the Defensive Sector of Lille, Colonel (now General de Brigade) Bertschi.

While defences continued to develop on the lines of the original plan, based on the close defence of the frontier, it was also necessary to organise the position.

The priority of work envisaged the eventual construction of three positions in the forward area, and a Corps reserve position was sited across the base of the Lille salient formed by the frontier. Further in rear, a second position had been sited, following the line of the Haute Deule, Sensée and La Bassée canals.

The whole scheme involved the immediate construction of field defences and the duplication of the anti-tank obstacle in the forward zone.

It was consequently necessary to construct at an early stage reinforced concrete "pillboxes" to afford protection to those weapons which formed the backbone of the fire defence throughout the whole depth of the position. In order to save time standard designs were prepared to accommodate both British and French weapons.

13. Work on these "pill-boxes" was begun by the Royal Engineers, assisted by other arms. Early in November a specially constituted force composed of twelve field companies of the Royal Engineers drawn from Territorial Army Divisions at home, and known as "X Force", arrived in the British Expeditionary Force area. This force had its own transport and special plant for the construction of reinforced concrete "pill-boxes" by mass production methods. It was accompanied by companies of the Auxiliary Military Pioneer Corps.

A special Excavator Company, equipped with mechanical excavators of various types, arrived at the same time as X Force. It has been employed in digging anti-tank ditches, burying signal cables, constructing breastworks, and other tasks.

A creation of such a defensive system demanded a quantity and variety of engineer stores far exceeding pre-war anticipations.

Bad weather in October and November, and a succession of frosts later, considerably delayed the work, but by the end of the period covered by this despatch the position had been developed in considerable depth. A large number of concrete "pill-boxes" had been completed and many others were under construction; new wire had been erected and existing wire strengthened, buildings had been reinforced, and many miles of anti-tank ditch dug.

The Saar Detachment.
14. In November 1939, I arranged with General Georges that a British infantry brigade should take its place in the line on the Saar front, under the command of a French Division.

The brigade took over the sector from the French 42nd Division on the 4th December without enemy interference and during the period under review conditions were quiet.

Since that date infantry brigades of the British Expeditionary Force have successively completed short tours of duty in this sector, and junior leaders have thus had valuable training in their day to day duties when in contact with the enemy.

The fortifications of the Maginot Line in the sector concerned continued to be manned by French fortress troops, the British battalions being disposed in depth in advance of the fortified line. The enemy positions were on the average one thousand five hundred yards distant from our foremost posts.

The British Army contains to-day very few regimental officers and other ranks who fought in the last war; much that was common knowledge and accepted practice then, must therefore be learned again. Nevertheless, events on the Saar front have proved beyond doubt that the young officer and his men, once they have had experience of active service, will be in every way worthy of their predecessors.

The Completion of the First Contingent.

15. During October and November, 15th and 17th Infantry Brigades were sent from home, and placed under command of 1st and 2nd *Corps* respectively. 13th Infantry Brigade was also relieved on the Lines of Communication by 25th Infantry Brigade.

On 1st and 2nd December, the French 51st Division was relieved by 4th Division and 17th Infantry Brigade, and withdrawn from my command: I was sorry to part with them and with their commander, who at all times gave me loyal support.

The plans for the despatch of the Force had envisaged that two divisions of the Territorial Army would be sent from home as soon as they were sufficiently trained. Since three regular infantry brigades had by now arrived, however, I decided on 27th October to form the 5th Division under the command of Major-General H. E. Franklyn. On the night of 29th–30th December the division took over a sector on the left of the 4th Division.

At this time the five divisions of the British Expeditionary Force were all in the line.

During the month of January the 48th Division (Major-General A. F. A. N. Thorne) arrived in France, and by 23rd January had completed its move forward. It was placed under 1st Corps, but held in G.H.Q. reserve.

By the end of January the Force, therefore, consisted of two corps, each of three divisions, with corps and army troops. The first stage in the development of the Force was thus concluded. The strength of the British Expeditionary Force at the end of January stood at two hundred and twenty-two thousand two hundred, all ranks, not including the men of the Air Component and of other units of the Royal Air Force for whose maintenance I am responsible.

Air Forces and Anti-Aircraft Defence.

16. Although development of the Air Forces and of the Air Defence organisations proceeded simultaneously with the despatch of the Force and with its subsequent moves, I have thought it convenient to describe this development separately.

The composition of the Force included a Component of the Royal Air Force under the command of Air Vice-Marshal C. H. B. Blount, Royal Air Force, consisting of two Army Co-operation Wings, one Fighter Wing and one Bomber Reconnaissance Wing.

The aircraft were flown to France according to plan at the outbreak of hostilities and came under my command from the dates of the disembarkation of their ground units. Later other units were added, and the Air Component now comprises, in addition to Headquarters, one Fighter Group Headquarters, eight Wings, a Communication Squadron, and certain administrative and other detachments.

The ground echelons were moved in advance of 1st and 2nd Corps to the aerodromes in the region to be occupied. In the early stages they were largely dependent on the assistance given to them by the French Région Aérienne under the command successively of General Jeauneaud and General Armengeaud.

On 14th and 15th September, the anti-aircraft units disembarked at the base ports and, in conjunction with fighter units of the Royal Air Force, undertook the task of protecting the disembarkation of the two Corps and their forward moves.

Once the concentration was complete, the available anti-aircraft resources were divided between forward defences and Lines of Communication. Besides the normal provision for the defence of headquarters and railheads, arrangements were made to protect certain important French installations in the British zone and a searchlight zone was also established as a protection against enemy night bombing.

On all occasions, the Air Officer Commanding has been greatly helped by General d'Astier, commanding the French Air Forces with the northern group of French Armies.

During the period under review, enemy air activity has been almost entirely confined to reconnaissance flights at great heights.

Air Reconnaissance.

17. The strategical plans for air reconnaissance were worked out in conjunction with the Air Ministry and with General Mouchard, commanding the Air Forces with the French Armies of the North East.

In accordance with these plans many reconnaissances have been carried out both by day and night. Much photography has been undertaken with useful results, both in information obtained and in experience gained in photographic and survey methods.

The work of the units of the Royal Air Force engaged in air reconnaissance deserves the highest praise, since it has been performed, as a rule, in the face of enemy opposition. Pilots have often been called on to carry out flights to the full limit of the range of their aircraft, flying over long and circuitous routes to avoid neutral territory; this rigorous duty has been boldly and cheerfully undertaken.

The preparation of Aerodromes.

18. It had been decided, before mobilisation, that the maintenance and construction of all aerodromes used by the Royal Air Force in France, as well as their signal communications, should be the responsibility of the British Expeditionary Force.

Many aerodromes and landing grounds had been placed at our disposal by the French authorities, but it soon became evident that the problems of construction and maintenance were far greater than had been contemplated before the war. A new policy had, therefore, to be formulated and comprehensive plans prepared. In most parts of France, permanent pasture does not exist, and this fact, in view of the weight of modern aircraft, has made it necessary to construct concrete runways, often of considerable extent, on the principal aerodromes in use. A number of special units of the Royal Engineers had consequently to be raised, and a large amount of plant, grass seed and materials had to be provided.

Frontier Control.

19. The sector of the frontier occupied by the British Expeditionary Force presented a very difficult control problem. There were initially over ten thousand Belgians working on the beet harvest in the British zone and on the average considerably more than twenty thousand local inhabitants passed the frontier daily on their normal business.

The strength of the frontier organisations charged with the control of the frontier traffic had been seriously reduced on mobilisation. It was therefore essential to supplement the normal machinery of control.

The system devised in co-operation with the 1st French Region and the commander of the fortified sector of Lille included a primary control on the frontier proper and a secondary control on the line of the foremost anti-tank obstacle wherever the latter did not coincide with the frontier.

Co-operation with the French authorities has been close and harmonious throughout. The Field Security Police have played an important role in this unusual and difficult task and have contributed largely to the success of the organisation.

Intelligence.

20. Conditions on the operational side of intelligence work in the field have naturally been abnormal. Much valuable preliminary work and re-organisation has been carried out and full advantage has been taken of the unusual situation, to complete the training of the Intelligence staffs. Co-operation with the French Intelligence service has been close and cordial.

It became apparent at an early date that the staff and organisation provided for dealing with wireless intelligence were inadequate for this increasingly important branch of operational intelligence. The expansion of the wireless intelligence units is now, therefore, in progress. Closest co-operation has been maintained with the French Wireless Intelligence Service.

It has been necessary to increase the air intelligence section of the Intelligence branch at General Headquarters, which has performed valuable work in the collection and distribution of information.

The problem of security has presented many unusual difficulties. This has been largely due to the long period of inactivity, the geographical position of the Force, the length of the Lines of Communication, and the congestion in the rear areas owing to the presence of evacuees. The French authorities have co-operated most closely in the matter of civil security and have throughout given all the assistance in their power.

Censorship.

The postal censorship discipline of the British Expeditionary Force is on the whole good. Very considerable increases in personnel have been found necessary in order to impose the requisite selective censorship on the abnormally large number of letters now despatched daily. Extremely useful reports on the outlook of the British Expeditionary Force as a whole and on its relations with the local French inhabitants are produced periodically. These are based largely on information supplied by the censorship organisation supplemented by reports from the Field Security Police.

Publicity and Propaganda.

The section of the Intelligence branch dealing with publicity and propaganda has worked in close co-operation with the organisations concerned both in England and France, and has fulfilled a role which has assumed far more importance than in previous campaigns. Much has been done to counter German propaganda. Material has been provided for the Miniform Committee in Paris in this connection, and information bulletins are issued periodically to all units of the British Expeditionary Force.

Cipher Personnel.

Up to date the whole of the cipher work in the Force has been carried out most efficiently by Army Educational Corps personnel. This personnel is now required to revert to its normal duties in the United Kingdom and is being replaced.

Press.

21. The significance and requirements of the Press and of the press and cinematographic publicity in the field in modern war have proved greater than was appreciated prior to the outbreak of hostilities. Shortly after mobilisation a Public Relations unit

was hastily formed and incorporated in the Intelligence branch of General Headquarters.

Since its formation in October this unit has administered and arranged facilities for a total of some fifty-five War Correspondents permanently accredited to the British Expeditionary Force, besides representatives of the principal news-reel companies. Some sixty visiting editors, correspondents, broadcasters and cinematographers, in addition to selected representatives of the neutral Press, have been given facilities for visiting the Force.

There has also been a small unit of the British Broadcasting Corporation with the Force since October, and facilities have been provided for selected official photographers to meet the requirements of the British Press.

The Newspaper Proprietors Association generously makes a large supply of papers available free daily for the Force. In the matter of distribution, close touch has been kept with them and with the "Continental Daily Mail," which supplies the troops with their latest news.

The Press and photographic censorship is now working efficiently and co-operation with the French is close and harmonious.

Development of the Rearward Services.
22. The work of the administrative staffs and services in back areas has in many respects been fully as heavy as it would have been if fighting had been in progress. It was their duty, while maintaining a continually growing force, to make and put into execution long term plans in preparation for the arrival of future contingents.

The initial scheme provided for the formation of temporary maintenance depots near the ports of Brest and Nantes, but it was soon evident that, with so long a line of communication, an advanced base was required.

The use of the port of Havre had at first been considered undesirable owing to certain geographical and technical difficulties in the air defence of the docks. These were, however, overcome in mid-November, and an Advanced Base area is now being established near this port with the co-operation of the French authorities, while Field Supply Depots are being set up further forward. By mid-December, the staff of the Movement Control were working some ninety stations, while fourteen ports were in use for landing personnel, animals and stores. Through these ports, a quarter of a million men, forty-five thousand mechanical vehicles and a monthly tonnage varying from sixty to one hundred thousand tons of stores of all kinds were imported and distributed to their various areas and reserve depots.

Works projects of great magnitude have been in progress from the outset, and the problems of accommodation have been many and complex. An extensive programme of building and hutting for depots, hospitals and reinforcement camps was put in hand, together with installations for electric light and power, the bulk storage of petrol and so on. A vast amount of minor work in connection with accommodation has been carried out by the Royal Engineers.

Railway construction at depots and aerodromes has been undertaken by the Transportation Services under very adverse weather conditions.

The complicated nature of modern military equipment has added greatly to the work of the Royal Army Ordnance Corps, as regards both storeholding and repair. Great difficulty has been experienced in finding suitable accommodation for depots and workshops at the bases, more especially since the whole of the resources of France are engaged at high pressure on her own war industries. New installations have therefore been planned and are now under construction.

The maintenance of mechanical vehicles has received constant attention and the number of road accidents, and consequently of repairs, has been greatly reduced through measures taken by the Provost Service to enforce road discipline.

The labour problem bids fair to become one of great magnitude, and its solution may be difficult. As no adequate labour force was available on mobilisation, the gap was filled by the temporary use of cavalry and infantry reservists. Later, the Auxiliary Military Pioneer Corps absorbed the various labour units already in France. This Corps has carried out cheerfully and efficiently the important, but often unexciting tasks allotted to its units.

I am grateful to the Government of India for the high standard of the animal transport units sent to France, which have proved their usefulness on many occasions.

Major General P. de Fonblanque, General Officer Commanding, Lines of Communication Area, has under his command the greatest part of the undertakings described above. They now cover almost one third of France, stretching from Dunkirk to Brest and from Cherbourg to Marseilles.

The Welfare of the Force

23. The health of the Force has been good and the number of troops in the care of medical units has never exceeded 2–8 per cent, of the strength of the Force, despite the unusually severe weather conditions in December and January.

I wish to express my appreciation of the work of the Royal Army Medical Corps under my Director of Medical Services, Major General J. W. L. Scott.

The arrangements for leave came into force on 18th December. The numbers permitted to be absent on leave at any one time are based on the percentage of strength which can be spared from the Force. By the end of January ten days' leave home had been granted to some sixty thousand of all ranks and compassionate leave had also been granted in deserving cases.

The question of leave was worked out in great detail by the Adjutant General, Lieutenant General Sir Douglas Brownrigg, and the members of his staff.

The Expeditionary Force Institutes have now established some ninety institutes open on the Lines of Communication and bulk stores have been established in forward areas to enable units to replenish their own canteens. The same organisation is providing concert parties and mobile cinemas, and a proportion of the troops are able to visit each week one of the entertainments provided by the Entertainments National Services Association.

I am likewise grateful to those organisations which have co-operated so whole-heartedly with the Royal Army Chaplains Department in attending to the welfare of the troops.

Amongst these are the Catholic Women's Guild, The Army Scripture Readers' Association, The Church Army, The Church of Scotland, Toc H, The Salvation Army, The Young Men's Christian Association, and the Young Women's Christian Association.

The despatch and delivery of mails takes place with regularity, and more than nine thousand bags of mail have been handled in one day by the Postal Service. The necessity for censorship is fully realized, but there has been no delay in the time taken in the transit of mail for an ever-increasing force.

The great distances between forward troops and the base made it necessary to depart from the old established procedure whereby the 2nd Echelon of the Adjutant General's Branch has always been located in the theatre of war. This office is now established in Margate, and the move has been fully justified by the increased speed with which matters are now handled.

Training and Organisation.
24. The absence of fighting has afforded opportunities to continue the training of the Force. Weapon training has been possible for

almost every unit, and thanks to the co-operation of the French Army, artillery practice camps have been held and other training facilities provided. Exercises with troops involving road movement on a large scale have been held and much progress has been made in the technique of co-operation with the Royal Air Force.

About eight hundred and fifty officers and non-commissioned officers have been sent home as instructors to assist in the training of new formations, while an equal number have been attached to the Force, for instruction, from units at home.

Despite the almost complete absence of battle casualties the supply of officers has caused me concern. Over four hundred candidates have been sent home for training as officers, while a further four hundred have been recommended for immediate commissions.

These have been drawn to a large extent from Warrant Officers Class III.

A large number of War Establishments, particularly for the Intelligence Corps and for units on the Lines of Communication, were found to need adjustment and steps have been taken to this end.

The existing War Establishment of an infantry battalion, which was not designed for Continental warfare, has called for modification and I am grateful that my recommendations for an increase have been accepted.

The Royal Corps of Signals has been put to great strain in providing communications not only for the Army, but for the whole of the Air Forces in France. The degree of dispersion required in modern warfare has materially added to their difficulties.

The success with which these demands have been met is due not only to the spirit in which the personnel of that Corps have faced and overcome difficulties, but to the successful arrangements for co-operation with the French military and civil organisations, and with the General Post Office. The Wireless Intelligence Staff have done valuable work, and the cipher duties of the Force have been most efficiently performed by personnel of the Army Educational Corps.

The Survey Directorate has been called upon to carry out a great deal of work under difficult conditions and has fulfilled all the demands made upon it.

Liaison with the French.

25. On the arrival of the British Expeditionary Force in France a French Military Mission was established at my headquarters to deal with French military and civil authorities and to act as a link with Grand Quartier General. In addition, officers and non-commissioned officers of the French Army are attached for liaison duties to the headquarters of each formation and unit as it arrives.

I wish to express my sincere gratitude to the chief of the Mission, General de Division Voruz, and to all his staff for their ever-ready help to the-British Army on all occasions.

Thanks to their efforts, matters relating to billeting, hire of land, and local purchase of material have been handled without friction. To them is due, in large measure, the friendliness of the relations which exist between the French population and the troops, and also as between French and British staffs and regiments.

A British Military Mission under Brigadier J. G. des R. Swayne was established with the Headquarters of General Georges under whose immediate command the British Expeditionary Force is serving.

Distinguished Visitors.

26. On 4th December His Majesty The King visited his troops in France and was received everywhere with enthusiasm. During the three days tour His Majesty was able to make a detailed inspection of forward and rear areas. On his return to England, His Majesty was graciously pleased to send a message to his Army which was warmly appreciated by all ranks.

The President of the French Republic has spent a day with the British Expeditionary Force.

The Prime Minister and other members of the War Cabinet, the Ministers from the Dominions, many members of the Army Council and seven Field Marshals are amongst those who have visited my Headquarters at various times.

Honours and Awards.

27. I am submitting separately the names of officers and other ranks whom I wish to recommend for reward or to bring to your notice for gallant or distinguished service.

I have the honour to be,

Sir,

Your obedient Servant,

GORT.

General,

Commander-in-Chief,

British Expeditionary Force

SECOND DESPATCH

(Covering the period from 1st February, 1940, to 31st May, 1940, with an Appendix covering operations of 1st Corps from 6 p.m. 31st May, to midnight 2nd/3rd June).[23]

---

23 The narrative portions of this despatch have been compiled from the war diaries and other records of the General Staff at G.H.Q. These have been supplemented by war diaries, including those of the Swayne Mission, and by diaries, notes and records made by various commanders and staff officers at the time, or within a few days of their arrival in England. The records of the General Staff at G.H.Q. are only partially complete for the period 10–18 May, owing to some papers having been destroyed at Boulogne, and a portion of the records for 31 May lost at sea. Some records of less

London, 25 July, 1940.
Sir,

1. I have the honour to submit a report on the employment of the British Expeditionary Force, and on the part which it played in operations in France and Belgium from 1ˢᵗ February, 1940, to 31ˢᵗ May, 1940, on which date I gave up Command of the Force.

The period under review may be divided into two distinct and sharply contrasting phases, namely, before and after 10ᵗʰ May, on which date active operations began. The active operations themselves can be divided geographically into two distinct parts; on the east, the advance to the River Dyle, and the withdrawal to the frontier; on the west, the defence of Arras and the organisation of the Canal line. Later, the two parts merged into one whole in the final phase of the withdrawal and embarkation of the Force.

No such clear definition can be made in terms of time; furthermore, the two operations, on the east and on the west, were closely interdependent, and the same reserves had to serve for both. For this reason the accounts of the operations on the two fronts cannot but be intermingled at certain points in the narrative. Broadly speaking, however, three distinct phases can be distinguished. First, the advance to the Dyle from

---

importance were burnt at Hazebrouck to avoid possible capture and others were destroyed in a lorry which caught fire near Cassel on or about 24 May.

2. The Appendix contains an account of the operations at Dunkirk from 6 p.m., 31 May, to midnight 2/3 June, which may conveniently be appended to this despatch, though they were not carried out under the orders of the Commander-in-Chief. It has been compiled by the General Staff at G.H.Q., from sources similar to those used for the despatch itself.

10th–16th May; then from 17th–26th May the withdrawal from the Dyle to the Escaut, the defence of the Belgian frontier and of the southern and western flanks; and finally the withdrawal and embarkation of the Force from 27th–31st May.

2. The narrative in my first despatch dated 25th April, 1940, concluded with the completion of the first contingent of the Force.

I had been informed that the expansion of the Force was to be continued by the despatch of 3rd Corps during the early months of 1940; the Armoured Division was to follow in May, and a fourth Corps, with 1st Canadian Division, during the late Summer; furthermore, it had been decided that the Force should be divided into two Armies, as soon as the number of divisions in the field, excluding the Armoured Division, rose above eleven.

Preparation for this expansion, which had been proceeding since the previous autumn, continued steadily until 1oth May.

Arrival of 3rd Corps in France.
3. 3rd Corps (Lt.-General Sir Ronald F. Adam, Bt.), consisting of 42nd Division (Major-General W. G. Holmes), 44th Division (Major-General E. A. Osborne) and 51st Division (Major-General V. M. Fortune) was due for despatch to France in February and March, and 51st Division arrived during early February. The 50th (Motor) Division (Major-General G. le Q. Martel) arrived in France at the same time and was allotted to 2nd Corps. It had been arranged that the front of the B.E.F. should be extended northwards to Croix de Poperinghe on the Belgian frontier, two miles north-east of Bailleul, and that 3rd Corps should go into the line on the left of the B.E.F. taking over 5th Division from 2nd Corps, and relieving 53rd French Division, between Armentieres and Croix de Poperinghe, with 51st Division. The Command of the new sector had passed to the B.E.F. at midnight 31st Jan./1st February, and the relief of the French troops was to take place about 12th February.

At this time, however, owing to the situation elsewhere in Europe His Majesty's Government found it necessary to postpone the despatch of 3rd Corps (excepting 51st Division) and also of certain anti-aircraft, administrative and labour units. I was also instructed to earmark one division for withdrawal from the B.E.F. if required; for this I selected 5th Division. It was evident that the programme of shipments of ammunition and other war material to France, on which I had counted to make up the serious deficiencies in stocks, would be severely curtailed in February and March.

4. These changes entailed a delay in the development of the Force which was naturally disappointing; moreover, it became impossible for me to take over the new sector to Bailleul, and at the same time to retain a proper proportion of divisions in reserve. I was, therefore, obliged to obtain the consent of the French to the indefinite postponement of the relief, and to accept the resulting congestion in the area of the B.E.F.

50th Division was temporarily accommodated in an area south-west of Amiens in G.H.Q. reserve.

At the end of March, however, the 3rd Corps was finally despatched to France; 51st Division duly relieved the French in the new sector on 28th March; 44th Division, on disembarkation, moved into 3rd Corps reserve in the St. Pol area, and 50th Division into 2nd Corps reserve, southwest of Lille; 42nd Division, on arrival, moved to the area south-west of Amiens, in G.H.Q. reserve.

5. The German invasion of Denmark and Norway on 9th April created a new situation; leave was stopped in the British and French Armies on 10th April, and 15th Infantry Brigade of 5th Division was despatched to England, *en route* for Norway, on 15th April; certain units of 42nd Division were also retained at home, but with a few exceptions despatched later. The remainder of 5th Division was left in France, but in War Office reserve, and was accordingly relieved in 3rd Corps by

42nd Division. Reports of enemy intentions to invade Holland and Belgium were received from different sources and at different times, and between the 11th and 22nd April certain troops were placed under short notice to move. Intensified air reconnaissance was ordered in the zone allotted to the Air Component which included part of the Ruhr and the area to the west of it, but apart from small bridging activity no positive results were observed.

The Saar Front.

6. During this period the detachment of one infantry brigade on the Saar front was maintained; at the outset the severe cold interfered considerably with the work of improving the defences in the forward area. Much required to be done, as regards increased protection, provision of alternative fire positions, covered approaches and improved communications; the wire required thickening and its tactical lay-out improving; the thaw, when it set in, was rapid and energetic steps had to be taken to maintain a proper standard of sanitation.

The tour of duty of each infantry brigade was raised in March to three weeks, and a pioneer battalion was included in the detachment.

At the end of March it was decided to increase the Saar force to a total of one division, with attached troops, including cavalry, machine guns, and pioneers. 51st Division was selected. The Division had concentrated in the Metz area by 30th April and by 7th May had relieved 7th French Division, thus extending the British front on the Saar on either side of the front originally held to a total of 12,000 yards from Guerstling exclusive to Remeling inclusive.

51st Division remained in the Saar area and took no part in the operations in Northern France. From 10th May therefore, it ceased to be under my effective command; the Saar Force was later moved to the Rouen area, where it took part in subsequent operations.

Patrolling, both by our own troops and by the enemy, grew steadily more active during this period; early on the morning of the 5th March, the enemy carried out a successful raid, supported with a box barrage of a type familiar in the war of 1914–18, on one of our front line positions in a wood known as the Hartebusch, then held by a battalion of the 4th Division (2nd D.C.L.I.). In this and subsequent encounters the enemy regularly suffered casualties, many of them at the hands of battalions of the 144th Infantry Brigade of the 48th Division, the first Territorial Army formation to meet the enemy in this campaign.

The sub-machine gun was taken into experimental use by patrols in the Saar front: its value had already been recognised and I trust that a weapon of this type will be permanently included in the armament of the infantry.

Preparation for Further Expansion.

7. In the meantime I had been preparing for the arrival of further troops, and, in particular, for the formation of Army Headquarters which were due to arrive in the latter part of June. On the assumption that the positions held by the B.E.F. were to remain the same, a lay-out had been prepared involving a move of G.H.Q. The construction of the new G.H.Q. and of the two Army headquarters was put in hand; this involved the laying of about 150 route miles of heavy armoured cable. Negotiations were in progress regarding the extension of the front of the B.E.F. on arrival of a fourth Corps, the French being anxious that this should be southwards rather than northwards.

Development of the Defensive Positions.

8. The development of the successive defensive positions and switch lines behind the Belgian frontier was continued steadily till 10th May. By this date over 400 concrete "pill-boxes" of

varying size had been completed with over 100 more under construction, while work on the improvement of field defences, wire and other obstacles proceeded continuously on the original front and in the sector north of Armentieres recently taken over from the French.

Chiefly by the use of excavator machinery over 40 miles of revetted anti-tank ditch had been added to that prepared by the French army in time of peace. Machines had also been used to assist the troops in constructing earthwork defences, mixing concrete and burying signal cables.

Training.

9. Training areas were being prepared to accommodate the Armoured Division and other formations; base reinforcement depots were rapidly taking shape in their new locations near Rouen, and their training staffs had assembled. Corps schools had been established, principally for the training of junior leaders, and a sniping school had been set up. Practice camps, both for field and anti-aircraft artillery had been developed with the help of the French and steps taken to continue the weapon training of selected units.

The practice undertaken with anti-tank weapons, to which special attention was given, was amply to prove its value when the time came.

The Equipment Situation.

10. The situation as regards equipment, though there was latterly some improvement in certain directions, caused me serious misgivings, even before men and material began to be diverted by the needs of operations elsewhere. I had on several occasions called the attention of the War Office to the shortage of almost every nature of ammunition of which the stocks in France were not nearly large enough to permit of the rates of expenditure laid down for sustained operations before the War.

There was a shortage of guns in some of the anti-tank regiments of the Royal Artillery, while armour-piercing shells for field guns had not, by 10th May, been provided.

There were also deficiencies in technical apparatus for light anti-aircraft requirements, such as Kenison Predictors, signal lights, technical and specialised vehicles of many types and a number of smaller items. The same difficulties in provision of equipment were no doubt the cause of delays in the despatch of new units to the B.E.F., particularly armoured and anti-aircraft units, and while it is to some extent true that the shortness of the campaign prevented the full effect of the shortages being felt, it is I think, justifiable to assume that the presence of the Armoured Division and of a complete Army Tank Brigade would have been an invaluable aid in the difficulties with which we were faced in meeting enemy armoured formations.

The Administrative Situation.

11. The development of the rearward installations had been proceeding systematically.

The medical base installations had been extended and a hospital area was in course of rapid development near Boulogne in addition to the original medical base sub-area at Dieppe.

The British Army requirements in the port of Brest, a French naval base, had been substantially reduced by the use of other ports such as St. Malo and Caen; by May, seventeen ports in all were being operated and 2,500 tons of stores were being despatched to railheads daily.

At the same time, the construction of semi-permanent depots of all kinds in the neighbourhood of Nantes, Rennes and Rouen was in progress; this would later on have led to more efficient and economical working than was possible in the temporary accommodation, taken up in September, 1939. By 10th May, seven ammunition depots were open, in addition to railhead dumps; all these were intended, in time, to be rail served; while the construction of the regulating station at Abancourt, by French railway troops on behalf of the B.E.F., was well advanced. It opened on a limited scale in the first week of May. A supply depot was being constructed close by so as to relieve the dangerous congestion at the ports of Rouen and Havre.

The progress of all these undertakings was adversely affected by the shortage of labour, to which I referred in my first despatch, and it was decided, in March, to send three Divisions to France to undertake labour duties and at the same time continue their training, albeit slowly. The Divisions selected were 12th (Major-General R.L. Petre), 23rd (Major-General W.N. Herbert) and 46th (Major-General H.O. Curtis). These arrived in April; 23rd Division was allotted for work on aerodromes in the forward area, and the remaining two to the Lines of Communication area.

Organisation.

12. The absence of actual operations up to 10th May gave opportunities to make a number of changes in organisation. Divisional cavalry regiments were grouped into Armoured Reconnaissance Brigades and the Lines of Communication area was re-organised into two districts.

Infantry battalions were filled up to the new and higher establishments, and action was initiated to raise the establishment of artillery units, including anti-aircraft. My Adjutant-General's branch, in conjunction with the Adjutant-General's branch at the War Office, had in hand plans for the more economical use of man-power, the elimination of fit men from sedentary or base duties and the reduction of tradesmen in War Establishments. Investigations made by the War Office, which had my full co-operation, were directed towards a more economical and more flexible system of replacement and repair of vehicles and equipment in the Force.

The Royal Air Force.

13. On 15th January, 1940, Air Marshal A.S. Barratt had assumed command of the British Air Force in France, including the Air Component which, however, was to remain under my operational control. Under this arrangement, in my opinion, the control of available air forces was better allocated to meet the needs not only of the British but also of the French Army for whom considerable aerial reconnaissance was being carried out. The development of the Allied Central Air Bureau and of its communications to the headquarters of higher formations in France and to the Royal Air Force at home, was likewise to prove its worth in the days to come as an organisation for co-ordinating information and requests for air action.

At the same time I felt that the resources of the Air Component would prove insufficient for the requirements of the Force during operations; so long, therefore, as this state of affairs existed it was of prime importance that the machinery for obtaining the allotment of additional bomber and fighter support should be as simple and as swift in operation as it could be made.

Throughout the period, construction of new aerodromes, landing grounds and communications for the British Air Force in France was proceeding as fast as resources would permit, concrete runways being constructed in the early part of the year until the season allowed for the sowing of grass. Upwards of 10,000 men were employed on this work, and forty-seven aerodromes and satellites (including 19 new aerodromes) were under development or construction. By 15th May eight of the nineteen new aerodromes were capable of use, and at least 50,000 tons of concrete had been laid. Constructional work was also undertaken on behalf of the Air Ministry at other R.A.F. installations in central France.

The Dyle and Escaut Plans.

14. Very shortly after the arrival of the B.E.F. in their positions on the Belgian frontier I had been invited by General Georges, commanding the French Front of the North East, under whose Command I was, to study the part to be played by the B.E.F. in the event of an advance into Holland and Belgium, or into Belgium alone. The question of such an advance was one of high policy with a political as well as a military aspect; it was therefore not for me to comment on it. My responsibilities were confined to ensuring that the orders issued by the French for the employment of the British Expeditionary Force were capable of being carried out; and indeed events proved that the orders issued for this operation were well within the capacity of the Force.

The subject presented difficulties greatly complicated by the policy of neutrality to which the Belgian Government were wedded. The French authorities were never in a position to obtain reliable and accurate details of the plans of the Belgian General Staff for the defence of their country in the event of an invasion by Germany; staff conversations were out of the question, yet plans had to be framed in such a way that they could be put into instant operation in the event of Belgium asking for military assistance from France or Great Britain when invasion had taken place or was imminent. Such slender contact as existed between the British and Belgian Military authorities was maintained through the Military Attaché at His Majesty's Embassy at Brussels and General Van Overstraeten, Military Adviser to the King of the Belgians.

15. Three alternative plans were decided on by the French High Command during October and November 1939, and I had agreed with General Georges on the part to be played in each of them by the B.E.F.

The first alternative was to occupy the frontier defences, pushing forward mobile troops to the line of the Escaut, while the French 7ᵗʰ Army on my left were to delay the enemy on the line of the Messines Ridge and the Yser Canal. This plan was soon discarded in favour of the second alternative, which was to secure and hold the line of the Escaut itself, from the point at which it crosses the frontier at Maulde northwards to the neighbourhood of Ghent where it was intended to effect a junction with Belgian forces.

Later, however, as information became available regarding the defences of the Belgian Army, and its readiness for war, the French High Command formed the opinion that it would be safe to count on the Belgian defence holding out for some days on the Eastern frontier, and the Albert Canal. It was also ascertained that the Belgians were preparing a *de Cointet* antitank obstacle running southwards from Wavre towards Namur.

The line of the river Dyle was from the military point of view a better one than that of the Escaut. It was shorter, it afforded greater depth and its northern portion was inundated. In addition, it represented smaller enemy occupation of Belgian territory.

On the other hand, it involved the B.E.F. in a forward move of some sixty miles against time, while it also necessitated the holding by the French on our right of the Gembloux gap which contains no natural anti-tank obstacle. This plan was twice discussed by General Georges with me on 13ᵗʰ October at my headquarters at Le Cauroy and again on 16ᵗʰ November at Folembray the headquarters of the French First Group of Armies; on this occasion there were also present General Billotte, who commanded the Army Group, and Generals Blanchard and Corap, Commanding the French 1ˢᵗ and 9ᵗʰ Armies. At this conference it was agreed that the frontage of the B.E.F. on the Dyle position was to be from Wavre to Louvain, both places inclusive, and a formal instruction to this effect was issued to me by General Georges on the following day. From this time onward, Commanders and Staffs were studying simultaneously two alternative plans for advances to the Dyle or the Escaut; these became known as plans D and E.

Both these plans were worked out in the greatest detail, and orders and instructions kept up to date as new divisions arrived and the role of divisions changed.

The Escaut plan was by far the simpler of the two; it involved sending armoured car reconnaissances to the river Dendre to be relieved by divisional cavalry, who were later, if necessary, to fight a delaying action backwards to the Escaut; demolitions were provided for on both rivers; for the remainder of the force, however, the advance appeared likely to be an easy one, well within a day's march on foot. The Dyle plan, on the other hand, involved an advance of some sixty miles, carried out at a time when every moment was of value over roads not previously reconnoitred, perhaps crowded with refugees moving counter to the allied armies. Much, too, depended on the resistance which the Belgians, and perhaps the Dutch, were able to offer to the enemy, who at such a time would certainly be making every effort to pierce the line of the Meuse and the Albert Canal.

16. The plans made in advance for the advance to the Dyle position actually worked to schedule in almost all respects. It may therefore be convenient to summarise them here.

The Allied forces were to advance to the line Namur-Wavre-Louvain-Antwerp, of which the B.E.F. Sector extended from Wavre to Louvain, both inclusive. On our right was to be the French 1st Army (General d'Armee Blanchard) under whose command was the French Cavalry Corps, and whose task it was to delay the arrival of the enemy on the Dyle position and to block with its main forces the Gembloux gap, with the Cavalry Corps pushed forward to the line Eghezee (8 miles north of Namur)-Tirlemont. On our left the French 7th Army (General d'Armee Giraud) was to advance to the general area Antwerp-Ghent, with the object of supporting Belgian resistance north of Louvain. The plans of this Army included a possible advance into

Holland as far as the line Turnhout-Breda, and this was actually carried out. It had been ascertained that a portion of the Belgian Army, if forced to withdraw from their frontier defences would come into line on the left of the B.E.F. on the general line from Louvain exclusive, thence northward to the fortified area of Antwerp, known as the National Redoubt.

The British front was to be occupied initially with 1st Corps (Lieutenant-General M.G.H. Barker, who had recently taken over command from General Sir John Dill), on a two-division front, on the right, and 2nd Corps (Lieutenant-General A. F. Brooke, now Sir Alan Brooke) on the left, on a front initially of one division.

The advance was to be made in four periods. In the first, 12th Royal Lancers (Armoured Cars) were to move to a general line some eight miles beyond the Dyle in observation of the approaches from the east; they were to be relieved by cavalry regiments of 1st and 2nd Corps when they arrived.

Behind them were to come, from right to left, 2nd Division (Major-General H.C. Loyd) and 1st Division (Major-General Hon. H.R.L.G. Alexander) of 1st Corps, and 3rd Division (Major-General B. L. Montgomery) of 2nd Corps. The whole of the move of these three divisions was to be made by motor transport, and troop carrying companies were allotted to Corps in such a way as to complete the move in 90 hours.

At the same time 44th Division was to march to an area north-west of Audenarde, with a view to organising the defence of the Escaut in this area.

Movement in the first phase was to be continuous by day and night. The French had decided to restrict the movements of their main bodies to the hours of darkness, but I judged the time factor to be of paramount importance and accepted the risk that our air support might be insufficient to prevent enemy interference with the move. Events proved that the risk was justifiable.

In the second period, to be completed by the end of the sixth day, 48th Division (Major-General A.F.A.N. Thorne) and 4th Division (Major-General D. G. Johnson, V.C.) were to move by march route and motor transport into 1st and 2nd Corps reserve respectively, while 1st Army Tank Brigade consisting of two battalions was to move chiefly by rail into 1st Corps area.

The third period was to be completed by the tenth day, and included the movement of 50th Division to 2nd Corps reserve, while 4th Division moved into the line on the right of 3rd Division.

The fourth period included the forward movement of 3rd Corps. 5th Division (Major-General H. E. Franklyn) was to move to positions in G.H.Q. reserve, along the river Dendre, north and south of Grammont; 42nd and 44th Divisions to the line of the river Escaut around Tournai and to the south of Audenarde respectively, to organise bridgehead positions pending orders for a further advance.

Detailed instructions had also been issued for the preparation of defences on the three river lines of the Dyle, Dendre and Escaut, as also for the necessary demolitions and inundations. Special arrangements had been made for the control of traffic, including refugees for whom routes had been allotted; definite bodies of troops were detailed for these tasks.

The Belgian Anti-Tank obstacle
17. Late in April and early in May, I received reports regarding the siting of the Belgian anti-tank obstacle; it appeared that, without informing either the French High Command or myself, they had sited the obstacle much further to the east than had originally been planned, namely on the line Namur-Perwez-Louvain: furthermore the obstacle was not as yet by any means completed. The matter was discussed with General Georges.

On the British front, the river Dyle was so far superior as an anti-tank obstacle to any artificial work further east which the Belgians might be preparing that I had no hesitation in urging adherence to the existing plan for the defence of the Dyle position.

On the front of the French 1st Army the situation was different: the absence of a natural obstacle forced them to rely on that prepared by the Belgians. To clear the matter up, information was demanded as to the true site of the artificial obstacle. These negotiations were begun through our Military Attaché on 8th May, but they were not destined to be concluded.

OPERATIONS—FIRST PHASE
(10th–16th MAY)

Belgium calls on Allies for assistance: advance to the River Dyle by British and French Armies: the Belgian anti-tank obstacle is found to be sited further forward than had been expected. The enemy penetrates the front of French 9th Army and crosses the Meuse. Action by Royal Air Force. General Billotte appointed to co-ordinate action of British, French and Belgians. The Dutch lay down arms.

10th May—The enemy invades Holland and Belgium.
18. The tension which had been increasing during April had lessened somewhat during the early days of May; during this period I had received reports of enemy activity from several sources of varying degrees of reliability, culminating in a report from the Hague, but it was not until the night of 9th–10th May that information was received of exceptional activity on the frontiers of Luxembourg, Belgium and Holland.

The weather was set fair, and with the exception of some heavy thunderstorms which had no effect on operations, remained so to the end of the month. At about 4.30 a.m. on 10th May, enemy aircraft appeared over my headquarters at Arras and bombs were dropped on aerodromes in the neighbourhood and on a number of towns including Doullens and Abbeville. At 5.30 a.m., a message was received from my mission with General Georges ordering "Alertes 1, 2 and 3," namely, instant readiness to move into Belgium. I at once sought, and obtained, the release of the 5th Division from War Office reserve, and henceforward it was employed under my orders. At about 6.15 a.m. I received instructions to put Plan D into effect.

It was ascertained that 12th Royal Lancers could be ready to cross the frontier at 1 p.m., and accordingly I laid down this time as zero hour.

At 1 p.m. I opened my command post at Wahagnies, midway between Douai and Lille. 1st and 2nd Corps experienced some delay in moving, due largely to the fact that owing to the short notice received, preliminary moves of transport had not taken place; apart from this, moves on this day proceeded according to plan; very little interference was experienced either from enemy aircraft or refugees and 12th Lancers reached the Dyle unopposed at 10.30 p.m.

The French armies on our light and left were reported as advancing on time.

The Belgian population received the allied armies in the most cordial manner, and in particular the leading troops were loudly cheered.

Operations between 11th and 15th May.
19. On 11th May, enemy air action increased somewhat, but did not interfere with the forward movement of troops, and during the afternoon and evening, the leading infantry brigades reached the Dyle, refugee traffic being handled successfully. The original arrangements, of which the Belgian Government were aware, included the use by the B.E.F. of roads passing through the northern and southern outskirts of Brussels, but not through the centre of the city. A series of requests was however received to discontinue the use of these roads on the ground that Brussels had been declared an open town and that British troop movements would prejudice its safety, but no adequate alternative routes to the Dyle were available and I was therefore

compelled to adhere to the original plan of using the outskirts of the city.

The 3rd Division, on arrival, reported that a Belgian division was holding the bridgehead at Louvain, although I had assumed that this should be a British responsibility. 2nd Corps therefore took up a narrow front on their right with a strong reserve in rear of Louvain.

5th Division, which was training in the area south-west of Amiens, was ordered to proceed by march route so as to shorten the move by motor transport in a later phase, and later occupied a position on the Senne.

The news from the Belgian army, of which King Leopold had assumed command on the outbreak of war, was not good. Belgian cyclist troops from east of the Meuse were falling back on Huy. At Maastricht, it was reported that they had been forestalled by enemy action from the rear and had been unable to demolish important bridges over the Albert Canal and the Meuse across which: the enemy had begun to move. Air bombing was requested and was extremely effective, but could not altogether deny the passage of the water obstacles to the enemy. On my right the French Cavalry Corps had reached their position on the line Huy-Hannut-Tirlemont and reconnoitred the Belgian anti-tank obstacle. They reported that, as I had supposed, there was no effective obstacle on the Gembloux line and that the obstacle on the Perwez line was not only unfinished but badly sited on a forward slope. I thereupon conveyed to General Georges a confirmation of my objections to pushing forward so as to make use of the obstacle in its unfinished state, notwithstanding the Belgians' anxiety that I should do so. Later that day I was informed that he had decided that the main line of resistance was to be on the Gembloux line as planned, but that the French were to push out advanced troops to the line of the obstacle. He expressed the hope that the B.E.F. would conform, and 1st and 2nd Corps accordingly reconnoitred the anti-tank obstacles reported to exist round the forest of Meerdael with a view to pushing forward detachments with anti-tank guns. They found them complete only in places.

20. The first phase of Plan D was successfully completed by 12th May, and the French 1st Army on my right then accelerated the programme governing their forward movement by moving by day as well as by night. The enemy progress across the Albert Canal had up to now been relatively small, due to a successful counter-attack by the French Cavalry Corps at St. Trend, but larger concentrations were now reported north of the Albert Canal. Disquieting news was received from the Ardennes, where a German thrust was reported as developing on the front of the French 9th Army, with at least two armoured divisions.

On this date I requested the War Office to expedite the despatch of the 1st Armoured Division to the greatest extent possible. I also asked that they should be shipped to the nearest available port and loaded tactically with a view to operations as soon as possible after landing.

The day was one of great activity in the air, and afforded great opportunities for the Royal Air Force to impede the enemy advance; but such opportunities were of a fleeting character, since the enemy established strong anti-aircraft defences soon after his arrival, particularly in towns at which roads converged. Tactical reconnaissance became virtually impossible without fighter support, and the demands made on the fighter group of the Air Component were extremely heavy. They had been met with unfailing skill and courage, and with marked success, but by now the group was reduced to some 50 aircraft, and although I had asked for four fresh squadrons from home, only one had arrived. In three days' operations, the British Air Force in France had firm reports of the destruction of 101 enemy aircraft, mostly fighters, against a loss of 78 of our own.

That afternoon a conference was held at the Chateau Casteau, near Mons which was attended by the King of the Belgians, General Van Overstraeten, M. Daladier, Generals Georges and Billotte, and my Chief of the General Staff (Lieutenant-General H.R. Pownall), as my representative in my absence. The primary object of the conference was to achieve some measure of co-ordination in the Belgian theatre of war. General Billotte's command included the French 1st and 7th Armies, between which lay the Belgian Army under the independent command of their King, and the B.E.F. which, though under the command of General Georges, was not under that of General Billotte. Whatever the nature of the operations, a common doctrine was clearly necessary and when General Georges enquired if the King of the Belgians and I would be prepared to accept co-ordination by General Billotte as his representative, General Pownall said he was sure that I would agree. The King of the Belgians likewise agreed.

21. On 13th May I moved my Command Post forward to Renaix; no event of major importance occurred during the day, but some small infantry attacks developed on the British sector. These were easily held. Movements of the main bodies of the French 1st and 7th Armies continued in accordance with their plans, and units of the latter were by now north of Antwerp on the Dutch border. It was, however, becoming increasingly evident that they would be unable to prevent the enemy occupation of Walcheren and Zuid Beveland which was developing from the north-east.

During the day and the following night the Belgian forces were in process of withdrawing their northern forces to the general line Louvain-Antwerp, and the Staff of the Belgian G.Q.G. expressed concern lest the simultaneous withdrawal of their Cavalry Corps and that of the French, north-west and south-west from their junction point at Tirlemont, would create a gap. There appeared to me to be little danger, but nevertheless

I ordered 12th Lancers to watch the situation, assisted if need be by divisional cavalry regiments.

22. On 14th May I went to Brussels, where at 12 noon I met the Commanders of 1st and 2nd Corps at the British Embassy. The Commander of 2nd Corps reported that the Belgian 1st Corps was now reforming in 4th Division area. I also discussed the organisation of the second position on the Senne canal and of a Corps reserve line east of Brussels. 5th and 48th Divisions were ordered to reconnoitre the Senne position on 15th May. That afternoon at 3 p.m. I visited H.M. the King of the Belgians and General Van Overstraeten and reached agreement that the Belgian 1st Corps should be withdrawn from the area of 2nd Corps and that the left boundary of the B.E.F. should be adjusted so as to allow the Belgians the use of the road Vilvorde-Alost for this purpose. I also stressed the importance of having fresh Belgian troops established early in position north of Louvain to continue the British line covering Brussels.

Further serious news came from the south where the enemy had crossed the Meuse between Sedan and Mézières, and further north he was reported to be surrounding the fortress of St. Héribert (4 miles S.S.W. of Namur).

The French Cavalry Corps on my right had on the previous day received orders to retire to the Perwez position whence they subsequently withdrew, according to plan, to the main position running through Gembloux.

At the request of Air Marshal Barratt I placed at his disposal for use on the French front three squadrons of fighters which I had only recently received in response to an urgent appeal to the Secretary of State for War.

23. On 15th May the Dutch Army laid down its arms; the immediate effect of this on the operations of the B.E.F. was small, for the British forces operating in Holland had at no time been under my command. I anticipated, however, that this would come as a shock to the Belgian Army.

The French 7th Army withdrew its advanced formations to the neighbourhood of Antwerp and on this day ordered divisions to move across my rear to fill the gap created further south. This move, however, did not take place till some three days later when it was accomplished, thanks to efficient traffic control, with little delay to our own movements.

On this day (15th May) I established a command post at Lennick St. Quentin, 6 miles west of Brussels. On the British front, the day passed quietly on the whole, 1st Corps was not attacked in strength; 3rd Division of 2nd Corps was attacked north-west of Louvain and its forward positions were penetrated, but a counterattack successfully restored the original line. There was considerable enemy bombing of rearward areas during the day, and the movement of refugees became increasingly difficult to control. This was, in part, due to the bombing of Tournai and other towns on the routes and to the French decision to close the frontier to pedestrian and horsed traffic. Despite my requests, made as early as 10th May, the Belgian authorities had done nothing to restrict the use of private motor cars or the sale of petrol.

During the day I received a request that I should take over part of the front held by the French division on my right. To meet this request I placed under the orders of this division a brigade of 48th Division; this step proved necessary since at about 6 p.m. the enemy had penetrated the French front, thus threatening the right of 2nd Division. By this tune, however, 48th Division, less one brigade, was in position in 1st Corps reserve behind 2nd Division, and I agreed with the commander of 1st Corps that the withdrawal of his right should take place to the River Lasne to join up with the French left. This movement was carried out on the night of the 15/16 May, closely followed by the enemy.

By the night of 15th May the movements envisaged in Plan D were all running ahead of schedule. 4th Division was moving into

Corps reserve behind 3rd Division; 5th Division was moving on to the Senne in place of 50th Division as originally planned, and the latter was now moving to G.H.Q. reserve along the River Dendre.

OPERATIONS—SECOND PHASE
(17th–26th MAY)
Withdrawal to the Escaut decided on; the threat to Arras and to the right flank; formation of Macforce and deployment of 23rd Division on the Canal du Nord. The enemy reaches the Somme and cuts communications with the Base; Calais and Boulogne invested: the administrative position. The organisation of the Canal line. Alternative lines discussed with French and Belgians, resulting in further withdrawal from the Escaut to the Frontier defences and fresh plans for attacks southwards in conjunction with French main forces. 5th and 50th Divisions counter-attack on 21st May. A further attack in conjunction with French planned for 26th May: this plan is abandoned owing to penetration of Belgian line on the Lys.
The beginning of the withdrawal (16th–17th May)

24. By 16th May, it became clear that a prolonged defence of the Dyle position was impracticable. The French 1st Army on my right were unlikely to make good the ground lost on the previous day, notwithstanding the support I had given them in the air and on the ground, and a further withdrawal seemed likely to be forced on them by events in the south.

On the other hand there had been no serious attack on the Belgian positions on my left; nevertheless, any withdrawal from our present positions would of necessity involve a withdrawal by the Belgian Army in the course of which Brussels, and probably Antwerp also, would be abandoned to the enemy.

Very early on 16th May therefore, I sent a representative to General Billotte who was co-ordinating the movements of the British, French and Belgian Forces; I asked that, if he intended to withdraw, he should let me know the policy and the timings at once, especially as the first bound back to the Senne canals involved a march of some fifteen to twenty miles.

At about 10 a.m. I received from him orders for a withdrawal to the Escaut, and for the occupation of the positions along that fiver originally planned. The operation was to begin that night (16/17 May), one day being spent on the Senne and one day on the Dendre positions; thus the Escaut would be reached on the night of 18/19 May, though the French orders did not rule out the possibility of staying for longer than one day on each bound.

That evening, I held a co-ordinating conference at 1st Corps Headquarters as a result of which I ordered 5th Division, which was on the way to join 2nd Corps, to the line of the Senne in 1st Corps reserve. Two brigades of 46th Division[24] which had been moved up from the Lines of Communication for the protection of vulnerable points, were ordered to relieve units of 1st and 2nd Corps on protection and traffic control of main routes in Belgium. Railheads, which had been advanced on 13th May to the general line Enghien-Ninove, were now moved back across the frontier.

During the night 16/17th May the withdrawal to the Senne positions began, and was successfully completed by the afternoon of the 17th. Some enemy tanks and motor cycle units had been reported on the right flank of 1st Corps, west of the forest of Soignies, and as a precaution, part of the 1st Army Tank Brigade, which had started to withdraw for entrainment, was turned about to meet the thrust.

By the time the tanks reached their entraining stations railway difficulties prevented the trucks being moved, and the remainder of the move was carried out by road; this gave rise to inevitable mechanical trouble later on.

By the early morning of 17th May the situation in the south had become grave, and enemy armoured and mobile forces were

---

24 One of the three divisions sent to France for pioneer duties.

reported to have crossed the Oise. At St. Quentin the situation was obscure, and though by this time General Giraud, lately commanding the French 7th Army, had been ordered to take command of the forces in that region, it was clear from reports and from visits of liaison officers that he had not yet succeeded in establishing effective control. A gap of at least twenty miles existed south of the Forest of Mormal in which there appeared to be no organised resistance. Later in the day information was received from the French that ten enemy armoured divisions were engaged in the battle.

During the whole of this period, communication with my liaison officer at General Georges' Headquarters was maintained so as to keep in touch with events as they developed. However, I received no information though this channel of any steps it was proposed to take to close the gap, which might have affected my own command.

It was not till later, on the night of 19th/20th May, that General Billotte informed me of the action which was being taken to this end by the French Armies in the south.

The defence of rearward areas.

25. Rear G.H.Q. at Arras had intensified the precautions already being taken against sabotage and air landing units, but on the early morning of 17th May a telegram was received from General Georges ordering 23rd Division to move at once to occupy the line of the Canal du Nord, on a frontage of fifteen miles from Ruyalcourt (10 miles north of Péronne) to Arleux (6 miles south of Douai).

The division, which, like the 12th and 46th Divisions had joined the B.E.F. for work in rearward areas, consisted of eight battalions only with divisional engineers, but no artillery, and signals and administrative units in no more than skeleton form. Its armament and transport was on a much reduced scale and training was far from complete.

Nevertheless, troops of these three divisions fought and marched continuously for a fortnight, and proved, were proof needed, that they were composed of soldiers who, despite their inexperience and lack of equipment, could hold their own with a better found and more numerous enemy.

23rd Division moved to their positions during 17th May; they were provided with about forty field, anti-tank, and anti-aircraft guns from ordnance reserves.

The enemy break-through was now offering an imminent threat to rear G.H.Q., to the communications over the Somme at Amiens and Abbeville, and to the base areas. To meet this, every available man and weapon was collected and orders were issued to the commander, Lines of Communication Area, for the remainder of 12th and 46th Divisions to be despatched to the forward zone. One brigade (36th Infantry Brigade of 12th Division) arrived during the day, and the leading battalion was despatched with four field guns to cover the north-western exits from Péronne, while engineer parties, organised by the Commander, G.H.Q. Troops, were sent to prepare for demolition the crossings over the Canal du Nord between the river Somme and the right of 23rd Division at Ruyalcourt. The remainder of 36th Infantry Brigade were moved forward to Albert, and the other two brigades of 12th Division ordered to the Abbeville area. These latter, however, arrived too late to come under my effective command, and their operations on the Somme were carried out under the Commander Lines of Communication Area.

Elsewhere in the area between Corps rear boundaries and the Somme, local defence schemes were put into operation under the orders of the Commanders of G.H.Q. Troops and of "X" Lines of Communication Sub-Area.[25] Few if any of these units

---

25 This Sub-Area had been formed to deal with units which, remained in the old G.H.Q. and Corps areas when the B.E.F. moved into Belgium.

or their commanders had any experience in fighting, but their determination was beyond all praise.

A mobile bath unit, for example, took part in the defence of St. Pol, while, both now and later, the General Construction Companies of the Royal Engineers, and many units of the Royal Army Service Corps, set to work to place their localities in a state of defence and manned them until they were overwhelmed, relieved or ordered to withdraw. Wherever possible, transport was collected or requisitioned to enable parachute detachments to be dealt with.

These many small delaying actions all contributed to gain the time required for the withdrawal of the main forces.

The defence of the town of Arras itself was entrusted to the O.C. 1st Bn. Welsh Guards who had under his command some units of the Royal Engineers, an Overseas Defence battalion (9th West Yorks), and various details including an improvised tank squadron.

Orders were issued for all administrative troops not required for defence to move forthwith north of a line Orchies-Lens-Frévent.

At the same time to guard against a more immediate threat to my right flank a force was organised consisting of 127th Infantry Brigade of 42nd Division, 1st Army Tank Brigade, a Field Artillery Regiment and the Hopkinson Mission,[26] all under the command of Major-General F. N. Mason-MacFarlane, my Director of Military Intelligence. The force was known as Macforce and its task was to cover the crossings over the Scarpe between Raches (3 miles N.E. of Douai) and St. Amand. It began to assemble at Orchies on the afternoon of 17th May.

---

26 The Hopkinson Mission, under the Command of Lieut-Colonel G.F. Hopkinson, had been formed to secure certain information for the R.A.F. and for G.H.Q. immediately on entry into Belgium.

Withdrawal to the Escaut begun.

26. It had now to be decided whether or not the withdrawal from the Senne to the Dendre was to begin on the night of 17/18 May, and the situation in the South was such that I felt that to spend a day on the Senne would be to risk being outflanked on the right and so imperil the force under my command to no good purpose. General Billotte had issued orders for withdrawal to the Dendre that night, but I had also seen an order from General Georges which envisaged remaining on the Senne for a further twenty-four hours. I therefore sent a liaison officer to General Billotte to represent my views. In the result, General Billotte's orders stood confirmed.

By 4 p.m. on 17th May therefore 1st and 2nd Corps were on the Senne with 5th, 1st and 4th Divisions in line right to left. 48th Division was covering the right flank from Enghien to Lembecq. 50th Division was on the Dendre, to which line 2nd and 3rd Divisions were now withdrawing, whilst 3 Corps was in position on the Escaut with 42nd Division (less one infantry brigade) and 44th Division.

27. On 18th May I held a conference at the headquarters of 1st Corps at which were settled the details of the withdrawal to the Escaut. This line was to be held with six divisions, right to left 1st Corps (48th and 42nd Divisions, less one infantry brigade, with 2nd Division in reserve), 2nd Corps (1st and 3rd Divisions with 50th Division in reserve), 3rd Corps (4th and 44th Divisions), on a front from the bridge over the Escaut at Bléharies to Audenarde, both inclusive 5th Division was in G.H.Q. reserve.

There was little pressure during the day on the British front or on that of the Belgians to the North. Owing to the late arrival of orders the Belgian Army had started their withdrawal after the B.E.F.; they had therefore asked for and received protection to their right flank at Brusseghem up to 7 a.m. and Assche up to 8 a.m. on 18th May. On withdrawal they effected a junction with the B.E.F. on the Dendre at Alost.

Southward from their junction with the B.E.F. the French line ran through Mons and Maubeuge, and enemy tanks were attacking the front of the French Corps on my immediate right. Enemy air action had by now intensified on the front of the B.E.F. and continuous fighter support was necessary during the hours of daylight, both to enable our reconnaissances to take place and to hold off enemy bombers. The enemy did not confine his attention to troops but attacked the long columns of refugees which continued to move westwards.

The position on the Canal du Nord.

28. The position on the Canal du Nord had caused some anxiety, partly on account of contradictory orders received. Shortly after orders had been issued on 17th May for the occupation of the position by 23rd Division, an order was received from G.Q.G. allotting to the B.E.F. the sector Péronne-Ruyalcourt instead of the sector Ruyalcourt-Arleux which was now to be occupied by the French. It was not however practicable to move the 23rd Division again and G.Q.G. were informed to this effect. Yet, by next morning no French troops had appeared either on the right of 23rd Division or to relieve them. Later in the day, however, an order was received by which the commander of the French 2nd Region was ordered to fill the gap. Enquiries by a liaison officer at Amiens, where the staff of the French 7th Army was in process of taking over from the 2nd Region, established that no troops would be likely to arrive for twenty-four hours at least.

By the afternoon, however, some enemy had reached Péronne, and were in contact with 36th Infantry Brigade.

On this day Major-General R. L. Petre, commanding the 12th Division, was given command of the troops engaged on this flank, namely 23rd Division, 36th Infantry Brigade and the garrison of Arras.[27]

---

27 Major-General Petre's command was known as Petreforce.

In the meantime an order issued by the French First Group of Armies had laid down the boundary between the French 1st Army and the B.E.F. through Maulde, Orchies, Raches and Hénin-Liétard. Arras was thus excluded from the zone of the B.E.F., but its defence was necessarily continued by British troops. All troops not required for defence left on the 19th, including rear G.H.Q. which moved in two echelons to Hazebrouck and Boulogne in accordance with plans prepared on 17th May when the threat to Arras became serious.

On the evening of 18th May I moved back my command post from Renaix to its previous location at Wahagnies.

Moves of the Royal Air Force.

29. On this day also, the bulk of the Advanced Air Striking Force moved from the neighbourhood of Rheims to Central France and the Air Component moved one of their main operational aerodromes from Poix to Abbeville. On the evening of 19th May enemy action obliged them to evacuate this aerodrome also. The Air Officer Commanding the Air Component then moved his headquarters to England, but an advanced landing ground was maintained at Merville until 22nd May.

From the 21st May onwards all arrangements for air co-operation with the B.E.F. were made by the War Office in conjunction with the Air Ministry at home. The air liaison work was carried out in England at Hawkinge and the targets selected in accordance with telephone or telegraphic requests from the B.E.F. so long as communications remained open, supplemented by information received from the Royal Air Force, and other sources.

Alternative plans considered.

30. On the night of 18/19 May, the 1st, 2nd and 3rd Corps completed their withdrawal to the line of the Escaut without interference, and prepared to defend the line of the river. Soon after arrival, however, the level of the water became dangerously

low, at places less than three feet deep. It looked, therefore, as if, apart from the unusually dry weather, some of the sluices in the neighbourhood of Valenciennes had been closed in order to produce inundations in the low-lying ground in that area, even if at the expense of the water on the front of the B.E.F.

The enemy had, during the previous day, penetrated as far as Amiens, and rail communication with the bases was severed at that point. Communications by road and rail over the Sorrime at Abbeville were still holding on 19th May and the town was being placed in a state of defence with such resources as were available, mainly, units of 12th Division. However, there was little doubt that enemy armoured forces in that area, which at the time I estimated at five armoured divisions, would shortly break through to the coast.

The force could then no longer be supplied through the ports south of the Somme, and the great bulk of the reserves, which were in the rearward areas, would shortly cease to be available to the force for the purposes of maintenance or replacement. Several days' reserve had, however, for some time past been maintained north of the Somme.

The prospect of securing the reinforcement of the Armoured Division had likewise become remote. I had been advised that two Armoured Brigades, of this division would disembark at Havre on 16th May, and were to concentrate at Bolbec, and I had therefore sent instructions by the hand of a staff officer to the Commander (Major-General R. Evans). He was to move the leading brigade on disembarkation with all speed to secure, the crossings of the Somme west of Amiens, from Picquigny to Pont Rémy, both inclusive, with a view to the concentration of the remaining brigade behind the Somme and the move of his division to join the main body of the B.E.F. However, in the meantime, orders had been issued locally to concentrate the Division south of the Seine, and the plan to cross the Somme and join the B.E.F. proved impossible to execute. The division therefore remained in the Lines of Communication Area and never came under my effective command.

About midnight on the 18th/19th May, General Billotte came to see me, and gave me an account of the situation as he saw it. He also told me of the measures which were being taken to restore the situation on the front of the French 9th Army, though clearly he had little hope that they would be effective. Reports from the liaison officers with French formations were likewise not encouraging; in particular I was unable to verify that the French had enough reserves at their disposal south of the gap to enable them to stage counter-attacks sufficiently strong to warrant the expectation that the gap would be closed.

Thus, in my opinion, there was an imminent danger of the forces in the north-eastern area, that is to say the French forces next to the sea, the Belgian Army, the B.E.F. and the bulk of the French 1st Army on our right, being irretrievably cut off from the main French forces in the south.

There were three alternative courses of action open to the northern forces under General Billotte: first, in the event of the gap being closed by successful counter-attacks made simultaneously from north and south it would in theory be possible to maintain the line of the Escaut, or at any rate the frontier defences, and thence southwards on one or other of the canal lines.

Secondly, there was the possibility of a withdrawal to the line of the Somme as far as its mouth. This plan had the attraction that we should be falling back on our lines of communication and if it was successful would not entail the abandonment of large quantities of equipment. It would obviously be unwelcome to the Belgians who would be faced with the alternatives of withdrawing with us and abandoning Belgian soil, fighting on a perimeter of their own, or seeking an armistice.

So far as I am aware, the French High Command had never suggested such a movement up to that date and it is doubtful whether even had they, decided on immediate withdrawal as soon as the French 9th Army front on the Meuse had been penetrated, there would ever have been sufficient time for the troops in the north to conform.

Thirdly there was the possibility of withdrawal north-westwards or northwards towards the Channel ports, making use of the successive river and canal lines, and of holding a defensive perimeter there, at any rate sufficiently long to enable the force to be withdrawn, preferably in concert with the French and Belgians. I realised that this course was in theory a last alternative, as it would involve the departure of the B.E.F. from the theatre of war at a time when the French might need all the support which Britain could give them. It involved the virtual certainty that even if the excellent port facilities at Dunkirk continued to be available, it would be necessary to abandon all the heavier guns and much of the vehicles and equipment. Nevertheless, I felt that in the circumstances there might be no other course open to me. It was therefore only prudent to consider what the adoption of such a plan might entail. On this day therefore at about 1.30 p.m. the Chief of the General Staff telephoned to the Director of Military Operations and Plans at the War Office and discussed this situation with him.

The Position of the French 1st Army and the British right flank reinforced.

31. The French 1st Army had by 19th May completed its withdrawal and was in touch with the right of 1st Corps. On the night of 19/20th May they took up positions on the line of the Escaut as far south as Bouchain; but at that point, instead of continuing to hold that river towards Cambrai (which according to my information was not held in strength by the enemy) they had drawn back westwards along the river Sensée. Thus in the quadrilateral Maulde-Valenciennes-Arleux-Douai, some nineteen miles by ten, there was assembled the bulk of the French

1st Army, amounting to three Corps of two divisions and two divisions in reserve—a total of eight divisions. The Commander of the French 3rd Corps, General de la Laurencie, remained that night in close touch with General Mason-MacFarlane, at the headquarters of Macforce.

Further west the French Cavalry Corps was assembling at Oppy, north-east of Arras.

None of these forces were being seriously pressed at this stage, but since the enemy had already penetrated, so deeply further south, I felt it necessary, without more delay, to strengthen the dispositions for the defence of what had become the bastion of Arras. It was also necessary to secure crossings westwards from the right of Macforce, along the line Carvin—La Bassée.

I therefore ordered 50th Division, then in G.H.Q. reserve, to send one Infantry Brigade (25th) to take up positions on the Canal on the line La Bassée-Carvin under the command of Macforce. The remainder of the division was moved that night (19/20th) to the same area, and was thus suitably placed for the counter attack in which they took part on 21st May.

I also ordered 12th Lancers with a field battery to move to Arras and carry out necessary reconnaissances south and south-westwards, and to gain touch with the outlying portions of Petreforce.

Arras was heavily bombed for the first time on 19th May, but 23rd Division, though in an exposed position, was not seriously attacked. However, at 5 a.m., 6th Royal West Kent, of 36th Infantry Brigade, on the Canal du Nord north-west of Péronne, had been attacked by enemy tanks and had been withdrawn to Sailly on the road to Albert.

General Petre that night issued orders for 23rd Division to withdraw from the Canal du Nord to the line of the Grinchon river south of Arras to join up at La Herlière with 36th Infantry Brigade which was to hold a line thence to Doullens. 23rd Division was, however, caught by enemy aircraft when embossed and finally occupied posts on the line of the Scarpe for some six miles East of Arras.

Thus, by the evening of 19th May, the situation was somewhat relieved in that the defensive flank had begun to take shape. On the other hand, the character of the operation had now radically altered with the arrival of German troops in Amiens. The picture was now no longer that of a line bent or temporarily broken, but of a besieged fortress. To raise such a siege, a relieving force must be sent from the south and to meet this force a sortie on the part of the defenders was indicated.

The attack of 5th and 50th Divisions.
32. On 20th May, the breach South of Arras deepened and widened. From indications received during the day the enemy armoured forces appeared to be directed on two main objectives; one down the valley of the Somme on Abbeville, the other by Hesdin and Montreuil, doubtless making for the Channel Ports. 12th Lancers, early in the day, reported tanks from the direction of Cambrai approaching Arras, where they were held off by the Welsh Guards; a strong request for bomber support was therefore made through the War Office to the Air Ministry. Later in the day enemy tanks were reported to be ten miles west of Arras, and all endeavours by 12th Lancers to reach Doullens had failed. By 6 p.m. they were back on the line Arras-St. Pol.

Early in the morning General Sir Edmund Ironside, the Chief of the Imperial General Staff arrived at G.H.Q.; he brought with him instructions from the Cabinet that the B.E.F. was to move southwards upon Amiens, attacking all enemy forces encountered and to take station on the left of the French Army. He was also to inform General Billotte and the Belgian command, making it clear to the latter that their best chance was to. move that night between the B.E.F. and the coast.

Similar information was to be given by the War Office to General Georges. During the day however, it appeared that operations were actually being directed by General Weygand who later, on 23rd May, announced in a General Order that he was now Commander-in-Chief in all theatres of war.

I discussed, these instructions with the C.I.G.S. at my Command Post at Wahagnies at 8.15 a.m.; I put to him my view that withdrawal to the south-westwards, however desirable in principle, was not in the circumstances practicable.

In the first place, it would involve the disengagement of seven divisions which were at the time in close contact with the enemy on the Escaut, and would be immediately followed up.

In addition to this rearguard action the B.E.F. in its retirement to the Somme would have to attack into an area already strongly occupied by the enemy armoured and mobile formations. Some of these indeed now appeared to be holding the line of the Somme whilst others were already within a short distance of the coast, and might turn northwards at any time. Thus the B.E.F. would be obliged to disengage its seven divisions in contact with the enemy, fighting a rearguard action, at the same tune to attack south-westwards, and finally to break through enemy forces on the Somme. During this manoeuvre both flanks would have to be guarded.

Secondly, the administrative situation made it unlikely that sustained offensive operations could be undertaken. Communication with the bases was on the point of being interrupted. The mobile echelons of gun and small arms ammunition were full, but once they were exhausted I could not safely reckon on being able to replenish them.

Lastly, though I was not in a position to judge, I had the impression that even if I had decided to attempt this manoeuvre, neither the French 1st Army nor the Belgians would have been in a position to conform.

Nevertheless, I told the C.I.G.S. that I fully realised the importance of an attack in a southerly direction and that I already had plans in hand to counter attack with the 5th and 50th Divisions to the south of Arras and that these divisions would be ready to attack on the following morning (21st May). These were the only reserves which I then had available, apart from one armoured reconnaissance brigade, and one infantry brigade of 2nd Division. To create a further reserve I had already begun negotiations with Belgian G.Q.G. for the relief of 44th Division on the Escaut, but these were not yet completed.

The C.I.G.S. agreed with this action and accompanied by the C.G.S. he left for Lens to meet Generals Billotte and Blanchard. At that interview the C.I.G.S. explained the action to be taken by 5th and 50th Divisions. General Billotte fully agreed to this plan, and said that the French would co-operate with two divisions.

On return to my headquarters, the C.I.G.S. sent a telegram to General Georges which made it clear that, in his opinion, General Billotte's Army Group would be finally cut off unless the French 1st Army made an immediate move on Cambrai or unless General Georges launched a counter-attack northwards from Péronne. My liaison officers with Generals Billotte and Blanchard conveyed a similar message from me to those commanders, making it clear that if our counter-attack was not successful the French and British Armies north of the gap would have their flank turned and could no longer remain in their present positions.

On 21st May I sent a formal acknowledgement of the instructions brought by the C.I.G.S. adding that, in my opinion, withdrawal to the south-west was entirely impossible until the situation had been retrieved on the front of the French 1st Army.

33. 5th Division was therefore ordered to join 50th Division in the Vimy area, and its commander, Major General Franklyn, was placed in command of all the British troops operating in and

around Arras. Frankforce, as it was to be known, consisted of 5th and 50th Divisions (each of two brigades only), 1st Army Tank Brigade[28] (previously with Macforce) together with Petreforce and the force under O.C. 12th Lancers. Petreforce was by this time very tired and widely dispersed.

My immediate instructions to General Franklyn were to occupy the bridgeheads on the Scarpe, east of Arras and thus to relieve the remains of 23rd Division. He would then be suitably disposed to advance south and south-east of Arras on the following day in conjunction with the French.

It will be convenient to conclude the story of Frankforce here.

During the evening of 20th May, General Franklyn completed his reconnaissances for an attack on the following day to secure the line of the rivers Scarpe and Cojeul: his intention was to exploit success by moving on 22nd May to the Sensée and thence towards Bapaume and Cambrai. In these plans he had the full co-operation of General Prioux, Commander of the French Cavalry Corps, but the light mechanised divisions were much reduced in strength and probably had no more than one quarter of their tanks fit for action.

However, one of these divisions was ordered to advance on each side of Frankforce, while 12th Lancers watched the right flank on the Arras-St. Pol road. The hope was not realised, however, that the French 5th Corps would also attack southwards from Douai with two divisions in co-operation with Frankforce on the 21st. A conference had been arranged at 6 p.m. on the 20th at General Franklyn's headquarters but no representative from that Corps attended. Finally, at 12.30 p.m. on the 21st I received a letter from General Blanchard to say that the Corps Commander, General Altmeyer, thought he could move on the 22nd or the following night.

––––––––––––

28 At this time their strength was reduced to approximately 65 Mark I and 18 Mark II tanks. By the end of the withdrawal from Arras there remained 26 Mark I and 2 Mark II tanks.

Time, however, was vital. General Franklyn adhered to his plans, and at 2 p.m. attacked with 1st Army Tank Brigade, 151st Infantry Brigade of 50th Division and 13th Infantry Brigade of 5th Division all under General Martel. The French 1st Light Mechanised Division cooperated, though its movements did not develop so widely to the flanks as General Franklyn had hoped.

The opposition was stronger than had been expected. Objectives for the day were reached, and in the evening there were heavy divebombing attacks by the enemy. Enemy tanks had been put to flight: over 400 prisoners had been captured: a number of enemy had been killed and many transport vehicles destroyed.

The tank brigade had, however, begun to suffer severely from mechanical trouble; the tanks had been on the road continuously since they detrained at Brussels, and the mileage covered had already far exceeded the estimated life of the tracks which were now beginning to break through wear.

It was clear therefore that the attack of Frankforce would not maintain its momentum unless it was reinforced and supported by the French on its left. During 22nd May, therefore, General Franklyn held his ground, and prolonged his right flank westwards, while the French Cavalry Corps took up a position at Mont St. Eloi. All day long pressure increased round his right flank, and an observation post of 12th Lancers on Mont St. Eloi could see at one moment as many as 48 enemy tanks.

Next day (23rd May) the enemy advanced steadily north-eastwards from the high ground of the Lorette ridge, and by evening they were reconnoitring the southern outskirts of Bethune and the road from Lens to Carvin. It was clear that Frankforce was becoming dangerously hemmed in. Two roads were still available for their extrication and at about 7 p.m. I decided that there was no alternative but to withdraw Frankforce. This withdrawal had necessarily to be in an easterly direction. 5th and 50th Divisions had been engaged with the enemy all day and had inflicted very severe losses; they were now ordered to withdraw to the area around Seclin, where they would be well placed to take part in any further counter-attack to the southward which might be staged. Petreforce was withdrawn to an area north of Seclin.

Thus concluded the defence of Arras, which had been carried out by a small garrison, hastily assembled but well commanded, and determined to fight. It had imposed a valuable delay on a greatly superior enemy force against which it had blocked a vital road centre.

21st May—The Organisation of the Canal line.
34. The time had now come to organise, as soon as possible, the further defence of the south-western flank of the force.

The enemy advance beyond Arras had hitherto been carried out almost entirely by armoured forces, supported by motorised infantry which was doubtless increasing in numbers every day. The situation regarding the enemy's normal infantry divisions was still uncertain. It was therefore of first importance to reinforce the organisation of the line of the canals from the Escaut to La Bassée, and to continue it to St. Omer and the sea. These canals offered the only anti-tank obstacle on this flank. They were, however, crossed by numerous bridges, many of which had already been prepared for demolition by our own engineers under my Engineer-in-Chief (Major-General R. P. Pakenham-Walsh), the Commander of Macforce, and the French Commanders' of the fortified sectors of Lille and Flanders (Généraux de Brigade Bertschi and Barthélémy).

It had been proved that even weak garrisons holding important road centres, such as Arras and Doullens, were of much value in imposing delay, for the initial advances of the enemy always followed the main roads. It was therefore decided to continue the policy of organising such "stops," not only along the canals but at all possible centres whether north or south of the canal line.

Macforce, which had been formed on May, had been augmented on 18th and 19th by 138th Infantry Brigade (46th Division) which went into line on the canal between Raches and Carvin, and on the following day 139th Infantry Brigade of the same division joined the force. On 21st May 127th Infantry-Brigade rejoined the 42nd Division and the sector from Millonfosse to St. Amand was handed over to the French.

Already on 20th May, I had ordered Major-General Curtis, Commanding 46th Division, to take command of the sector of the canals between Aire and Carvin. General Curtis force was known as Polforce, and was to consist of four battalions – of 46th Division, 25th Infantry Brigade of 50th Division (in line between La Bassée and Carvin) and one field battery, together with a number of engineer and other units of G.H.Q. troops which had been moving northwards and were collected on the Canal. It had originally been intended that part of this force should hold St. Pol, Frévent and Divion, but the railway trains in which were the remaining three battalions of 46th Division failed to reach that town in time and remained south of the Somme. The defence of these localities south of the Canal had therefore to be abandoned.

Further to the north-west the defence of the canal line was being organised by Brigadier C.M. Usher, Commander of X Lines of Communication Sub-area. On 22nd May he reported that the enemy had already reached the left bank of the river Aa between Gravelines and St. Omer. 23rd Division had been ordered to move to this area and its leading battalion (6th Green Howards) arrived at Gravelines. Brigadier Usher therefore held the right bank of the river from St. Omer to Gravelines with this battalion and five batteries of heavy artillery used as infantry, in conjunction with certain French troops of the Secteur Fortifié des Flandres.

The front of Macforce was covered by the French, 3rd, 4th and 5th Corps, who were still in their quadrilateral on the line of the Escaut and the Sensée. Here, however, information was frequently lacking and could only be obtained by reconnaissance.

Thus, by 22nd May, the canal line was occupied in the sense that the whole of the length of 85 miles from the sea at Gravelines to Millonfosse (West of St. Amand) was divided into sectors for each of which a British commander was responsible. The total strength of the troops on the Canal line did not on this day exceed 10,000 men, and the number of anti-tank weapons was barely adequate to cover all the crossing places: certainly there could be no question of being able to keep an effective watch against small parties of infantry crossing the canal between the bridges. The barges, however, had almost all been moved away or at any rate to the bank furthest from the enemy, and bridges were fast being prepared for demolition.

21st May—The Situation on the Belgian Front.
35. On 21st May at 4.45 p.m. I met the three Corps Commanders. I told them what had happened on the southern flank and how, in order to take the initiative and encourage the French 1st Army to do likewise, I had gone to the length of committing practically the whole of my reserve.

From the Corps Commanders I learned that the line was thinly held and that attacks had taken place at several points. At Petegem on the front of 44th Division the enemy had secured a bridgehead 1,000 yards deep on a front of 3,000 yards, and at the junction with the French near Maulde on the front of 1st Division a number of enemy had crossed the river disguised as refugees, but had been detected and driven out with the bayonet. The Corps Commanders all felt that they could hot how hold on for more than twenty-four hours. We discussed a withdrawal to our old frontier defences, where advantage could be taken of the existing blockhouses and trenches, and of the anti-tank ditch. This move would have little effect on the French on our right since it would pivot on the junction point, where the Escaut crossed the frontier, but would seriously affect the Belgians, who now held the line of the Escaut from Audenarde to Ghent and of the canal from Ghent to the sea at Terneuzen.

I had also to consider the pressing need to stiffen the defence of the canal line westwards to Gravelines and to form a new reserve to replace the divisions now committed to counter-attacks southward from Arras.

A provisional decision was therefore reached to withdraw to the frontier defences on the night of 22ⁿᵈ/23ʳᵈ May, details being left until I had reached agreement with the French and the Belgians.

General Weygand had visited General Billotte during the day and the latter indicated that an attack was being planned for the following day (22ⁿᵈ May), northwards from the direction of Roye, with the object of closing the gap. At 8 p.m. on 21ˢᵗ May I went to Ypres where in the Burgomaster's office I met H.M. the King of the Belgians and General Billotte. There were also present General Van Overstraeten, General Champon, the head of the French Mission with Belgian G.Q.G., General Pownall and others.

I explained the situation which was developing on the Escaut about Audenarde, and the difficulty of maintaining positions there since the water in the river was so low as no longer to form an obstacle. It was then agreed that on the night of 22ⁿᵈ/23ʳᵈ May the Escaut should be abandoned and that the Allied armies should occupy a line from Maulde northwards to Halluin, thence along the Lys to Courtrai and Ghent.

I discussed the possibility of reserves. It appeared that the available divisions of the French 1ˢᵗ Army were all too tired to take part in offensive operations in the immediate future. It was therefore agreed that the French should take over a further sector of the defensive positions northwards from Maulde, so that the 2ⁿᵈ and 48ᵗʰ Divisions could be withdrawn into reserve on leaving the line of the Escaut. The French took up these positions on 22nd May. On the north, 44th Division on withdrawal from the Escaut were to hold the sector Halluin-Courtrai, but it was hoped that a Belgian formation would relieve them on the night of 23rd/24th May.

When these moves were complete the Allied line would run slightly west of north to Halluin, and then almost at right angles, north-eastwards along the Lys. It was evident that sooner or later the Belgian army would have to swing back to a line in rear, pivoting on their right of Halluin. Accordingly at the end of the conference General Billotte asked the King of the Belgians whether if he were forced to withdraw he would fall back on to the line of the Yser. His Majesty agreed, though evidently with some regret, that no alternative line existed.

On return from the meeting, orders were issued to implement these decisions, and that evening I moved my command post to the Chateau de Premesques, midway between Armentières and Lille.

The final severance of the L. of C. and the investment of Boulogne.
36. During the 21st May the enemy penetration into the rearward areas increased and communication across the Somme was finally severed. Since the 17th May the Commander of the Lines of Communication Area (Major-General P. de Fonblanque) had been taking energetic steps for its defence, in so far as it was possible with the few and scattered troops available.

These consisted, apart from Armoured Division and 51st Division now returning from the Saar, of those portions of 12th and 46th Divisions (some nine battalions in all) which could not be despatched forward, three unbrigaded infantry battalions and the contents of the reinforcement depots, together with troops of the Auxiliary Military Pioneer Corps and of the administrative services.

On 23rd May, however, the War Office appointed Lieutenant-General Sir Henry Karslake to command the defences on the Lines of Communication and I was not concerned in the operations which ensued. Nevertheless, I did not immediately abandon hope of the Armoured Division breaking through, and I urged the War Office to use their best endeavours to this end and to prevent its being used piecemeal in local operations at the request of the French Command.

At about 3.30 p.m. on the 21st May, I received information that an enemy column of all arms was approaching Boulogne. The rear element of G.H.Q., consisting largely of the Adjutant-General's Branch and of headquarters of Services, which had been sent to that town on 17th and 18th May, had been moved to Wimereux on 20th May as a result of enemy bombing.

All possible steps had been taken to put Boulogne in a state of defence with the troops available, consisting of labour units and the personnel of rest camps. On 19th May, an endeavour was made to bring up troops from beyond the Somme, to hold the line of the Canche; but the time for this was past and the troops could not get beyond Abbeville. The hospitals in the Etaples area were now evacuated, and on 21st May a party of Engineers, supervised by my Director of Works, Brigadier W. Cave-Browne, demolished most of the bridges over the Canche.

As soon as the news of this new threat was received, the War Office was asked for bomber support, which was at once forthcoming. Enemy tanks were located and bombed at Hesdin and Fruges, but no good targets were obtained on the coast road. The War Office was also asked to send a detachment of Royal Marines for the defence of Boulogne but had already done so. Early on the 22nd May, 20th Guards Brigade (Brigadier W.A.F.L. Fox-Pitt) of two battalions with an anti-tank battery landed, thus establishing the defence of the town and enabling those troops who were not required for the defence to be evacuated in good order.

By the evening of 22nd May, the enemy armoured forces were within nine miles of Calais. Boulogne was now isolated and its final evacuation was carried out under the orders of the War Office, being completed on the night of 23/24th May.

The Administrative Situation.

37. During the whole of this period I had been kept in the closest touch with the administrative situation by the Quarter-Master-General (Lieutenant-General W. G. Lindsell). Up to 16th May the administrative arrangements which formed part of Plan D had worked well, and although enemy air action steadily intensified during the period, there was no serious interference with the maintenance of the force.

On 17th May, however, the Quarter-Master-General decided, in view of the situation south of Arras, to discontinue the use of the railway from the regulating station at Abancourt via Amiens and Arras, and to switch all traffic via Eu and Abbeville to Bethune. He also ordered forward every available trainload of ammunition to the Hazebrouck area.

On 19th May, directly after the C.G.S. had spoken to the War Office as to the possibility of enforced withdrawal, the Q.M.G. telephoned to the War Office to discuss the opening of new bases. On the same day, one of his staff officers left for London to arrange an emergency shipment programme for supplies and stores to the ports of Boulogne, Calais and Dunkirk. It was to prove none too soon, for the railway at Abbeville was cut on 21st May. A new plan had to be put into operation at once for the maintenance of the force north of the Somme, estimated at 250,000 men and requiring a daily lift of ammunition, supplies and petrol, of some 2,000 tons.

The petrol situation, fortunately, gave no cause for concern since, although the dumps forward of the Somme had been destroyed on evacuation, together with a large civil storage plant near Douai, there still remained a large army bulk filling station near Lille.

The supply situation was however, bad, and on 21st May, Corps had only three days R.A.S.C. supplies in the forward area. Matters might, at any time, have become serious had it not been for the success of the measures taken between 23rd and 26th May, to organise the supplies in Lille belonging to the Expeditionary Force Institutes and to civilian firms. The decision to maintain the force through the northern ports was finally taken on 21st May and the headquarters of a Base Sub-Area established at Dunkirk, together with a section of Q.M.G.'s staff, in close touch with the British and French Naval authorities.

Rail communication in the area was by now precarious, and plans were worked out on the basis of establishing dumps, one in each Corps area, which could be wholly maintained by road. The position was, by this time, greatly complicated by the numbers of improvised forces which the quickly changing situation had made necessary: most of these, like the three divisions for pioneer duties, had no proper administrative echelons. Some were within reach of Corps, but others were not and these had to be dependent on fortuitous sources of supply, or else live for a time on the country.

The situation had grown even worse by 22nd May, when the ports at both Boulogne and Calais were out of action, and the greater part of the Railhead Mechanical Transport Companies had been captured. Furthermore, a reconnaissance of Ostend had shown that the port could not be worked for military requirements at short notice. A certain number of rations and small arms ammunition was sent by air up to 23rd May, but from then onwards it became impossible for aircraft to land. On 23rd May therefore, on the advice of the Q.M.G., I decided to place the B.E.F. on half rations.

Dunkirk, though its water supply was destroyed, remained available for unloading supplies till 26th May, but constant air raids imposed a well-nigh unbearable strain on the stevedore battalions. However, they remained at duty until, in the end, all the quays and cranes were put out of action. Thereafter supplies could only be landed on the beaches. Lighters arrived to embark troops loaded with a portion of supplies, ammunition and water, and these were unloaded and distributed by Corps. The delivery of supplies to Corps was maintained, albeit irregularly, up till 30th May when the last convoy went forward from the supply depot on the beach at La Pane.

By 20th May all the General Hospitals had been cut off from the forward area and improvised arrangements had to be made for the evacuation of casualties. Some of the Casualty Clearing Stations had to be diverted from their normal function and used as Hospitals. Hospital ships continued to berth at Dunkirk till the night 31st May/1st June and casualties were evacuated to them by road and by rail. Ambulance trains were running as late as 26th May.

Further proposals for an attack Southwards.
38. On 23rd May the French 1st Army pushed forward some elements southwards from Douai. On the same day, 5th and 50th Divisions, which had attacked two days before, were themselves being attacked on the Scrape and had already lost most of their tanks through mechanical wear.

The threat to their rear was increasing hourly and they were thus unable to make any further advance or to assist the French, except in so far as they were able to engage troops who might otherwise have threatened the right flank of the French advance. The French approached the outskirts of Cambrai meeting with little opposition but withdrew later on being attacked by dive-bombers.

On the same day I received a copy of a telegram from the Prime Minister to M. Reynaud, which read as follows:-

"Strong enemy armoured forces have cut communications of Northern Armies. Salvation of these Armies can only be obtained by immediate execution of Weygand's plan. I demand that French Commanders in North and South and

Belgian G.Q.G. be given most stringent orders to carry this out and turn defeat into victory. Time vital as supplies are short."

I was not sure whether the situation which was developing for the allied armies in the north could be accurately appreciated except on the spot. I therefore telegraphed to Sir John Dill asking him to fly over that day.

The next day, however (24th May), the Prime Minister again conferred with M. Reynaud and General Weygand in Paris, and I received the following telegram from the Secretary of State describing that conference:-

"Both are convinced that Weygand's plan is still capable of execution and only in its execution has hope of restoring the situation. Weygand reports French VII Army is advancing successfully and has captured Péronne, Albert and Amiens. While realising fully dangers and difficulties of your position which has been explained to Weygand it is essential that you should make every endeavour to co-operate in his plan. Should however situation on your communications make this at any time impossible you should inform us so that we can inform French and make Naval and Air arrangements to assist you should you have to withdraw on the northern coast."

It will be noted that, according to the telegram General Weygand informed the Prime Minister that Péronne, Albert and Amiens had- been recaptured. It later transpired that this information was inaccurate.

The Weygand plan, as it came to be known, was for a counter offensive on a large scale.

From the north the French 1st Army and the B.E.F. were to attack south-west at the earliest possible moment with about eight divisions and with the Belgian Cavalry Corps supporting the British right.

The newly formed Third French Army Group was reported to be organising a line on the Somme from Amiens to Péronne with a view to attacking northwards.

A new cavalry Corps was assembling south of the Somme near Neufchatel and was to operate on the line of the Somme west of Amiens, in touch with the British Armoured Division on their left.

I fully appreciated the importance of attacking early before the enemy could bring up his infantry in strength, but facts had to be faced. The 5th and 50th Divisions were on this day (23rd May) still closely engaged with the enemy, and 2nd, 44th and 48th Divisions, would not become available for a further 48 hours, since the French and the Belgians though they had arranged their relief, could not complete it earlier. The ammunition immediately available, to the B.E.F. was of the order of 300 rounds per gun and with communications cut with the main base, the prospect of receiving any further supply was remote.

The French light mechanised divisions and our own armoured units had already suffered serious losses in tanks which could not be replaced. Such information as I had received of the Belgian cavalry did not lead me to take an optimistic view of the prospect of their being able to engage, at short notice, in a battle forty miles away and on French soil.

Experience had already shown the vital importance of close co-ordination of the allied armies in any operation. General Billotte had been appointed the co-ordinator at the conference at Mons on 12th May, but in practice, the measure of co-ordination fell far short of what was required if the movements of the three allied armies were to be properly controlled.

Except for the issue of orders to retire from the Dyle (obtained only after I had sent Major-General Eastwood to General Billotte's headquarters to represent my views), I received no written orders from the French First Group of Armies, though at the meetings between General Billotte and myself which took place from time to time, we always found ourselves in complete agreement. Unfortunately, however, General Billotte had been seriously, and as it turned out, fatally injured in a motor accident returning from the conference which he and I had attended at Ypres on the night of 21st May. General Blanchard succeeded him in command of the French First Group of Armies, and presumably succeeded to the function of co-ordination although this was never officially confirmed.

I telegraphed to the Secretary of State pointing out that co-ordination was essential with armies of three different nations, and that I personally could not undertake any measure of co-ordination in the forthcoming operations as I was already actively engaged on my Eastern and Southern fronts and also threatened on my Lines of Communication.

Nevertheless, I saw General Blanchard and proposed to him that to implement our part of the Weygand plan, we should stage an attack southwards with two British divisions, one French division and the French Cavalry Corps. So far as we were concerned the attack could not take place till the 26th at the earliest owing to the reliefs which were in progress, and the need to assemble 5th and 50th Divisions. I also asked General Blanchard to enquire from G.Q.G. how such an operation could be synchronised with the attack from the line of the Somme which was said to be in process of preparation. These negotiations, as will be seen, were later continued by Sir Ronald Adam on my behalf. I emphasised, both to the Secretary of State and to General Blanchard, that the principal effort must come from the south, and that the operation of the northern forces could be nothing more than a sortie.

I never received any information from any source as to the exact location of our own or enemy forces on the far side of the gap; nor did I receive any details or timings of any proposed attack from that direction.

23rd May–Further development of the Canal line.
39. On 23rd May the organisation was continued of "stops" behind the Canal line. At Hazebrouck, where the organisation of defences had been begun on 21st May by the staff of the Major-General R.A. at G.H.Q. the garrison was now about 300 strong and included eighteen French light tanks and some Belgian machine gunners.

Cassel was occupied by 13/18th Hussars, less one squadron, and on the same afternoon (23rd) Brigadier Usher's force took over the defence of Bergues.

On the night of 22/23rd May the withdrawal to the frontier defences had been carried out. The French had taken over the sector northwards from Maulde and the right boundary of the B.E.F. was now Bourghelles-Seclin both inclusive to the French. This change of boundary did not however affect the dispositions which the B.E.F. had taken on the Canal line by which the rear of the French positions was protected.

On the left of the B.E.F. the Belgians, who had previously agreed to relieve the 44th Division after withdrawal to the Lys on the night of 23rd/24th May, ordered one of their divisions to occupy the sector Halluin-Courtrai on the night of 22nd/23rd May. 44th Division was concentrated in G.H.Q. reserve on the morning of 23rd May.

On the right, 2nd and 48th Divisions passed through the French on the night of 22nd/23rd May and also concentrated in G H.O reserve.

These moves left only four divisions on the frontier defences and made it possible to withdraw the headquarters and Corps troops of 3rd Corps for employment on the Canal line where they were badly needed. This was done at 4 p.m. on 23rd May, leaving 1st Corps with 42nd and 1st Divisions and 2nd Corps with 3rd and 4th Divisions.

2nd, 44th and 48th Divisions came under 3rd Corps and that night made a march westwards. I had decided to employ 2nd and 44th Divisions on the Canal line facing west, but their move required a farther twenty-four hours to complete.

Meanwhile the canal defences required stiffening as much as possible. And accordingly, Polforce temporarily assumed control of the whole front between St. Omer and Raches, and two regiments of 2nd Armoured Reconnaissance Brigade were placed under its command. Polforce also undertook the responsibility for demolitions as far north as Watten including no less than 43 bridges.

The sector eastward from Raches was now handed over to the French, the British demolition parties being left on the bridges at the disposal of French 3rd Corps.

Macforce, now comprising four field batteries, half an anti-tank battery and one battalion, withdrew from the line Carvin-Raches on 23rd May and was moved to a rendezvous in the eastern end of the Forest of Nieppe where it was joined by Headquarters and one regiment of 1st Armoured Reconnaissance Brigade. 139th Infantry Brigade (46th Division) continued to hold the sector from Carvin to Raches until 26th May.

The situation on the canal line deteriorated during 23rd May and the enemy established bridgeheads at Aire, at St. Omer (which seems to have changed hands twice during the day) and near Watten. His tanks were reported as harbouring in the forest of Clairmarais, and during the day his armoured fighting vehicles came within three miles of Hazebrouck. By the evening, however, these movements had been checked and steps taken to keep. The enemy out of the Forest of Nieppe.

The enemy had also been active that day on the canal line at Béthune, where they had been driven off and had then moved towards Carvin. Here the defenders had been reinforced by further artillery under C. R. A. 2nd Division (Brigadier. C.B. Findlay), and the crossings were firmly held.

On 23rd May Calais was finally isolated. Its garrison; had been reinforced under the orders of the War Office, by 30th Infantry Brigade (Brigadier C. Nicholson) and 3rd battalion Royal Tank Regiment-a cruiser tank regiment. I had intended to move the latter within the canal line, but it was already too late. After two attempts they were driven back into Calais, with the exception of three tanks which eventually reached Dunkirk by way of Gravelines. The remainder of the gallant defence of Calais was conducted under the orders of the War Office. It was finally concluded on the night of 26/27th May.

Information received at this time indicated that two enemy armoured divisions were converging on Calais and two more, supported by a motorised. S. S. (Schutz-Staffel) division, on St. Omer. A fifth armoured division appeared to moving on Béthune

24th May. Preparations for counter attack and strengthening of canal defences.

40. During 24th May, I had simultaneously to prepare for a counter-attack southwards on the 26th and also to press forward with the strengthening of the canal line.

To make the detailed arrangements for the counter-attack I appointed the Commander of the 3rd Corps, Lieutenant-General Sir Ronald Adam, who, on my behalf, continued negotiations with General Blanchard, and with the Commander of the French 5th Corps, General Altmeyer.

The final plan was for a counter attack with three French and two British divisions under the command of General Altmeyer. As a first stage, on the evening of 26th May, bridgeheads were to be established south, of the Scarpe, and the main attack was to start the following morning, with the objective Plouvain-Marquion-Cambrai. Sir Ronald Adam with three divisions (two British and one French) was to advance east of the Canal du Nord, and General Altmeyer with two French divisions to the west of the Canal du Nord, his right being covered by the French Cavalry Corps. This attack was never carried out for reasons which will presently appear.[29]

On the same day, I issued orders to dissolve the various improvised forces on the Canal line, and their units were absorbed by the formations in the areas of which they now were. I appointed Major-General Eastwood[30] to take command of the defences on the Canal line, and he assumed command early on 25th May.

The position on the Canal line was considerably strengthened – during 24th May. 44th Division began to move into the line between the forest of Clairmarais and Aire, with 2nd Division on its left between Aire and La Bassée, and 46th Division (lately Polforce) from La Bassée to Raches. It was not till the evening however that 2nd and 44th Divisions gained contact with the enemy and for most of the day the defence of the sector still remained under the Commanders of Macforce and Perforce.

Fighting of a somewhat confused character went on for most of the day in and south of the Forest of Nieppe, and the enemy also began heavy bombing and shelling of Cassel. The remainder of Macforce, which included field and anti-tank artillery, was therefore sent to reinforce the 13/18th Hussars.

48th Division (with under its command part of 23rd Division in the area Gravelines-St. Omer) was ordered to send one "infantry brigade to Dunkirk and one to Cassel and Hazebrouck. 145th Infantry Brigade completed its relief of the improvised garrisons of the two latter places on 25th

---

29 See para 43.
30 Major-General T. R. Eastwood had recently arrived in France to take command of a division, and, pending a vacancy, was attached to the Staff of G.H.Q.

May, but General Thorne found that the French had already made complete dispositions for Dunkirk, and had informed the British Base Commandant. He therefore decided to send 144th Infantry Brigade to Bergues and Wormhoudt. He established his H.Q. at Bergues, which he rightly regarded as the vital point of defence.

The French reinforce Dunkirk.

41. The local defences of Dunkirk, in accordance with French practice, were under the Admiral du Nord, Admiral Abrial, whose command included Boulogne, Calais and Dunkirk. Under his authority the command of military forces in these areas was assumed on 24th May by Général de Corps d'Armée Fagalde, commanding the French 16th Corps which up to now had been fighting on the left of the Belgian Army.

The French defences of Dunkirk were based on the peace time organisation of the Secteur Fortifié des Flandres, and extended only as far as the Belgian frontier. They comprised an inner and an, outer sector, the inner on the line of the old Mardyck Canal to Spyker, thence by Bergues to the frontier and so to the sea; the outer on the line of the river Aa to St. Omer thence by Cassel and Steenvoorde to the frontier. General Fagalde had at his disposal certain regional troops in numbers equivalent to a weak division, who were located in the outer sector from Gravelines to the Forest of Clairmarais and whose dispositions had been roughly co-ordinated with those of Brigadier Usher. About this time the 68th French Division arrived at Dunkirk from Belgium and took over the inner sector.

On the 24th and 25th May the British posts on the river Aa were taken over by the French, who also began to operate the inundations, which formed part of the defence scheme of Dunkirk and extended each side of Bergues and as far as the Belgian frontier north of the Bergues-Furnes canal.

25th May – Attacks on the Canal Line and on the Belgian Army.
42. On 25th May, enemy activity intensified. Two enemy Corps were reported to be attacking the French in the area Denain-Bouchain; the enemy was also across the canal at St. Venant, and was developing the bridgeheads between that place and Aire and also at St. Omer, whilst further north the situation on the river Aa was still obscure.

At about 7 a.m. on 25th May, news was received that in the late evening of 24th May the enemy had attacked the Belgian 4th Corps on the Lys with a force reported to be of four divisions, supported by tanks. The attack penetrated to a depth of 1.5 miles on a front of 13 miles between Menin and Desselghem.

It was fast becoming a matter of vital importance to keep open our line of communication to the coast through a corridor which was hourly narrowing. It was no longer possible to count on using the main road Estaires-Cassel-Dunkirk, while the news which had just been received made it certain that before long, the whole area east of the Yser canal would be in the hands of the enemy, since there was, in fact, no satisfactory defensive position between the Lys and the Yser canal. There seemed, therefore, to be a serious risk of the Belgian right becoming separated from the British left at Menin, and of the Belgian Army being forced to fall back in a northerly, rather than in a westerly direction. I considered it vitally urgent to prolong the British front without delay northwards to Ypres, along the old Ypres-Comines canal, now practically dry, and round Ypres itself to the line of the Yser canal.

As an immediate step, 12th Lancers were sent off early on 25th to watch the left flank of 2nd Corps on the Lys, and gain touch with the right flank of the Belgians.

The remaining infantry brigade of 48th Division (143rd) was later placed under 2nd Corps, and a pioneer battalion sent to begin preparations for the defence of Ypres in case Belgian measures for the purpose should prove inadequate.

The Belgians had at this time one division in reserve between Menin and Ypres, and this was ordered to counter-attack at 2 p.m. However it is doubtful whether it was found possible ever to launch this counter-attack. Orders were also issued for the Belgian 1st Corps to come into line on the right of their 4th Corps between Ghelewe and Ledeghem; this move was carried out on the 26th May.

Sir John Dill (who had now become C.I.G.S.) and whom I had asked to visit me, arrived on the morning of 25th May, and I explained the position to him. He then telegraphed to the Prime Minister and to the Secretary of State, that there could be no disguising the seriousness of the situation. He added that in his opinion the proposed counter-attack to the south could not be an important affair in view of the enemy attacks which had penetrated the Belgian defences.

General Blanchard arrived during Sir John Dill's visit and took part in our discussions.

During the day the Belgians continued to withdraw in a north-westerly direction under enemy pressure. Reports also indicated that a fresh enemy attack would take place next day on the northern end of the Lys position.

OPERATIONS—THIRD PHASE
26th–1st MAY
The decision taken, in agreement with the French, to withdraw behind the Lys. H.M. Government authorises withdrawal to the coast. The Dunkirk perimeter organised by Sir Ronald Adam. The Belgians ask for an armistice. General Blanchard at first determines to remain in position but later French 3rd and Cavalry Corps withdraw to Dunkirk. Occupation of perimeter completed. Problems of embarkation of British and French troops. Withdrawal of 2nd and 3rd Corps. G.H.Q. closes and C.-in-C. embarks for England.

The decision to Withdraw.

43. By 6 p.m. that night (25th May) I was convinced that the steps I had taken to secure my left flank would prove insufficient to meet the growing danger in the north.

The pattern of the enemy pincer attack was becoming clearer. One movement from the south-west on Dunkirk had already developed and was being held; the counterpart was now developing on the Belgian front.

The gap between the British left and the Belgian right, which had been threatening the whole day, might at any time become impossible to close: were this to happen, my last hope of reaching the coast would be gone. At this tune, it will be recalled, I had no reserves beyond a single cavalry regiment, and the two divisions (5th and 50th) already earmarked for the attack southwards.

The French 1st Army, which was not affected in the same way as the B.E.F. by the situation which was developing on the Belgian front, had, it will be remembered, agreed to provide three divisions and the Cavalry Corps for this attack. Therefore, even if no British divisions could be made available, the possibility of carrying out the operation would not be entirely precluded. I did realise however that the French Were unlikely to take the offensive unless British support was forthcoming.

Even so, however, the situation on my northern flank was deteriorating so rapidly that I was convinced that there was no alternative but to occupy, as quickly as troops could be made available, the line of the Ypres-Comines canal and the positions covering Ypres. I therefore issued orders to 50th Division to join 2nd Corps at once, and shortly afterwards I ordered 5th Division to follow. 2nd Corps placed 5th Division on its left flank northwards from Halluin along the Ypres-Comines canal with 50th Division on its left around Ypres. At this time also, the greater part of the medium and heavy artillery of 1st and 2nd Corps was grouped under 2nd Corps, and the successful defence of the positions on the Ypres-Comines canal and around Ypres, which was maintained during the next three days; was greatly assisted by these artillery units, which remained in action till they had fired all their ammunition.

The Commander of 3rd Corps, who was no longer required to take part in the attack southwards, was now ordered to take over the command of the front from St. Omer to Raches from Major-General Eastwood, whom he relieved on 26th May.

I immediately communicated my decision to the headquarters of the French First Group of Armies, but I was unable to get-into personal touch with General Blanchard that evening as he was visiting the Belgian G.Q.G. at Bruges. However, I went to see General Blanchard at his headquarters at Attiches early next morning (26th May), at a moment when the enemy was attacking at Carvin and had penetrated the front of a North African Division near Bois d'Epinoy. I found that General Blanchard also feared the collapse of the Belgian Army and felt that the time for a counter attack southwards was past. Indeed he had already decided that the situation on both flanks made it necessary to withdraw.

After an hour's discussion, we arrived at a joint plan for the withdrawal of the main bodies behind the line of the Lys. These arrangements were subject to there being no further deterioration in the Belgian situation.

With this decision, there vanished the last opportunity for a sortie. The layout of the B.E.F. was now beginning to take its final shape. Starting from what could be described as a normal situation with Allied troops on the right and left, there had developed an ever lengthening defensive right flank. This had then become a semi-circular line, with both flanks resting on the sea, manned by British, French and Belgians. Later the position became, a corridor in shape. The southern end of this corridor was blocked by the French 1st Army; and each side was manned, for the greater part of its length, by British troops. Next to the sea were French troops on the west, and French and Belgian troops on the eastern flank.

The immediate problem was to shorten this perimeter. British and French forces were together holding a front of 128 miles of which 97 miles were held by British troops, though some sectors were held jointly with the French. The virtual closing of Dunkirk as a port of entry was making the supply situation ever more difficult, and the ammunition situation permitted only of very restricted expenditure.

The Plan for Withdrawal.

44. Later, on 26th May, I discussed the plan for withdrawal with the Corps Commanders, and issued orders for the operation in accordance with the agreement reached with General Blanchard that morning. The plan, as agreed with the French First Group of Armies, envisaged the reservation of certain roads for the exclusive use of the B.E.F. In fact, however, French troops and transport continued to use them, and this added very considerably to the difficulties of the withdrawal of British troops. The roads were few and for the most part narrow, and for the next three days they were badly congested with marching troops and horsed transport of French formations, and with refugees.

On the night 26th/27th May, 1st and 2nd Corps, leaving rearguards in the frontier defences, were to swing back to the old divisional reserve position with their right at Fort Sainghin (5 miles south-east of Lille), while the French prolonged this line from Thumeries to the canal at Pont-à-Vendin, linking up there with 2nd Division. The following night (27th/28th May), main bodies were to withdraw behind the Lys, leaving rearguards on the Deule canal up to its junction with the Lys at Deulemont: these rearguards were to stay there until the next night (28th/29th May). The immediate effect of these dispositions would be to shorten the total perimeter by some 58 miles, but on the other hand I had to face the possibility of having to occupy the front from Ypres to the sea, some 25 miles long, which was still the responsibility of the Belgian Army.

There remained the question of the future. I had not so far discussed with General Blanchard a further withdrawal to the sea. However, the possibility could not have been absent from his mind; nor was it absent from mine, for, although up to now no instructions had been given authorising me to undertake such an operation, I had, as I have said, foreseen the possibility of such a move being forced upon us.

I returned from the conference at General Blanchard's headquarters at about 10.30 a.m. on 26th May to find a telegram from the Secretary of State which read:-

"I have had information all of which goes to show that French offensive from Somme cannot be made in sufficient strength to hold any prospect of functioning with your Allies in the North. Should this prove to be the case you will be faced with a situation in which the safety of the B.E.F. will predominate. In such conditions only course open to you may be to fight your way back to West where all beaches and ports east of Gravelines will be used for embarkation. Navy will provide fleet of ships and small boats and R.A.F. would give full support. As withdrawal may have to begin very early preliminary plans should be urgently prepared... Prime Minister is seeing M. Reynaud to-morrow afternoon when whole situation will be clarified including attitude of French to the possible move."

I replied that a plan for withdrawal northwestward had been agreed with the French that morning; I added that the news from the Belgian front was disquieting, and concluded by saying:-

"I must not conceal from you that a great part of the B.E.F. and its equipment will inevitably be lost even in best circumstances."

Later in the day, I had a further telegram from the War Office which read as follows:-

"Prime Minister had conversation M. Reynaud this afternoon. Latter fully explained to him the situation and resources French Army. It is clear that it will not be possible for French to deliver attack on the south in sufficient strength to enable them to effect junction with Northern Armies. In these circumstances no course open to you but to fall back upon coast. . . . M. Reynaud communicating General Weygand and latter will no doubt issue orders in this sense forthwith. You are now authorised to operate towards coast forthwith in conjunction with French and Belgian Armies."

The Situation, of the Belgian Army.

45. The situation on the Belgian front was causing me ever increasing anxiety. At the conference at Ypres on the evening of 21st May, His Majesty the King of the Belgians had agreed that, if forced to abandon the positions on the Lys, he would withdraw to the Yser, maintaining touch with the left of the B.E.F. Now, however, signs were not wanting that the Belgian Army were being forced to withdraw northwards and away from the Yser canal. If so, the task of defending the whole line as far as the sea appeared likely to fall on ourselves and the French, as actually did happen.

Admiral of the Fleet Sir Roger Keyes, who had been carrying out liaison duties with H.M. the King of the Belgians since the operations began, came to G.H.Q. on the morning of 26th May, and I expressed to him my earnest hope that the Belgian Army would fall back towards the Yser. Sir Roger Keyes took this message back to the Belgian G.Q.G. at Bruges, where he saw His Majesty. Later he telegraphed to me saying that the Belgians would do their best, but that His Majesty considered that the only method of avoiding immediate and complete disaster was a strong and immediate counter offensive between the Lys and the Escaut. Such an operation was, however, quite out of the question since, now that 5th and 50th Divisions had been committed, my reserves were again reduced to one weak cavalry regiment.

The indication that the Belgian Army would withdraw northwards and not to the Yser, was confirmed in a note, a copy of which I received, sent on 26th May by General Michiels, the Chief of the Staff of the Belgian Army, to General Neissens, head of the Belgian Mission with G.K.Q.

This note contained the following passage:-

. . . "To-day, 26th May the Belgian Army is being attacked with extreme violence on the front Menin-Nevele,[31] and since the battle is now spreading to the whole of the area of Eecloo, the lack of Belgian reserves makes it impossible to extend our boundaries, which were notified yesterday, further to the right.

We must therefore, with regret, say that we have no longer any forces available to fill the gap in the direction of Ypres.

As regards the withdrawal to the Yser the idea must be ruled out since it would destroy our fighting units more quickly than the battle now in progress, and this without loss to the enemy."

On receipt of this information, on the morning of 26th May, I asked the Secretary of State to bring strong pressure on the Belgian Government to withdraw their Army westwards and to maintain touch with the B.E.F. I also communicated in the same sense to Sir Roger Keyes, but his reply never reached my Headquarters.

---

31 Eight miles west of Ghent.

26th May—The Southern and Western fronts.

46. On the remainder of the front 26th May was marked by heavy air action everywhere. The enemy attack on the French North African division at Carvin which was in progress when I visited General Blanchard at Attiches, was driven back by the prompt action of two battalions of 50th Division which were deployed behind the French troops. 2nd and 44th Divisions reacted against the enemy and both succeeded in advancing some distance westwards from Merville and Hazebrouck respectively towards the Canal.

Further north, the French had completed the relief of all our troops on the river Aa from St. Momelin northwards but had themselves begun in places to withdraw towards the Mardyck Canal. It therefore became the more necessary to strengthen further the defences of Bergues, and this was carried out under the orders of 48th Division.

Plans for final withdrawal.

47. On this evening (26th May), I put in hand my plans for a final withdrawal. I was uncertain how far I should be successful in withdrawing the whole of the B.E.F. within the bridgehead at Dunkirk, nor could I judge how much fighting my troops would have to undertake during the withdrawal.

I had, therefore, asked the War Office whether it would be possible to send out an infantry brigade of the 1st Canadian Division so as to provide a nucleus of fresh and well trained troops on the bridgehead position. This request was at once agreed to, and orders were given to despatch the Brigade to Dunkirk on the night 26th/27th May. These orders were, however, cancelled on 28th May.

The contraction of the B.E.F. area and the shortening of its Lines of Communication was now making it possible to dispense with a number of the rearward units. I had already issued orders for the embarkation of a number of key personnel who could be spared so as to ease the supply situation which was becoming acute; I now ordered the withdrawal of all units which were not required to continue the battle. This policy involved leaving most of the fighting troops until the last, but if full use was to be made of the shipping available, and congestion avoided on the beaches, no other course was possible.

The task of organising a bridgehead at Dunkirk, and of arranging the details of embarkation was likely to prove an exacting one: work had to begin at once, and my own headquarters were fully occupied with the withdrawal of the forward troops.

I therefore appointed Lieut-General Sir Ronald Adam to undertake this duty, and sent with him my Quarter-Master-General and other staff officers from G.H.Q. He was to take command of the troops already in the area, make arrangements for the troops of 1st, 2nd and 3rd Corps who would be withdrawing into the bridgehead and arrange for the embarkation. He was to act in conformity with the orders of General Fagalde, provided that these did not imperil the safety and welfare of British troops.

Sir Ronald Adam accordingly handed over command of the 3rd Corps to Major-General S.R. Wason (till then Major-General R.A. at G.H.Q.), and took up his duties on the morning of 27th May.

At 7 a.m. that morning he attended a conference at Cassel as my representative. At this conference there were present Admiral Abrial and General Fagalde from Dunkirk, General Blanchard, General Prioux, now in command of the French 1st Army, and General Koeltz who was representing General Weygand Sir Ronald Adam and General Fagalde arrived early, and before the conference began they had the opportunity to reach general agreement on the organisation of the bridgehead position.

The perimeter was to extend from Gravelines south-eastwards to the Canal de la Colme, along the canal to Bergues and thence by Furnes and Nieuport to the Belgian coast. In fact, the French were by now evacuating Gravelines and the western part of the perimeter, and in process of going back to the line of the Mardyck Canal from the sea to Spyker, on the Canal de la Colme. The French were to be responsible for the defence of the western half of the perimeter as far as Bergues inclusive, and the British for the eastern half. By this time, the position of the Belgian Army was so obscure that the possibility of its being included in the bridgehead was not taken into account, though the perimeter could of course have been extended eastwards to include them if necessary.

Sir Ronald Adam then explained to General Fagalde his plan for Corps boundaries, assembly areas and the layout of beaches. He specially stressed the importance of avoiding traffic congestion in the perimeter and said that he had decided to allow no British transport north of the canals except such as was strictly necessary for tactical, supply or medical purposes. He urged General Fagalde to issue similar orders to the French troops under his command. He also suggested that the French troops entering the bridgehead position should all be located in the western part of the perimeter. However, it appeared that these orders did not reach all the French troops, who brought a quantity of transport into the sector.

These matters were later reviewed at the full conference, but the principal business was the issue by General Koeltz of an order of the day by General Weygand.

This enjoined a resolute attitude on the part of every leader, and the counter-offensive wherever possible. General Koeltz then proceeded to urge Generals Blanchard and Fagalde to attempt the recapture of Calais and, though at the time they had nothing available save the 68th Division and the regional troops, they did not demur.

However, so far as I am aware, no action was ever taken in this respect.

Description of the Dunkirk Perimeter.

48. The British sector of the Dunkirk perimeter had its right at Bergues, and thence followed the canals to Fumes and Nieuport. These places were old-fashioned fortified towns, easy to defend but affording good bombing targets. The destruction of the bridges presented no difficulty, and all were in fact blown in time by British or French troops except that at Nieuport which was wide and solid, and could not be demolished before the arrival of the enemy. Two natural switch lines were available: the canal from Bergues to Dunkirk and the Canal des Moeres from Dunkirk south-east towards Hondschoote.

Immediately north of this line came the inundations, extending from Bergues over the district of the Moeres to a width varying from one to three miles. Except in a few places, they did not cover the roads but were designed to leave them clear, while preventing deployment. They did, however, sometimes prevent troops from digging themselves in. On the Belgian side of the frontier the order to begin the inundations was not given by Belgian G.Q.G. till the morning of 26th May and they never became effective.

To the north of the inundations was more low-lying land; then came the Bergues-Furnes Canal, and the main lateral road from Fumes to Dunkirk. Finally there was the narrow strip of dunes giving way to a wide, open beach running the whole length of the position and shelving very slowly to the sea. There were no quays or piers whatever except those at Dunkirk itself. At intervals of about a mile along the shore lay the seaside resorts of Coxyde, La Panne, Bray Dunes and Malo-les-Bains.

Layout of the Sector and Problem of Traffic Control.

49. Sir Ronald Adam, on leaving Cassel, went at once to the headquarters of the 48th Division at Bergues to find out the latest situation and in particular what troops were immediately available either to hold the perimeter or to control the traffic. He learnt that the enemy were advancing north eastwards from the Forest of Clairmarais: there could therefore be no question of using any of the reserves of 48th Division, and the only troops immediately available were certain engineer units. General Thorne, however, lent his C.R.A. (Brigadier Hon. E.F. Lawson) who was instructed to lay out the defence of the perimeter, and to use for the purpose such troops as were on the spot, or were entering the perimeter.

The position was then divided into three Corps areas, each including a collecting area outside the perimeter, a sector of the canal line and a sector of the beach.

Already it was seen that the traffic problem was going to assume formidable proportions. Ever since the 10th May it had been a potential source of trouble, but it had been kept in hand in the early stages by strict adherence to prearranged plans and by the use of infantry for traffic control. Once the withdrawal from the Dyle began, the problem became acute in France as well as in Belgium. Refugees began to leave their homes in northern France before the French Government put into operation the plans they had made. The French organisations were not available and no British troops could be spared to control the traffic. The refugee problem had therefore become increasingly acute, and the tide which at first set westwards from Belgium had now met the enemy again in the Somme area and had begun to turn back on itself. Scenes of misery were everywhere, and the distress of women, children and aged people was pitiable. Fortunately the fine weather and warm nights mitigated their plight to some degree and though the outbreak of famine was expected at any moment it did not actually occur in the area of the B.E.F. Little, unfortunately, could be done to help the refugees, since supplies for the troops were still seriously short. Moreover their presence on the roads was often a grave menace to our movement. It had been necessary to give Corps a free hand in handling them: on occasions it had been necessary to turn vehicles into the fields in order to keep the roads clear.

During the 27th May, troops and their transport began to withdraw into the perimeter on the fronts of all three Corps; and where the troops had received the necessary orders, vehicles were disabled and abandoned in the assembly areas. The few troops who could be spared for traffic control did not, however, prove sufficient for the purpose, and consequently a great number of British and French vehicles entered the perimeter and the town, of Dunkirk when they should have remained outside. There was inevitably a large number of vehicles which had become detached from their units, and a number of cases also occurred that day in which units became separated from their formations and arrived within the perimeter without sufficiently clear orders. These were sent to reinforce the defence of the perimeter, or embarked, as seemed best to those in control.

Next day (28th May) when Corps started to take charge in their areas, the difficulties with the British traffic were cleared up, only to be replaced by difficulties with the French traffic.

The French 60th Division began to arrive from Belgium, and at the same time rearward elements of their light mechanised divisions appeared from the south-east and south. These were soon followed by the transport of the French 3rd Corps, mainly horsed. None of these appeared to have received orders to leave their transport outside the perimeter: seldom did they do so unless compelled by British traffic control posts.

By the 28th, Brigadier Lawson, using the greatest energy, had succeeded in the urgent task of manning the perimeter from Bergues to Nieuport with troops from a number of units, chiefly artillery.

50. The Admiralty had placed the naval arrangements for embarkation in the hands of the Dover Command. A Senior Naval Officer had been sent to Dunkirk to work out detailed plans, and steps had been taken to collect a large number of small ships, and of boats for taking troops from the beach out to the ships.

On 27th May, however, these arrangements had not had time to take effect, nor had it yet been possible to provide sufficient naval ratings to man the beaches. Yet a start was made; beaches were organised at La Panne, Bray Dunes and Malo-les-Bains, one being allotted to each Corps; and military beach parties were improvised on each Corps beach. They carried on without naval assistance for two days, but were hampered by a shortage of small boats and by a lack of experience in their use. The troops were unable to handle boats on a falling tide, and during daylight on the 27th, when only one destroyer and two whalers were available for work on the beaches, not more than two hundred men were embarked.

Dunkirk, which for some days had been heavily bombed, received a particularly severe attack on 27th May; lorry columns had been set on fire in the town and a pall of black smoke from the burning oil tanks hung continuously over the town and docks, impeding the air defence.

Though the outer mole could still be used the inner harbour was now blocked except to small ships.

Dunkirk was therefore cleared of all troops and they were sent to the dunes east of the town to await embarkation. The port itself was kept under the control of G.H.Q. and manned by naval ratings. At one time it seemed likely to go out of use at any moment, but troops were in fact embarked there till the end, in numbers which far exceeded expectations.

Supplies, water and ammunition were despatched from England to the beaches, and on 28th May the first convoy arrived. Unfortunately a high proportion of these stores were destroyed on the way over or sunk when anchored off the shore. Nevertheless considerable quantities were landed at Coxyde and La Panne and served to create a badly needed reserve.

During 27th May, the move of 5th and 50th Divisions was completed and the left flank thus extended as far as Ypres. On the front from Bergues to Hazebrouck enemy pressure steadily increased.

On the same afternoon, G.H.Q. moved from Premesques to Houtkerque (six miles W.N.W. of Poperinghe). Communications were difficult throughout the day since Corps headquarters were all on the move, and it had not yet been possible to re-establish line communications which hitherto had run through Lille.

The Belgian Armistice.
51. During 27th May, I received a further telegram from the Secretary of State which read "...want to make it quite clear that sole task now-is to evacuate to England maximum of your force possible". It was therefore very necessary to discuss further plans with General Blanchard, for no policy had yet been laid down by G.Q.G. or any other French higher authority for a withdrawal northward of the Lys. I had no idea what plans either he or Admiral Abrial had in mind.

In the evening, I left my headquarters at Houtkerque with the C.G.S. and the French liaison officer from General Blanchard's headquarters to try and get into touch with General Blanchard. I failed to find him at La Panne, so I went on to Bastion No. 32 at Dunkirk to visit Admiral Abrial, only to find that both he and General Fagalde were equally unaware of his whereabouts.

While at the Bastion, General Koeltz asked me, shortly after 11 p.m. whether I had yet heard that H.M. the King of the Belgians had asked for an armistice from midnight that night. This was. the first intimation I had received of this intention, although I had already formed the opinion that the Belgian Army was now incapable of offering serious or prolonged resistance to the enemy. I now found myself suddenly faced with an open gap of 20 miles between Ypres and the sea through which enemy armoured forces might reach the beaches.

Owing to the congestion on the roads, I did not get back to my headquarters at Houtkerque until about 4.30 a.m. on 28th May. There I found that a telegram had been received from the War Office at 1.30 a.m. saying that H.M. the King of the Belgians was capitulating at midnight.

Withdrawal to the Sea.
52. Next morning (28th May), General Blanchard arrived at my headquarters at Houtkerque at about 11 a.m., and I read him the telegram which I had received the previous day from the Secretary of State. It was then clear to me that whereas we had both received similar instructions from our own Government for the establishment of a bridgehead he had, as yet, received no instructions to correspond with those I had received to evacuate my troops. General Blanchard therefore could not see his way to contemplate evacuation.

I then expressed the opinion that now the Belgian Army had ceased to exist, the only alternatives could be evacuation or surrender. The enemy threat to the North-Eastern flank appeared certain to develop during the next forty-eight hours. The long South-Western flank was being subjected to constant and increasing pressure, especially at Cassel and Wormhoudt, and the arrival of the enemy heavy columns could not be long delayed. These considerations could not be lightly dismissed. While this discussion was taking place, a liaison officer arrived from General Prioux, now in command of the French 1st Army, to say that the latter did not consider his troops were fit to make any further move and that he therefore intended to remain in the area between Bethune and Lille, protected by the quadrangle of canals.

I then begged General Blanchard, for the sake of France, the French Army and the Allied Cause to order General Prioux back. Surely, I said, his troops were not all so tired as to be incapable of moving. The French Government would be able to provide ships at least for some of his troops, and the chance of saving a part of his trained soldiers was preferable to the certainty of losing them all. I could not move him. Finally he asked me formally whether it was my intention to withdraw that night to the line Cassel-Poperinghe-Ypres.

I replied in the affirmative and informed him that I now had formal orders from His Majesty's Government to withdraw the B.E.F. and that if I was to have any hope of carrying them out I must continue my move that night. General Blanchard's parting was not unfriendly, and when he left I issued my orders for withdrawal to provide for that change of mind on the part of the French High Command for which I so sincerely hoped and which in fact took place later.

1st and 2nd Corps were to withdraw on the night of 28th/29th May to a horse-shoe position on the line Proven-Poperinghe-Ypres-Bixschoote, with outposts on the line Ypres-Godevaersvelde. The position of 3rd Corps was more difficult and obscure. 2nd Division, now reduced to less than the strength of an infantry brigade, had fought hard and had sustained a strong enemy tank attack. It was already in process of withdrawing from the line and orders were issued for it to fall back in the direction of Beveren and Proven, prolonging the right flank of 1st Corps. 48th and 44th Divisions were in contact with the enemy on a front of over twenty miles from Bergues through Cassel to Vieux Berquin, in touch with the French

1st Light Mechanised Division, west of the latter place. The French 1st Army had 3rd and 4th Corps in line between Merville and Sailly-sur-la-Lys, but were out of touch with their 5th Corps.

The orders to 48th Division were to stand for a few hours longer. They withdrew that night under pressure from the enemy, with the assistance of the armoured vehicles of the Hopkinson Mission. The garrison of Wormhoudt was extricated together with such portions of the garrison of Cassel as could disengage from the enemy. 44th Division was also ordered to disengage that night, and to move north-eastwards towards the old frontier defences. 46th Division, which had moved on the night 26th/27th May from the Seclin area to Steenvorde, was to move into the Dunkirk perimeter.

Before he received this order, the Commander of 44th Division (Major-General Osborne) had visited headquarters of the French 4th Corps, where he learned of the Belgian armistice; and heard that General Prioux had orders to stand his ground. He, too, had endeavoured to convince General Prioux that the only hope for his army lay in withdrawal.

Later, on 28th May fresh orders were issued by the French 1st Army. They were to the effect that General Prioux himself would remain with the 4th Corps in its present position, and that General de la Laurencie, with his own 3rd Corps and the Cavalry Corps, would withdraw so as to arrive within the Dunkirk perimeter on 30th May. No copy of this order reached General Osborne, who learned of the change of plans when, at 10.30 p.m. that night, he visited the headquarters of the French 1st Army. As General de la Laurencie had decided to begin his move at 11.30 p.m., General Osborne had some difficulty in conforming, but succeeded in doing so. I was genuinely very glad to learn that part, at any rate, of the French 1st Army would now be sharing in the withdrawal, however great the difficulties might be.

Occupation of the Perimeter Completed.

53. 1st and 2nd Corps were now free to proceed with the occupation of their sectors of the Dunkirk perimeter, and both Commanders met Sir Ronald Adam on 28th May. 2nd Corps had, that morning, ordered Headquarters, 2nd Armoured Reconnaissance. Brigade, to take over the sector from Fumes exclusive to the sea at Nieuport, and now ordered 4th Division to move from the line of the Ypres-Comines Canal to relieve them. 3rd Division was to follow as soon as possible and take over the sector between the French-Belgian frontier and Furnes.

These two divisions had been in the line at Ypres since 25th May. They had held positions on the historic ground of the Ypres-Comines Canal, Zillebeke and the eastern outskirts of Ypres, and on these positions, the infantry, well supported by the artillery, had stubbornly held their ground in the face of strong and determined attacks by the enemy.

1st Corps also ordered 1st Division to move into their sector of the perimeter; on the same day 1st Corps was ordered to reinforce the garrison of Bergues with one battalion. This order could not be carried out that day, but next day (29th May) a battalion of 46th Division (9th Foresters) was sent there.

During this time it had been, a constant anxiety to G.H.Q. lest those enemy forces released by the Belgian armistice should forestall our occupation of the perimeter. There had been no time to lose. Early on the 28th the leading enemy mobile troops and tanks had reached Nieuport, and they would have arrived there unopposed had it not been for the work of a troop of 12th Lancers. The state of the roads, congested as they were with refugees and Belgian troops, must also have played their part in delaying the enemy. Throughout the day, however, the defensive positions were improved and a number of additional troops from various units, chiefly Royal Artillery, were collected and organised to occupy them.

On 29th May, troops of 12th Infantry Brigade and Corps Artillery began to arrive; that night 4th Division relieved the mixed detachments which up to now had been holding the sector. Throughout the 29th May the enemy had been attempting to cross the canal between the French-Belgian frontier and Nieuport. At the latter place, where the bridge had not been blown, they established a bridgehead in the town. Everywhere else they were driven back. Some attempted to cross in rubber boats; others were disguised as civilians, even as nuns, and attempted to cross with the refugees, horses and cattle. On this day enemy forces advancing near the coast were shelled by H.M. ships.

Thus, once again the enemy had been forestalled just in the nick of time, and the prompt and gallant action of the troops on the spot had gained the few vital hours which were to make it possible, against all expectation, to embark practically the whole force.

54. On the afternoon of 28th May, I moved my headquarters from Houtkerque to La Panne, which was in direct telephonic communication with London. On arrival I heard reports from Sir Ronald Adam and the Quarter-Master-General.

These reports were not optimistic. No ships could be unloaded at the docks at Dunkirk, and few wounded could be evacuated. There was no water in Dunkirk and very little on the beaches. The naval plans were not yet in full operation, and some 20,000 men were waiting to be taken off the beaches, 10,000 having been taken off in the last two days, chiefly from Dunkirk. The area was congested with French and Belgian troops and their transport, as well as with refugees.

They gave it as their opinion that, given a reasonable measure of immunity from air attack, troops could gradually be evacuated and supplies landed. If, however, intensive enemy air attack continued, the beaches might easily become a shambles within the next forty-eight hours.

I communicated the gist of this report to the C.I.G.S. and I asked that H.M. Government should consider the policy to be followed in the event of a crisis arising, as well it might.
In reply, I received two telegrams which read:-

". . . H.M. Government fully approve your withdrawal to extricate your force in order embark maximum number possible of British Expeditionary Force.... If you are cut from all communication from us and all evacuation from Dunkirk and beaches had, in your judgment, been finally prevented after every attempt to re-open it had failed you would become sole judge of when it was impossible to inflict further damage to enemy."

I also received a gracious telegram of encouragement and good wishes from His Majesty, The King, which I communicated to all ranks.

General Weygand telegraphed on this day appealing personally to me to ensure that the British Army took a vigorous part in any counterattacks necessary; the situation, he added, made it essential to hit hard. When he sent this message, he could have had no accurate information of the real position or of the powers of counter-attack remaining to either the French or the British. General Koeltz had not, as yet, had time to return to G.Q.G. with a first-hand report on the situation, and in any case the time for such action in the northern theatre was long past.

French troops arrive: Problems of embarkation.
55. By 29th May, the naval arrangements were beginning to bear fruit: however, during the day, the enemy began to shell Dunkirk from the south-west, and the port and the beaches were constantly bombed.

Owing to a misunderstanding, the personnel of certain anti-aircraft units had been embarked instead of being retained for the defence of the port-of Dunkirk. Therefore, I was the more dependent on the action of fighter aircraft, and I made this clear to the War Office. I realised how heavy was the demand to be made on the Royal Air Force for the remainder of the operation, and how impossible it would be to expect that they could succeed completely in preventing air action on the beaches. Yet they did succeed in intercepting a large part of the enemy attacks, and those which arrived, though at times serious, were never able to impede our embarkation for long.

French troops were now arriving in the perimeter in large numbers, and, unfortunately, brought with them much transport. The congestion created within the perimeter was well-nigh unbearable and for two days the main road between La Panne and Dunkirk became totally blocked with vehicles three deep. The French were in process of withdrawing all their troops behind the defences on the Belgian frontier, and for the next two days their dispositions were superimposed on those of the British troops in that part of the perimeter between the frontier and Bergues. The French military forces, within the perimeter or now approaching it, consisted of two weak divisions of the 16th Corps (60th and 68th), General Barthélémy's regional troops, General de la Laurencie's 3rd Corps of two divisions (12th and 32nd), and the Cavalry Corps, together with some artillery.

The arrival of these troops, though welcome from so many points of view, raised the question of embarkation in an acute form. Admiral Abrial had apparently received no orders from his Government that the whole of the British troops were to be embarked, and he professed great surprise when he heard of my intentions. He had, it seems, imagined that only rearward elements were to be withdrawn, and that British troops would stay and defend the perimeter to the last, side by side with the French. I therefore sent Sir Ronald Adam to see the Admiral. He explained the orders to extricate my Force which I had received from His Majesty's Government and which had been confirmed the day before.

Meanwhile, the French troops were expecting, to embark along with their British comrades, notwithstanding that no French ships had so far been provided: the beaches were becoming crowded with French soldiers, and difficulties might have occurred at any time. I urged the War Office to obtain a decision as to the French policy for embarkation and asked that the French should take their full share in providing naval faculties. However, to permit embarkation of the French troops to begin at once, I decided to allot two British ships to the French that night, and also to give up the beach at Malo-les-Bains for their sole use.

Medical arrangements.
56. Hospital ships worked continuously till 31st May though continuous bombing made their berthing difficult and they frequently had to put to sea before they were fully loaded. Walking wounded were taken on board personnel ships from Dunkirk or the beaches, but to prevent delay in embarking fit men, orders were issued that the most serious cases should only be embarked on hospital ships. Casualty Clearing Stations had been established at Dunkirk and at the beach at La Panne. Some of the wounded were, however, too ill to move. They had been collected into two Casualty Clearing Stations, one at Crombeke and one at Rosendael, where they were to be cared for till the enemy should arrive.

The Evacuation of 3rd and 2nd Corps.
57. The 3rd Corps Sector included the canal from Dunkirk to Bergues, with the town of Bergues, and a little more than two miles of front west of the town. By the evening of 29th, 3rd Corps had withdrawn 44th and 2nd Divisions from their positions and Corps headquarters were now embarked. 44th and 48th Divisions

were ordered to be transferred to 1st Corps, and 2nd, 23rd and 46th Divisions to proceed to Dunkirk for embarkation, ist Corps was also ordered to embark what remained of 42nd Division, except for 126th Infantry Brigade. Subsequently a change was made, 44th Division being embarked and 46th Division remaining with 1st Corps.

During the 29th and 30th May, 5th and 50th Divisions came into the 2nd Corps, area: the former, sadly reduced in numbers, was withdrawn from the line, while the latter occupied a sector between the Belgian frontier and the right of the 3rd Division.

On the evening of 29th May, therefore, the organisation of the perimeter was complete, and Sir Ronald Adam's task was successfully accomplished. He himself embarked that night. By 30th May, there remained in the area, at an estimate, 80,000 British troops for evacuation and I had now to complete the plans for the final withdrawal of the Force. I had received a telegram from the Secretary of State, which read as follows:-

"Continue to defend present perimeter to the utmost in order to cover maximum evacuation now proceeding well... If we can still communicate with you we shall send you an order to return to England with such officers as you may choose at the moment when we deem your command so reduced that it can be handed to a Corps Commander. You should now nominate this commander. If communications are broken you are to hand over and return as specified when your effective fighting force does not exceed equivalent of three divisions. This is in accordance with correct military procedure and no personal discretion is left to you in the matter... The Corps Commander chosen by you should be ordered to carry on defence and evacuation with French whether from Dunkirk or beaches..."

The problem was to thin out the troops, while maintaining a proper defence of the perimeter, yet at the same time not to retain a larger number of men than could be embarked in one lift.

I had received orders from home that French and British troops were to embark in equal proportions. Thus it looked at one time as if the British would have to continue holding a perimeter, either the existing one or something smaller, at least another four or five days, to enable all the troops to embark. Yet the enemy pressure was increasing and there was no depth in our position. A line on the dunes could only be held during the hours of darkness to cover the final phase of the withdrawal.

I discussed the situation with the Commanders of 1st and 2nd Corps on 30th May. Embarkation had gone well that day, especially from Dunkirk, but enemy pressure had increased at Furnes and Bergues and it was plain that the eastern end of the perimeter could not be held much longer. The enemy had begun to shell the beach at La Panne. I was still concerned lest the arrangements for embarking the French should for any reason prove inadequate. I therefore motored to Dunkirk to inform Admiral Abrial of my views and to assure myself that the arrangements for embarking British and French troops in equal proportions were working smoothly.

The Admiral assured me of his agreement about the evacuation of the sector, and we then discussed the problem of embarkation.

I had already agreed with General de la Laurencie to evacuate 5,000 picked men from his 3rd Corps, which had fought alongside us and of the fighting value of which I had a high opinion. However, the Admiral told me that he had had orders from General Weygand that the personnel of the Cavalry Corps were to be embarked in priority to others. The matter was settled in a most friendly atmosphere and I satisfied myself, so far as it was possible, that no trouble was likely to arise in practice over the sharing of the berths at the Dunkirk mole.

I judged that it would be imprudent to continue to maintain our position on the perimeter outside the permanent defences of Dunkirk for more than twenty-four hours longer, and I therefore decided to continue the evacuation by withdrawing 2nd Corps on the night of 31st May/1st June.

Orders were accordingly issued for 2nd Corps to withdraw 3rd, 4th and 5th Divisions to the beaches and Dunkirk. 50th Division was to fall back to the French defences on the Belgian frontier, and come under command of 1st Corps, together with the British Base staff at Dunkirk. These moves began to take place on the morning of 31st May; by this time there had been a general thinning out of the whole force, and I felt that, however the situation might develop, valuable cadres had been withdrawn which would enable the fighting units of the B.E.F. to be quickly reformed at home.

58. The remains of the B.E.F., on being withdrawn inside the area of the French defences, now came under the orders of Admiral Abrial, and the time had therefore arrived for me to hand over my command, in accordance with the instructions I had received, and to embark for England. I invited Generals Blanchard and de la Laurencie to join me on the journey. To my regret they were both unable to do so, though I was able to arrange for some of the staff of General de la Laurencie's 3rd Corps to sail with that of G.H.Q.

I had selected Major-General Hon. H.R.L.G. Alexander to remain in France in command of 1st Corps, now numbering less than 20,000 men in all. On the afternoon of 31st May I gave him his instructions, which were based on those I had myself received from H.M. Government. He was to operate under the orders of Admiral Abrial, and to assist the French in the defence of Dunkirk. At the same time he was to occupy himself with arrangements for the evacuation of his command, and I stressed the importance of the French sharing equally in the facilities which were provided for evacuation.

I agreed with Major-General Alexander on the night 2nd/3rd June as a provisional date for evacuating his force.

That evening, therefore, at 6 p.m., my headquarters closed, and after handing over command to Major-General Alexander,[32] I embarked in H.M.S. Hebe, and sailed for England about 2 a.m. on 1st June. At this time the withdrawal of 2nd Corps was proceeding according to plan, but under increasing enemy pressure by land and air; the troops were moving to their places on the beaches steadily and in good order. The plans made by the Admiralty to provide small craft were by now in full operation; embarkation was proceeding far more smoothly than it had yet done, and was favoured by a calm sea that night.

In all, 211,532 fit men and 13,053 casualties were embarked at Dunkirk and the beaches, in addition to 112,546 allied troops.[33]

SOME LESSONS OF THE CAMPAIGN
The importance of equipment; the time factor; liaison; defence in depth; the employment of air forces; river crossing and demolitions; signal communications; traffic control; security; supply and transport; the behaviour of the troops.

59. So ended a campaign of 22 days which has proved that the offensive has once more gained ascendency in modern war when undertaken with an army equipped with greatly superior material power in the shape of air forces and armoured fighting vehicles.

The British Expeditionary Force had advanced sixty-five miles from the frontier to the Dyle: then the same distance back from the Dyle to the frontier: finally a further fifty miles to the sea at Dunkirk. A frontal advance had become a flank defence; a flank

---

32 An account of events after Major-General Alexander assumed command is given in Appendix 1.

33 These figures have been obtained from the War Office.

defence the defence of a perimeter which at times exceeded one hundred miles, with my force of nine[34] divisions and parts of three semi-trained and partially equipped divisions sent to France for labour duties. Finally had come the withdrawal to the sea and the shrinkage of this wide front to the twenty-four miles of the Dunkirk bridgehead.

The series of situations which the B.E.F. had to face was not brought about by failure on their part to withstand enemy attacks when holding a position of their own choosing: it was caused. by the enemy breaking through completely on a front many miles away from that held by the B.E.F. Nevertheless this break through, once it began, was destined to involve in its ill-fated consequences both the French 1st Army and the B.E.F. In the withdrawal which ensued both these armies lost the whole of their artillery and transport.

It would not be appropriate in this Despatch to discuss questions affecting the higher command of the Allied forces: on these matters I received orders from H.M. Government and through the French commanders under whom I was placed.

Nor is this Despatch the place to deal at length with the military lessons of the Campaign; I have already conveyed my detailed views to the proper quarter.

There are, however, certain matters which it may be convenient to mention, in broad outline, in this Despatch since they may serve in some respects to amplify and to explain the narrative of events. They are dealt with in the paragraphs which follow.

The paramount importance of equipment.
60. It was clear from the outset that the ascendency in equipment which the enemy possessed played a great part in the operations. He was able to place in the field and to

---

34 Excluding 51st Division on the Saar Front.

concentrate no less than ten armoured divisions in the area which he selected and later, to employ at least five of these against the British rearward defences. On the other hand, the British armoured forces in the theatre of war amounted to seven divisional cavalry regiments equipped with light tanks, one regiment of armoured cars of an obsolete pattern, and two battalions of infantry tanks, the latter, except for twenty three Mark II tanks, being armed each with one machine-gun only.

Our anti-tank armament was more ample than that of the French, but did not extend further back than the division. No guns were available for the defence of Corps or rearward areas or for the three "Pioneer" divisions, except by withdrawing weapons from the formations to which they had been allotted in War Establishments.

These instances amongst many others which might be quoted serve to indicate the vital necessity for an expeditionary force, if it is to be used in a first-class war, being equipped on a scale commensurate with the task it is to be called upon to fulfil.

The days are past when armies can be hurriedly raised, equipped and placed in the field, for modern war demands the ever increasing use of complicated material. Indeed the scientific side of warfare has been evolving at a very rapid rate even since the end of the war of 1914–18 and is continuing to do so. Modern equipment requires time to design and produce, and once it is produced, further time is required to train troops in its technical and tactical uses. Improvised arrangements, made at short notice, can only lead to the shortage of essential equipment, the production of inferior articles, and the unskilful handling of weapons and vehicles on the battlefield.

The Time Factor.
61. The speed with which the enemy exploited his penetration of the French front, his willingness to accept risks to further his

aim, and his exploitation of every success to the uttermost limits emphasised, even more fully than in the campaigns of the past, the advantage which accrues to the commander who knows how best to use time to make time his servant and not his master.

Again, the pace of operations has been so accelerated by the partnership between offensive aircraft and modern mechanised forces that the reserves available for the defence are of little use unless they are fully mobile or already in occupation of some reserve position. For instance, had it not been that eight Troop Carrying Companies, R.A.S.C., were available, the attack south of Arras could never have been mounted, nor indeed could the flank defences on the canal have been organised in time to forestall the enemy.

We had already foreseen, and taught at the Staff College, that the methods of staff duties in the past war would prove too slow for modern requirements. Headquarters of formations were so frequently on the move that conferences, supplemented by Operation Instructions or messages, usually replaced the formal orders which had been the accepted procedure in past campaigns.

Full use was also made of liaison officers of all grades, who had been provided by the War Office on a generous scale. In the period before active operations began, they were of real value in settling matters of detail and in reconciling points of view which did not always at first coincide; during the fighting, they were more often than not the actual bearers of Operation Instructions, and performed most valuable service to their commanders in ascertaining the exact state of affairs in forward or flank units. The junior liaison officers, known as Motor Contact Officers, likewise showed determination and resource in carrying out their duties.

The liaison with flanking French formations was carried out by the exchange of bilingual liaison officers. I was particularly fortunate in the French officers who were attached for these duties from neighbouring formations.

I would also like to take this opportunity of recording my thanks to Général de Division Voruz and the staff of his Mission with G.H.Q. for their unfailing helpfulness at all times.

Defence in Depth.

62. Closely allied to the question of the time factor is that of defence in depth. The speed at which armoured units can advance, once they have, broken into a position, calls for a more elastic conception of defence than would be necessary were it designed solely to hold up a marching enemy. Consequently, frontages may, in the future, be considerably shorter than those which the French High Command required the B.E.F. to hold in France.

In more rearward areas, schemes must be prepared for the manning, at short notice, of centres of communication and other important denies. Therefore, all units, even those designed for purely administrative purposes, must be prepared to take their part in the battle, and they must receive the necessary preliminary training.

Anti-tank defence is a science as well as a craft. It is a science in that it is necessary to perfect armour-piercing weapons and anti-tank tactics. It is a craft in that troops must be trained to stalk tanks by day, to keep track of their movements, and to attack them in their harbours at night.

The Employment of Air Forces.

63. It was clear from the reports of the Spanish war, confirmed by those of the Polish campaign, that the enemy would employ his air forces to further the offensive operations of the army by the use of dive bombers and parachute troops. The latter, though effectively employed in Holland, were less used against the B.E.F.; however, the nuisance value of those which were employed,

by their interference with railway, telephone and telegraph communications in rearward zones, Was altogether out of proportion to their numbers. There were seldom troops available to isolate and search the areas where they landed, usually at dusk, and no French civil organization existed for the purpose.

The enemy bombers, both high level and low flying, were a more serious menace. Their control by the German command was most efficient, capable of bringing the aircraft to their objective by wireless call at short notice.

Attack by dive bombers was a new experience for British troops. Even those who had grown accustomed to heavy shell fire in France during 1914–18 found that this form of attack, when first encountered, placed a strain on morale. As had been anticipated, it was soon realised that those who were properly entrenched and had perfected the drill of taking cover when on the move, suffered relatively little danger.

Ground anti-aircraft defence, both gun and light automatic, improved in accuracy as time went on and it accounted for the destruction of over 500 aircraft in addition to its effect in breaking up formations of enemy aircraft. But being purely defensive, it can never prove the complete antidote to enemy bombers and reconnaissance aircraft, even when available in sufficient strength. A commander must have at his call sufficient fighters to intercept and attack the enemy.

The commander must, likewise, dispose of a sufficient bomber force to be able to engage opportunity targets of vital tactical importance. Such targets were the enemy mechanised columns at Maastricht, Sedan and Boulogne. The machinery for their control must be efficient enough to ensure that aircraft can be despatched in time.

River Crossing and Demolitions.
64. The skill and speed of the enemy in crossing water obstacles was very apparent as was also the excellence of his equipment

for the purpose. On the other hand, the paramount importance of demolitions on such obstacles as a means of imposing even a short delay, was established: during the operations the B.E.F. destroyed over 500 bridges, and there were few failures. From the number of demolitions which it was found necessary to carry out, it is clear that every engineer unit, no matter what its normal role, must receive the necessary training to execute such work.

Signal Communications.
65. During the operations a very heavy strain was thrown upon the Royal Corps of Signals: not least upon those responsible for the communications of G.H.Q. The problem was twofold: first to provide the normal communications within the force, secondly to provide the long-distance communications required to enable G.H.Q. to remain in constant touch with French G.Q.G., the War Office and the Royal Air Force. The latter considerations made it necessary to the moves of G.H.Q. Communications within the B.E.F. demanded mobility and rapidity of construction combined with the need to deal with a heavy volume of traffic. The frequent moves, and the time lag which occurred when cipher had to be used, resulted in a heavy demand on despatch riders.

Traffic Control.
66. The vital importance of controlling movement by road was emphasised over and over again during the operations.

The movements of mechanised columns depend for their success on the proper reconnaissance and allotment of roads, the avoidance of traffic blocks and the power to divert the flow of traffic quickly and without interruption whenever an obstacle occurs. The danger of interference by enemy bombing is always present, but it can be minimised by the employment of fighter aircraft, by an adequate layout of anti-aircraft guns, by the provision of facilities for clearing breakdowns and the repair of roads, and by the training of troops in a proper drill when attacked from the air.

The movement of refugees, as has been described above, laid a further burden on the Provost service. Though the greatest efforts were made by all ranks to cope with the task, it was evident that our organisation required considerable expansion. Recommendations for the creation of a road control organisation under the Quarter-Master-General, on the lines of that in use in the French Army, had already been submitted, but unfortunately too late for more than preliminary results to be achieved.

Security.

67. Akin to the foregoing problem is that of security. Until 10th May the work of the Intelligence Service in this respect had been heavy and constant, but when operations began, it assumed almost unmanageable proportions. This was due to the opening of the Belgian frontier, the mass movement of refugees, and the arrival of enemy saboteurs and agents by parachute.

The troops, however, soon became aware of the danger and realised the importance, of security measures and the paramount need for discretion.

Supply and Transport.

68. As has been already indicated in this. Despatch, the operations showed clearly how complete reliance cannot be placed on any one channel of movement or maintenance. Enemy action by mobile forces or by air may put important road or railway routes out of action for hours or days at a time, or even completely sever communications with the bases.

The proportion of reserves held forward, and under load, on rail or on lorry, must therefore be high, despite the resultant extravagance in transport. The War Office had provided Lines of Communication Railhead Companies, R.A.S.C., to operate in the event of a railhead being out of action for a time, and these units fully justified their existence.

During the final phases of the operations, the civilian employees of the French and Belgian railways were often not to be found, and the Railway Operating Companies, R.E., had to take over the working of the trains at short notice.

The change of bases made necessary after 20th May was a fine example of quick decision, flexible administration, and the power of the administrative staffs at home and in France to improvise at short notice.

The Behaviour of the Troops.
69. Most important of all, the Campaign has proved beyond doubt that the British Soldier has once again deserved well of his country. The troops under my command, whatever their category, displayed those virtues of steadiness, patience, courage and endurance for which their corps and regiments have long been famous.

In addition to the fighting troops, the rearward units, as well as the three divisions sent to France for pioneer duties, all found themselves, at one time or another, engaged with the enemy although often incompletely trained and short of the proper complement of weapons.

Time and again, the operations proved the vital importance of the good junior leader, who has learned to encourage, by his example, the men whom he leads, and whose first care is the well-being of the troops placed under his command. Firm discipline, physical fitness, efficiency in marching and digging, and skill at arms, old fashioned virtues though they may be, are as important in modern warfare as ever they were in the past.

APPRECIATIONS
The Royal Navy; the Royal Air Force; Commanders and Staffs

The Royal Navy.
70. I have already referred to the embarkation of the Force from Dunkirk and its transport to England which evoked the wholehearted admiration of the Army. The operation was carried out in accordance with the finest traditions of the Royal Navy. The plan involved the use of hundreds of privately-owned small craft, and was put into execution at short notice and at a time when Naval resources were severely strained by demands elsewhere. It was carried through regardless of danger and loss by enemy bombing. My deep gratitude is due to all concerned, particularly to Vice-Admiral Sir B.H. Ramsay, Vice-Admiral at Dover, Rear-Admiral W.F. Wake Walker, who superintended the actual embarkation and Captain W.G. Tennant, R.N., the senior naval officer ashore. Nor can the Army forget the sterling work of all those members of the Merchant Navy and the civilian owners of small craft, in many instances volunteers, who unhesitatingly and regardless of dangers gave their services to the British Expeditionary Force.

The Royal Air Force.
71. Successful operations on land depend more than ever before on the closest co-operation between aircraft and troops on the ground, and the B.E.F. owes a deep debt of gratitude to the Royal Air Force for their work throughout the operations. Pilots returned to the air again and again to carry out essential tasks for both French and British Armies, when they were long overdue for rest and sleep.

The embarkation of the Force would have been well-nigh impossible but for the fighter protection afforded. The toll taken[35] of the enemy aircraft on this and earlier occasions has once again established the individual superiority of the British airman in the air.

I wish specially to record my thanks to Air-Marshal A. S. Barratt (now Sir Arthur Barratt), Air Officer Commanding-in-Chief, British Air Forces in France, and to the Air Officer Commanding my Air Component, Air-Vice-Marshal C. H. B. Blount.

Commanders and Staffs.

72. The course of operations in May afforded very unequal opportunities for the several branches of the Staff, Services and departments to show their efficiency, and it would, therefore, perhaps, be invidious to deal with their work in detail to a greater extent than I have already done in this Despatch. Some, however, were required with their Staffs to bear a specially heavy and prolonged strain of responsibility and I wish to refer particularly to the valuable services of my Chief of the General Staff (Lieut.-General H. R. Pownall), my Quarter-Master General (Lieut.-General W. G. Lindsell), and my Engineer-in-Chief (Major-General R. P. Pakenham Walsh), my Signal Officer-in-Chief (Major-General R. Chenevix-Trench), and my Military Secretary (Brigadier Sir Colin Jardine, Bart.).

From the narrative of events, it will be evident how great is the debt I owe to the Commanders of my three Corps. Lieut.-Generals Sir Alan Brooke, M. G. H. Barker and Sir Ronald Adam, Bart. The sudden turn of events on 17th May threw a violent and unexpected strain on the Commander, Lines of Communication Area (the late Major-General P. de Fonblanque), and I wish to record my sincere appreciation of his good and devoted work during the time that he was serving under my command.

---

35 On one day, 77 enemy machines were shot down at the loss of only 16 of our own.

Finally, I desire to express my thanks and good wishes to all those officers in the French Army whose duties brought them into contact with the British Expeditionary Force, and whose goodwill, understanding and personal friendship did so much to foster the good relations which existed between the two armies.

Honours and Awards.

73. I am submitting separately the names of officers and other ranks whom I wish to recommend for reward or to bring to your notice for gallant or distinguished service.

I have the honour to be Sir,
Your Obedient Servant,
GORT,
General, Commander-in-Chief, British Expeditionary Force.

APPENDIX TO SECOND DESPATCH OF C.-IN-C., B.E.F. OPERATIONS OF 1ST CORPS FROM 6 P.M. ON 31st MAY TO MIDNIGHT 2ND/3RD JUNE, 1940

Major-General Hon. H. R. L. G. Alexander, on taking over command of 1st Corps, handed over command of the 1st Division to Brigadier M.B. Beckwith-Smith. He then proceeded to Dunkirk to see Admiral Abrial, who informed him that he intended to hold the perimeter till all the troops were embarked. A French Corps on the right was to hold the sector from Gravelines to Bergues (Gravelines however had not apparently been in French hands for some days) and a mixed French and British Corps under command of Major-General Alexander was to hold a line from Bergues to Les Moeres, and thence to the sea.

Major-General Alexander at once told the Admiral and General Fagalde that in his view this plan did not take account of the true naval and military situation which was serious and deteriorating rapidly. The fighting condition of the troops was now such that prolonged resistance was out of the question and the present front could riot in his opinion be maintained after the night 1st/2nd June: furthermore the line to be held was so close to the beach and to Dunkirk that the enemy might soon stop all further evacuation by short range artillery fire. He gave the same opinion to the Secretary of State and received a reply that the British force should be withdrawn as rapidly as possible on a basis of equal numbers of British and French continuing to be embarked from that time onward. This he showed to Admiral Abrial and General Fagalde informing them that he would hold the sector allotted to him till midnight 1st/2nd June and then withdraw under cover of darkness. They agreed that in the circumstances no other plan was feasible.

The naval situation had by now grown worse, and the Channel from Dunkirk was under direct artillery fire. It was therefore evident that the force could not be evacuated completely on the night 1st/2nd June. Major-General Alexander therefore agreed on a modified plan with Admiral Abrial and General Fagalde at 8 a.m. on 1st June. He arranged to hold his present line till midnight 1st/2nd June; thus he would cover Dunkirk and so enable the French to evacuate as many of their troops as possible. He would then withdraw to a bridgehead round Dunkirk with all available anti-aircraft and anti-tank guns and such troops as had not yet embarked.

During the 1st June, heavy enemy attacks developed on the British sector, supported by bombing and artillery fire. The garrison of Bergues (1st Loyals) were forced to withdraw to the line of the canal north of the town, and to the west, 46th Division, 126th Infantry Brigade of 42nd Division and 1st Division were forced back north of the canal for about 1,000 yards. 50th Division had also to meet enemy penetration from the east, but by nightfall on 1st June the enemy advance had been checked on a line Bergues-Uxem-Ghyvelde, thence due east to the frontier and along the frontier defences to the sea.

Embarkation was temporarily stopped at 3 a.m. on 2ⁿᵈ June to prevent casualties in daylight; by that time there remained in the Dunkirk area about 3,000 men of various artillery and infantry units, with seven antiaircraft guns and twelve anti-tank guns. They held the outskirts of Dunkirk throughout 2ⁿᵈ June with little interference save heavy shelling and bombing of the beaches.

By midnight on 2ⁿᵈ/3ʳᵈ June, all the remaining British troops had been embarked. Major-General Alexander, with the Senior Naval Officer (Captain W. G. Tennant, R.N.) made a tour of the beaches and harbour in a motor boat and on being satisfied that no British troops were left on shore, they themselves left for England.

THE BRITISH EXPEDITIONARY FORCE AND WITHDRAWAL FROM WESTERN FRANCE JUNE 1940

Introduction and Summary

Operation Dynamo and the withdrawal of British forces from Northern France and Belgium did not signal an end to the Battle for France. Some elements of the BEF had withdrawn to the South and the British and French General Staffs hoped an effective front against German forces could be reconstituted in Central and Western France. To this end, a number of units were sent to Western France on 12 June to try to shore up French resistance. The day was inauspicious as, at the same time, a large part of the 51st Highland Division, caught at St Valery-en-Caux, was forced to surrender. Most of the Division was taken prisoner. With that, resistance against the Germans in Northern France was effectively over.

The 2nd British Expeditionary Force arrived at Cherbourg on 13 June to find it painfully apparent that it would be impossible to reconstitute a front line against the German advance and that the French Armies were effectively operating under local command. It was simply a matter of time before they were defeated. Arrangements for the withdrawal of British forces were thus speedily put in place. Under Operation Ariel from 15–25 June, British units and other groups wishing to escape the Nazis (including Poles, Czechs and those Frenchmen who would form the nucleus of the Free French movement) were embarked from ports in Western France.[36]

This withdrawal was not accomplished without significant losses. For example, the liner *Lancastria* carrying several thousand evacuees from St Nazaire was sunk on 17 June by Luftwaffe bombers. The precise number of casualties on board the *Lancastria* will never be known, but conservative estimates place the death toll at over 3,500.

Submitted 22 June 1940 by Lieutenant-General, Sir Alan Brooke (23 July 1883 – 17 June 1963 – KG, GCVO, CBE, DSO & bar), Commanding II Corps, British Expeditionary Force
TNA: CAB 106/244. Published as supplement 37573 to *The London Gazette*, 21 May 1946, pp.2443–2449.

WEDNESDAY, 22 MAY, 1946
The War Office,
May, 1946.
OPERATIONS OF THE BRITISH EXPEDITIONARY FORCE, FRANCE
FROM 12TH JUNE, 1940 TO 19TH JUNE, 1940.
I have the honour to report that, in accordance with the instructions of 10th June, 1940, received by me from the Secretary of State for War, I duly left Southampton by ship at

---

36 For further reading Brian Bond, *Britain, France and Belgium 1939–1940*, (London: Brassey's Publishing, 1990); Martin Evans, *The Fall of France: Act with Daring*, (Oxford: Osprey, 2000); Alistair Horne, *To Lose a Battle: France 1940*, (London: Macmillan, 1969); Basil Karslake, *1940 The Last Act: The Story of the British Forces in Franc after Dunkirk*, (London: Leo Cooper, 1979); Philip Warner, *The Battle of France, 1940: 10 May – 22 June*, (London: Simon & Schuster, 1990).

1400 hours on 12th June, and reached Cherbourg at 2130 hours the same evening.

For reasons connected with local French orders, it was not possible to disembark until 0030 hours on 13th June, when Brigadier G. Thorpe (Base Commandant) came out to the ship in a tug and took me ashore with my staff.

2. At 0800 hours 13th June I left Cherbourg by car, and reached Le Mans at 1400 hours after a journey much hampered by the crowds of refugees on the roads.

There I was met by Lieutenant-General Sir Henry Karslake, Major-General P. de Fonblanque, G.O.C., Lines of Communication Troops, and Brigadier J. G. des R. Swayne. I at once took command of all British troops in France from General Karslake. I instructed him to return to England, which he did by plane that afternoon.

3. At 1500 hours I left Le Mans with Brigadier Swayne for an interview with General Weygand and, after a journey of some 170 miles, reached the Headquarters of No.1 Mission[37] (Major-General Sir Richard Howard-Vyse) at 2000 hours that evening.

General Weygand was away at a Cabinet meeting, but, on his return, he sent a message to say that he would see me at 0830 hours on 14th June.

4. I had left my staff at Le Mans to get in touch with the situation as it was known by General Karslake and Major-General de Fonblanque. The general inference of the enemy's intention seemed to be that, after crossing the Seine south of Rouen, the bulk of the troops engaged would move South in order to encircle Paris.

The situation on the front that evening, so far as it was known, was that the Tenth French Army, which included the

---

37 No. 1 Mission, under Major-General Sir Richard Howard-Vyse, represented British interests at the French Army Headquarters (Chief of Staff, General Weygand) in Paris.

157th Infantry Brigade of the 52nd Division, Armoured Division (less one Brigade) and Beauman Force[38], was holding a line from the sea West of the Seine to Neubourg and thence to Conches. Between the Southern flank of the 157th Infantry Brigade and Damville, there was a gap of some 8 miles, which was only lightly held by elements of the 3rd D.L.M. South of this area the Army of Paris was supposed to be holding a line from Dreux to Bonnecourt on the Seine, but there was no confirmation that this Army was actually in position.

14th June.

5. At 0830 hours I saw General Weygand. He spoke most frankly and explained the situation to me. He said that the French Army was no longer capable of organised resistance, that it had now broken up into four groups – one of which was the Tenth Army (General Altmayer), with which the B.E.F. was operating – and that considerable gaps existed between the groups.

The Armies, he explained, would continue to fight under the orders of their own Commanders, but co-ordinated action of the force as a whole would no longer be possible. Reserves were exhausted and many formations worn out.

He then informed me that, in accordance with a decision taken by the Allied Governments, Brittany was to be defended

---

38 The Beauman Division was an improvised formation which on 13th June, was organised as follows:-

"B" Bde.- formed of personnel from auxiliary military Pioneer Corps.

"C" Bde.-Formed of personnel from infantry base depots.

4 Provisional Battalion-Formed from reinforcement personnel.

"E" Anti-tank Regiment (improvised).

"E" Field Battery (improvised).

212 Army Troops Company, Royal Engineers.

213 Army Troops Company, Royal Engineer.

by holding a line across the peninsula in the vicinity of Rennes. He suggested that we should proceed to General Georges' Headquarters to discuss with him the details of this project.

We then went to General Georges' Headquarters, at Briare, where we continued the discussion. I pointed out that the length of the proposed line was some 150 kilometres which would require at least fifteen Divisions. I gathered from both General Weygand and General Georges[39] that they did not consider the Brittany project to be a feasible proposition with the forces that now remained available in the Tenth French Army including the B.E.F. General Weygand referred to the project as "romantic," and said that it had been adopted without military advice. General Weygand stated, however, that, since the Allied Governments had issued instructions for the defence of Brittany he must carry out their orders. Consequently, in consultation with General Georges, he had drawn up instructions for the participation of the B.E.F. in the scheme. Being under the impression that H.M. Government had approved this plan, I signed the document which prescribed the role of B.E.F. in it. (Copy attached at Appendix 'A').

6. In view of the gravity of the situation which General Weygand had described to me, I immediately sent a telegram to inform the C.I.G.S. I also requested Major-General Sir Richard Howard-Vyse to proceed to the War Office as soon as possible to report more fully to the C.I.G.S., and to take to the C.I.G.S. a copy of the document reproduced in Appendix "A".

7. I then returned to my Headquarters at Le Mans, arriving at 1615 hours. I spoke to the C.I.G.S. by telephone at 1630 hours and explained the situation. I asked whether the Brittany scheme had H.M. Government's approval and told him that both Generals Weygand and Georges appeared to consider it

---

39 General Georges was C.-in-C., North Eastern Theatre of Operations

impracticable with the force available. The C.I.G.S. informed me that he knew nothing of the Brittany scheme, but said he would refer the matter to the Prime Minister.

I told the C.I.G.S. that, in view of the general state of disintegration which was beginning to spread in the French Army, I considered that all further movement of troops and material to France should be stopped, and that arrangements should be started for the evacuation of the B.E.F. from available ports. The C.I.G.S. informed me that orders had already been issued to stop the dispatch of further troops and material to France.

8. An hour later (1715 hours) the C.I.G.S. telephoned to say that the Prime Minister knew nothing of the Brittany plan, and that all arrangements were to start for the evacuation of those elements of the B.E.F. which were at that time not under the orders of the Tenth French Army.

As H.M. Government had not been consulted with regard to the Brittany scheme, and the withdrawal of the B.E.F. had been approved, I considered that I was no longer in a position to carry out the dispositions settled with Generals Weygand and Georges. I therefore requested the C.I.G.S. to inform General Weygand, and I understood this was to be done. The instructions which I received later (see paragraph 10 below), stating that I was no longer under General Weygand's orders, confirmed this opinion.

Orders outlining the arrangements for the evacuation were at once issued, and an officer was dispatched to Lieutenant-General J. H. Marshall-Cornwall requesting him to come to my Headquarters.

9. The C.I.G.S. telephoned again at 2015 hours and said that it was most important that everything should be done to ensure good relations between ourselves and the French, and to avoid, in every possible way, giving the impression that the B.E.F. was deserting them. I replied that I would most certainly see that this was done, that I was moving no troops engaged with the

Tenth Army but that I was arranging to move back all other troops and material towards the ports.

At this stage the Prime Minister himself spoke and asked about the employment of those elements of the 52nd Division which were hot under the orders of the Tenth French Army. I assured him that I considered that no useful purpose could be served by adding them to the forces already with that Army. They could not possibly restore the situation on that front, nor could they close the gap of some 30 miles which now existed between the Tenth French Army and the Army of Paris.

The Prime Minister then agreed to my proposal that the troops under orders of the Tenth French Army should remain fighting with that army for the present, whilst the withdrawal of the remainder of the B.E.F. should, proceed.

Moves to ports of embarkation were therefore continued, Canadian forces moving on Brest, corps troops on St. Malo 52nd Division. (less elements with Tenth French Army) on Cherbourg, L. of C. troops and material on St. Malo, Brest, St. Nazaire, Nantes and La Pallice. Finally those elements with Tenth French Army were to embark at Cherbourg when the situation admitted of their withdrawal from that Army.

10. At 2235 hours I spoke to the C.I.G.S. and told him of the Prime Minister's approval for evacuation. The C.I.G.S. informed me that I was no longer under the orders of General Weygand, and that the B.E.F. was to act as an independent force. I was, however, to continue to co-operate in every way possible with the Tenth French Army.

11. During the night of 14th/15th June, my staff and myself were busily engaged in perfecting the arrangements for the embarkation and evacuation of approximately 150,000 personnel, with large stocks of vehicles and material which had been accumulated since September, 1939. Major Macartney of the Quartermaster General's Movement Staff arrived from the War Office that night. He brought with him a

list showing the order of priority for shipment of stores, etc., and a suggested outline plan for evacuation. A Senior Naval Officer also arrived early next morning.

15th June.

12. At 0315 hours Lieutenant-General J. H. Marshall-Cornwall reported to me, and we discussed the situation. I placed all British troops with the Tenth French Army under his command, and gave him orders to co-operate with that Army until an opportunity arose to disengage his troops and withdraw them to Cherbourg for embarkation to the United Kingdom.

The subsequent operations of Lieutenant-General J. H. Marshall-Cornwall's troops (Norman Force[40]) are described in that officer's report which is attached at Appendix "B".

13. The withdrawal of B.E.F. started in the early hours of 15th June. The flights of the Canadian Division which had arrived in the Concentration Area were sent back to Brest for embarkation, corps troops were reembarked at St. Malo, and various L. of C. troops in the Le Mans area were moved nearer the port areas.

14. Information as to the position of the enemy on the front of the Tenth French Army and southwards was very meagre as bad visibility prevented air reconnaissance, and there were no ground troops to reconnoitre between Alencon and Tours.

The general inference, however, was that there was little enemy activity west of Rouen, but (hostile infantry were engaging the 157th Infantry Brigade in the area of Conches.

---

40 Norman Force, was an improvised formation which, on 15th June, comprised:-

3rd Armoured Brigade.

157th Brigade Group (157th Infantry Brigade; 71st Field Regiment R.A.; Troop-Carrying Company, 52nd Division).

Beauman Division (see previous footnote 38).

A British pilot of a Bomber aircraft, who had made a forced landing, reported that he had run into heavy anti-aircraft fire about Evreux and that he had seen a column of all arms moving south in that area. This report seemed to confirm previous information that the Fourth German Army was moving South with its left on Chartres.

15. At 0810 hours I considered that my position at. Le Mans was too exposed, since there was no known body of troops covering that area. I therefore moved my Headquarters back to Vitre, just west of Laval. I took with me the G.O.C. L. of C. Area, a part of whose staff I had amalgamated with my own since I was entirely dependent on L. of C. Signals for my communications. My own staff consisted only of four officers and two clerks, the remainder having been stopped at St. Malo and sent back to England.

16. At 1230 hours the C.I.G.S. telephoned to say that the Prime Minister was anxious about the withdrawal of the 52nd Division (less the detachment with Tenth French Army). The Prime Minister wished the embarkation to be cancelled, as he feared the effect of such a withdrawal on the morale of the French.

I pointed out that my plans had already received approval, that orders had been issued for the move, and that any alterations now would complicate the embarkation at Cherbourg and might well endanger it. The C.I.G.S., however, said that the Prime Minister did not wish, the division to be embarked without the approval, of His Majesty's Government.

17. At this time the complete absence of any information of the whereabouts of the enemy on the Le Mans front caused me some anxiety, as any penetration of enemy troops towards Laval and Rennes would have seriously endangered the safety of the B.E.F.

18. I spoke again to the C.I.G.S. at 2150 hours. I explained to him the situation as I knew it, and I once more impressed on him the need to evacuate 52nd Division (less the detachment

with Tenth French Army). The necessary shipping was available at Cherbourg and was being kept idle. The air situation was also at that time favourable.

An hour and a half later the C.I.G.S. gave permission to embark one field regiment, one field company and other details of 52nd Division which were not needed to support the infantry of the Division. Orders implementing these instructions were at once issued.

19. Later that night another battalion and a troop of anti-tank guns from 52nd Division were put under General Marshall-Cornwall's orders for the protection of the Cherbourg peninsula at St. Sauveur.

No information of the enemy's movements could be obtained, but he did not appear at the moment to have exploited the gap at Le Mans.

20. During the preceding 24 hours just over 12,000 troops were reported to have been evacuated from the different ports.

16th June.

21. At 0700 hours the C.I.G.S. rang me up and said that all arrangements could be made for the evacuation of 52nd Division (less the detachment with Tenth French Army), but that no actual movement was yet to take place. At 0830 hours, however, he rang up again and confirmed that 52nd Division (less the detachment with Tenth French Army) could now begin to embark: Norman Force itself was to continue to co-operate with the Tenth French Army. I then asked the C.I.G.S. what the policy should be with regard to troops of the French Army who might wish to embark at Cherbourg. He informed me that they would be allowed to do so. Orders for the embarkation of 52nd Division (less the detachment with the Tenth French Army) were issued.

I issued orders to G.O.C. L. of C. to the effect that work of re-embarkation of personnel, stores, and vehicles was to continue at all ports as long as the tactical situation permitted.

22. Owing, once more, to poor visibility no air reconnaissance was possible, but reports from Motor Contact Officers and from Norman Force showed that the enemy was in contact with the Tenth French Army along its front but that he was attacking seriously only against 157th Infantry Brigade. Further to the South enemy movement seemed to be directed on Chartres.

Information was received later from captured orders which showed that the Fourth German Army was to attack that day with the ultimate object of gaming Cherbourg and Brest.

23. The C.I.G.S. telephoned at 1325 hours to confirm that 52nd Division (less the detachment with Tenth French Army) could now embark. He said that he was. still unable to give orders as to the future of Norman Force, which was to continue in the meantime to co-operate with the Tenth French Army. I pointed out that that Army was carrying out the Brittany plan and had been ordered to withdraw on Laval and Rennes. I therefore asked that Norman Force should be allowed to disengage and withdraw on Cherbourg.

The C.I.G.S., however, was not prepared to give the decision, and asked that I should ring him up again on my arrival at my new Headquarters.

24. At 1430 hours, I moved my Headquarters S.W. from Vitre to Redon, which lies about 30 miles N. of St. Nazaire, and reached Redon soon after 1615 hours. I then rang up the C.I.G.S. who said that it had been decided that Norman Force was to stay with the Tenth French Army until that Army started to disintegrate, when General Marshall-Cornwall could withdraw his force for embarkation either to Cherbourg or the nearest available port.

25. I had previously arranged that 90,000 rations, as well as ammunition, should be sent up to Cherbourg, as this was the port on which Norman Force would be based. Any alterations to this plan at this stage would have caused a breakdown

in the supply arrangements which were very difficult because the roads were congested and the railways working spasmodically.

26. During that evening I was in touch with Major-General J. S. Drew commanding the 52ⁿᵈ Division. He informed me that he had embarked one of his brigades and expected to get the other away the next day.

I gave him orders to proceed to the United Kingdom with his second brigade.

27. Brigadier J. G. des R. Swayne, Head of No. 2 Mission[41], reported to me on this way to the United Kingdom. I also dispatched Brigadier N. M. Ritchie, B.G.S., 2ⁿᵈ Corps, to the United Kingdom that night, as there was no longer need for his services in France on account of the reduction of the number of troops.

28. Throughout the day the Germans maintained their pressure on the Tenth French Army. In the evening a message was received from General Marshall-Cornwall in which he gave it as his opinion that the Tenth French Army would disintegrate if it were seriously attacked. This opinion was confirmed by his G.S.O.I (Lieutenant-Colonel R. Briggs, R.T.R.) who called at my Headquarters about 2300 hours that night. On the rest of the front the German advance continued, and the gap between the Tenth French Army and the Army of Paris was well over 50 miles wide. What German forces were in this gap it was impossible to say, as no Allied fighting troops were in the area and air reconnaissance was much hampered by low cloud and thunderstorms.

29. During the previous 24 hours about 47,000 troops and 250 vehicles of all kinds were reported to have been embarked.

---

41 No. 2 Mission had been attached to the Headquarters of General Georges (C.-in-C. North-Eastern Theatre of Operations).

17th June.

30. Early that morning I received a message from General Marshall-Cornwall to the effect that the Tenth French Army was in full retreat on Laval and Rennes, and that he was withdrawing his troops to Cherbourg. His own Headquarters were moving to Avranches and would go next to Cherbourg. At 1015 hours I spoke to the C.I.G.S. and explained the situation to him.

On receiving General Marshall-Cornwall's report I ordered Air Commodore Cole-Hamilton – Commanding the Air Component – to move with two fighter squadrons and his one flight of reconnaisance aircraft to the Channel Islands whence he was to co-operate with Norman Force by carrying out reconnaissance tasks and by protecting the embarkation of that Force at Cherbourg. As soon as he had completed these tasks he was to proceed to the United Kingdom. The remaining Fighter Squadron was to operate from Brest to give close protection to that port during the embarkation of the B.E.F.

31. At 1130 hours, I spoke to Air Marshal Barratt, and explained my plan to him. I also discussed with him the arrangements for the withdrawal from La Rochelle of his party, which was defending Nantes and St. Nazaire during the evacuation. He expressed himself as satisfied with the arrangements that were being made.

32. At 1300 hours the C.I.G.S. telephoned and informed me that the B.B.C. had reported that the Pétain Government had asked the Germans for an Armistice (this was subsequently confirmed by Capitaine Meric of the French Mission). He agreed that, in view of this, all efforts should now be directed to getting personnel away and afterwards, if the situation allowed it, as much material as possible. He further agreed that I should leave with my staff for the United Kingdom that evening. I said that I would ring up again about 3 p.m. to see if there were any final orders and that, if I should be unable to communicate owing to the cable being cut, I would embark as arranged.

I then saw General de Fonblanque and the Senior Naval Officer (Captain Allen, R.N.), explained the situation and ordered them to make every effort to get all personnel away, and also as many guns and vehicles as possible.

33. At 1445 hours I rang up the C.I.G.S. as arranged, but he had not returned to the War Office. At 1530 hours I rang up again, but was informed by Signals that all communications with London had been cut at Rennes, and that it was also impossible to get in touch with any port except Nantes. I, therefore, decided to leave Redon – which I did at 1615 hours – and proceeded with my staff and the G.O.C. L. of C. Area and the Senior Naval Officer to a point about 4 miles outside St. Nazaire. There I remained until 2045 hours.

34. At 2130 hours I left St. Nazaire in the armed trawler H.M.S. "Cambridgeshire." The destroyer which had been sent, for my use. By the Commander-in-Chief Western Approaches was not "available as she was being used to assist in carrying survivors from the "Lancastria," which had been sunk by enemy aircraft that afternoon. The "Cambridgeshire " remained in the harbour during the night. During that time, three enemy air raids took place, but no damage was done, although a few bombs were dropped ashore.

18th June.

0300 hours. The "Cambridgeshire" sailed as escort to a slow convoy.

19th June.

1800 hours. The "Cambridgeshire" reached Plymouth. I went up to the Commander-in-Chief's house where I rang up the C.I.G.S. and reported my arrival in the United Kingdom.

That evening, with my staff, I caught the midnight train to London and reported to the C.I.G.S. at 0900 hours on 20th June.

APPENDIX A.
Commandement en Chef
Du Front Nord-Est.
Au Q.G. Nord-Est 14 Juin, 1940.
10h. 30.

NOTE.
Etat-Major
3e Bureau
Secret.
No. 2063 3/Op.
Le Général Brooke Cdt. le Corps Expéditionnaire Britannique a pris contact le 14 Juin matin avec le Général Weygand Cdt. l'ensemble des Théâtres d'Opérations et le Général Georges Cdt. le Front N.E. pour prendre des directives en ce qui concerne l'emploi des troupes britanniques en France. Dans le cadre de la décision prise par les gouvernements britannique et francais, d'organiser un réduit en Bretagne, il a été décidé:

1e). Que les troupes britanniques en cours de debarquement (E.O.C.A.[42] Brooke, fin de la 52e division et D.I. canadiénne) seront concentrees a Rennes.

2e). Que les troupes britanniques engagées à la Xe Arme'e (D.I. Evans, D.I. Bauman et 52e D.I. non compris ses éléments non encore débarqués) continueront leur mission, actuelle sous les ordres du General Cdt. La Xe Armée.

Leur emploi dans la manoeuvre d'ensemble de cette Armée devra les amener autant que possible & agir dans la région du Mans pour faciliter leur regroupement ultérieur avec les forces du Général Brooke.
Signé BROOKE.
WEYGAND et GEORGES.

---

42 Eléments Organique Corps d'Armée

Pour copie conforme:

Pour le Général Cdt. en Chef.

sur le front Nord-Est.

Le Général Chief d'Etat Major.

APPENDIX 'B.'

SUMMARY OF OPERATIONS OF B.E.F. IN FRANCE FROM
1ST TO 18TH JUNE, 1940.

1. After the evacuation of the main British Expeditionary Force from Flanders in the first week of June the only British troops remaining in France were the 51st Division, which had been holding a sector of the Sarre Front, and the incomplete 1st Armoured Division, which had begun its disembarkation on 20th May and had been rushed up piecemeal in a desperate effort to relieve the sorely tried right flank of the B.E.F. By the 1st June this attenuated Division, which was incomplete when disembarked and had lost heavily in its first engagement on the Somme, could only muster roughly one-third of its quota of tanks.

2. These two formations, the 51st Division and the 1st Armoured Division, the only British fighting formations remaining in France, were placed under the orders of General Altmayer, commanding Tenth French Army, which held the left sector of the Somme front from Amiens to the sea. The handling of the British troops, which had been delegated to General Altmayer by General Weygand, was co-ordinated and supervised by a British Military Mission at Tenth Army Headquarters.

3. The frontage allotted to the 51st Division on the Somme sector was sixteen miles in extent, an excessive amount, but probably not much greater than that which many French divisions were holding at the time owing to their depleted resources. The Division had already been in action on the Sarre front, and had had a long and arduous journey from the Eastern frontier to its new sector. On 4th June the 51st Division Commander was ordered to carry out an attack on the

Abbeville bridgehead, for which operation the newly arrived French 31st Division was placed under his orders, as well as 160 French tanks and a considerable reinforcement of French artillery. The attack, however, was not a success, mainly owing to the difficulty of arranging effective co-operation between British and French infantry, guns and tanks at such short notice, and the 51st Division suffered fairly heavy casualties.

4. On the following day (5th June) the Germans launched a powerful offensive against the whole front held by the Seventh and Tenth French Armies, from St. Quentin to the sea. The 51st Division was by this time in an exhausted condition, after 12 days of continual movement and battle, and was holding too wide a front to be able to resist effectively. The Tenth Army Commander, when asked to relieve the Division from the front, replied that he had no reserves available. The Division fought bravely, but was forced back by German infiltration between its widely scattered posts. Owing to the extent of its frontage the division had no depth in its defences, and had no time to organize rearward defences, nor any reserves with which to counter-attack. It was forced back to the line of the river Bresle, the next natural obstacle, 15 miles in rear.

5. Meanwhile the 1st Armoured Division was re-fitting south of the Seine. Its tanks were in poor mechanical condition, owing not only to battle casualties, but also to the long road distances they had been forced to cover and to the lack of opportunity for adequate maintenance. It was in fact in no condition for offensive operations.

6. On the 7th June the Germans put in a smashing attack with their 5th and 7th Armoured Divisions on the point of junction between the two Corps of the Tenth French Army. This drive was directed from west of Amiens on Rouen and the lower Seine, with the object of splitting the Tenth Army and cutting off its IX Corps between the Seine Estuary and Dieppe. The IX French Corps then comprised the British 51st Division on

the extreme left, and then further east the 31st and 40th French Divisions and the 2nd and 5th Light Cavalry Divisions. The whole of this force was completely sundered from the X Corps on its right by the penetration of the German tanks.

7. Meanwhile, owing to the threat developing to the British base at Rouen, General Sir Henry Karslake, G.O.C. the Lines of Communication, had scraped together an improvised force for its local defence. This force comprised nine infantry battalions of a sort; they consisted partly of second line Territorial units sent out to France for pioneer duties and partly composite units made up from miscellaneous reinforcements at the base. They had no war equipment except rifles and a few odd Bren guns and anti-tank weapons, which they had never fired before. They were without artillery, means of transport and signal equipment. They were placed under the command of Brigadier Beauman, in charge of the North District, Lines of Communication. Very unfortunately this heterogeneous collection of untrained and ill-equipped units was given the title of a Division. The French were thus misled into thinking that it was a fighting formation, complete with artillery and ancillary services. Beauman's so-called Division had been given the task of holding a back line along the rivers Bethune and Andelle covering Rouen, and had done good work in organizing the defence of this position.

8. While the German armoured attack was at its height on the afternoon of the 7th June, General Weygand personally visited Tenth Army Headquarters east of Rouen and impressed on General Altmayer, and on General Evans commanding the British Armoured Division, the necessity for holding the German attack on the Seine at all costs as this was "the decisive battle of the war."

It was now becoming obvious that to enable the IX Corps to fall back in good order to the line of the Lower Seine, a cover position would have to be held along the river Andelle, some 12 miles east of Rouen. General Evans, therefore, at once ordered his 3rd Armoured Brigade (in fact reduced to some four weak squadrons of 30 tanks in all) to stiffen up the right flank of Beauman's defensive line.

9. On the 8th June the German armoured drive continued on the axis Amiens-Rouen, and succeeded in penetrating the weak British defences on. the watershed between the rivers Andelle and Bethune, west of Forges-Les-Eaux. Beauman's ill-equipped units, with the British tanks supporting them, fell back to the line of the Seine. That night German armoured units penetrated into Rouen, and the French Tenth Army lost all touch from then onward with its IX Corps in the Rouen-Dieppe cul-de-sac.

10. The 51st Division was thus completely cut off from its proper line of retirement via Rouen. This was mainly due to the failure or inability of the French High Command to withdraw their left wing while there was still time and space for this manoeuvre. Throughout all these operations it was becoming clear that the French High Command was issuing "die in the last ditch" orders, which their troops had no intention of carrying out. From this time onwards, until the final evacuation of the B.E.F. on the 18th, it was obvious that the spirit of the French Army was crushed and that it had little intention of offering serious resistance. This spirit was also shared by the higher commanders; beginning on the 8th June, the Tenth French Army Headquarters literally ceased to function for 48 hours; it had lost all touch, and its X Corps was broken and in full retreat.

11. The Germans had on the 9th June reached the line of the Seine and had established bridgeheads at several points. The 3rd Armoured Brigade and Beauman's fragmentary units were withdrawn to reorganize, and the 2nd Armoured Brigade, which had been refitting at Louviers, was put in to support General de la Laurencie's III Corps which was trying to hold the Seine crossings south of Rouen. It was now apparent that the German armoured units and air force were being employed elsewhere, while three army corps were detached to drive southwest

towards Alençon with a view to separating the Tenth French Army from the Armée.

12. It was at this critical juncture that the 52nd Division was hastily sent out to France. Its leading brigade, the 157th, under an able and cool-headed commander, Brigadier Sir John Laurie, was rushed up and placed under the orders of the Tenth French Army. On the night of 12th/13th June it took over the right sector of the III Corps front east of Conches, in a very exposed position, with a gap of eight miles on its right, and two newly arrived French battalions on its left west of Evreux.

As none of the 52nd Divisional Artillery had yet arrived, the 157th Brigade was given the support of some French batteries.

13. On 14th June the Germans renewed their pressure on the Tenth French Army front, but most of their tanks and aircraft appeared to have been diverted on a south-easterly axis towards Paris. A fairly sharp infantry attack developed on the left flank of the 157th Infantry Brigade, which suffered some 50 casualties, and the French infantry on their left, as well as the French artillery supporting them, retired hastily, leaving the brigade in the lurch. As a result of this pressure the Tenth French Army withdrew south-west a distance of 30 miles to the wooded area north-west of Mortagne. As the Armée de Paris was retiring almost due south on the Loire, this divergence of the lines of retreat of the two armies created a gap of some 30 miles on the right flank of the Tenth Army.

14. In conformity with this withdrawal the 157th Brigade moved back and took up a front of eight miles astride the Mortagne-Verneuil road, with the French Cavalry Corps on its right. On the night of the 14th/15th I was placed by General Brooke in command of all the British troops operating with the Tenth French Army, and was ordered to withdraw them towards Cherbourg for re-embarkation, whilst still co-operating, so far as possible, with the French withdrawal. It had been my intention

to leave the 157th Brigade in the line until mid-day on the 16th before withdrawing it, in order to allow General Altmayer to readjust his front. I notified General Altmayer of this intention on the 16th, and he appreciated the respite granted him.

15. On the 16th June, however, the German motorized columns had already followed up swiftly the French withdrawal, and the 157th spirit of the French Army was crushed and that Brigade was attacked all day. The French units on its right and left retired without making any serious resistance, and the British Brigade was exposed to serious danger by both its flanks being turned. As a result of this enemy pressure, the Tenth Army issued orders for a general retirement on the axis Alençon-Rennes, with a view to withdrawing into Brittany. As co-operation with such a movement would have been contrary to my own instructions, I at once issued orders to Beauman's Force, the 3rd Armoured Brigade (which had once again relieved the 2nd) and the 157th Infantry Brigade, for a withdrawal north-westwards to Cherbourg.

16. In the case of Beauman's Force and the 3rd Armoured Brigade, neither of which were in contact with the enemy, this was a comparatively simple operation, although it involved moving at right angles across the simultaneous line of retreat of the XIV Corps of the Tenth Army. The 157th Brigade, however, was still engaged with the enemy, and it was only due to the cool handling and tactical ability of its Brigadier that it was extricated from its dangerous situation, embussed by midnight on the 16th/17th, moved 200 miles by roads encumbered by columns of troops and refugees and embarked 24 hours later at Cherbourg.

17. In order to protect the embarkation at Cherbourg, I had asked for a fresh battalion of the 52nd Division to be left to occupy a covering position some 20 miles to the south. This, combined with the five French battalions of the Cherbourg garrison, ought to have provided ample security, and I had hoped to continue the embarkation until the 21st in order to remove all

the stores and mechanized vehicles. The enemy, however, again upset our calculations by the speed with which he followed up our rapid withdrawal. At 9 a.m. on the 18th, a column of 60 lorries, carrying motorized German infantry, reached the covering position near St. Sauveur. Finding resistance there, they turned west to the sector held by French troops, and succeeded in penetrating the position by the coast road. The French made little attempt to resist, and I had to make the decision at 11.30 to complete the evacuation by 3 p.m. The covering battalion (5th Bn. K.O.S.B.) was withdrawn between 12 noon and 3 p.m., and the last boat left at 4 p.m. All weapons were removed, except one 3.7 in. A.A. gun, which broke down and was rendered unserviceable, and one static Bofors gun which could not be removed in the time. Two Anti-Tank guns also had to be abandoned during the withdrawal. When the last troopship left, the Germans had penetrated to within three miles of the harbour.

(Sgd.) J. H. MARSHALL-CORNWALL,

Lieutenant-General.

20th June, 1940.

LONDON

THE BATTLE OF BRITAIN

Introduction and Summary

For British historians the Battle of Britain began on 10 July and came to an end around 31 October 1940.[43] In its latter phases it blended into the London Blitz, which lasted until the early summer of 1941. German historians incorporate this period of bombing into their definition of the Battle of

43 For further reading see Paul Addison, Jeremy Crang, *The Burning Blue: A New History of the Battle of Britain*, (London: Pimlico, 2000); Patrick Bishop, *Fighter Boys: The Battle of Britain, 1940*, (New York: Viking, 2003); Garry Campion, *The Good Fight: Battle of Britain Wartime Propaganda and The Few*, (Basingstoke: Palgrave Macmillan, 2010); Garry Campion, *The Battle of Britain, 1945–1965: The Air Ministry and the Few*, (Basingstoke: Palgrave Macmillan, 2015); Matthew Cooper, *The German Air Force 1933–1945: An Anatomy of Failure*, (New York: Jane's Publishing Incorporated, 1981); Phil Craig, Tim Clayton, *Finest Hour: The Battle of Britain*, (New York: Simon & Schuster, 2000); Patrick G. Eriksson, *Alarmstart: The German Fighter Pilot's Experience in the Second World War*, (Stroud: Amberley, 2017); David Fisher, *Summer Bright and Terrible: Winston Churchill, Lord Dowding, Radar and the Impossible Triumph of the Battle of Britain*, (Emeryville [CA]: Shoemaker & Hoard, 2005); John Foreman, *Battle of Britain: The Forgotten Months, November And December 1940*, (Wythenshawe [Lancashire]: Crécy

Britain. On 2 July 1940, as the German High Command wrestled with how to force the British into defeat or a negotiated peace, the Luftwaffe was given two tasks:

The interdiction of the Channel to merchant shipping, to be carried out in conjunction with German naval forces, by means of attacks on convoys, the destruction of harbour facilities, and the sowing of mines in harbour areas and the approaches thereto.
The destruction of the Royal Air Force.[44]

Publishing, 1989); Peter Haining, *The Chianti Raiders: The Extraordinary Story of the Italian Air Force in the Battle of Britain*, (London: Robson Books, 2005); Peter Haining, *Where the Eagle Landed: The Mystery of the German Invasion of Britain, 1940*, (London: Robson Books, 2004); Richard Hough, *The Battle of Britain: The Greatest Air Battle of World War II*, (New York: W.W. Norton, 1989); T. C. G. James, *The Battle of Britain* (Air Defence of Great Britain; vol. 2), (London: Frank Cass Publishers, 2000); T. C. G. James, *Growth of Fighter Command, 1936–1940* (Air Defence of Great Britain; vol. 1), (London: Frank Cass Publishers, 2000); T. C. G. James, *Night Air Defence During the Blitz*, (London: Frank Cass Publishers, 2003); Lynne Olson, and Stanley Cloud, *A Question of Honor: The Kościuszko Squadron: Forgotten Heroes of World War II*, (New York: Knopf, 2003); John Ray, *Battle of Britain*, (London: The Orion Publishing Co., 2003); John Philip Ray, *The Battle of Britain: Dowding and the First Victory 1940*, (London: Cassell & Co., 2001); John Philip Ray, *The Battle of Britain: New Perspectives: Behind the Scenes of the Great Air War*, (London: Arms & Armour Press, 1994).

44 Werner Kreipe, 'The Battle of Britain' in Werner Kreipe [et. al.], *The Fatal Decisions* (London: Michael Joseph, 1956), p.11.

Disrupting the flow of UK trade was the primary means by which the German High Command hoped to force Britain out of the war. If that failed Britain was to be faced with the threat of invasion and/or the devastation of major cities by aerial bombardment. Both these objectives would be materially assisted by the destruction of the Royal Air Force. Hitler did not wish to wage total war against the British if he could avoid it. He regarded the British as a fellow superior race and was an admirer of the British Empire. His endorsement of the decision to halt the panzers as they neared Dunkirk may have been, at least in part, in line with a desire not to force the British into a humiliating defeat. The evidence suggests that with the bulk of the British Army back across the English Channel, Hitler continued to hope that the British would, at some point, see sense and make peace with him. The attack on Britain would be ramped up gradually. Securing aerial supremacy over southern England, as the precondition to an invasion, was not the immediate goal as the High Command order of 2 July demonstrates. Indeed, it may well be that Hitler never considered an invasion as desirable, or likely to succeed if it was attempted, especially since the *Kriegsmarine* had been badly mauled during the Norwegian campaign. Hitler's primary objective was the destruction of Soviet Communism – not the destruction of the British Empire. He hoped that with British trade being disrupted, Britain's cities bombarded from the air, and with the Luftwaffe gaining aerial superiority over southern England, the British would make peace rather than risk a German invasion. This would allow him to move German forces to the East in preparation for an attack on the Soviet Union.

Whatever Hitler's intentions, in the Battle of Britain the RAF had a number of significant advantages over a Luftwaffe tasked with gaining air superiority. Fighting over southern England and the English Channel, supported by an early warning network comprising radar and the Royal Observer

Corps, the aircraft of RAF Fighter Command enjoyed a form of home field advantage while German fighters operated at the limit of their capabilities. The radar and reporting system acted as a force multiplier meaning that the more carefully controlled and directed aircraft of RAF Fighter Command were about twice as effective as their German counterparts. With the system of detecting, reporting and directing developed by the head of RAF Fighter Command (Air Chief Marshal Sir Hugh Dowding) the front-line squadrons of Spitfires and Hurricanes found their targets 75 per cent of the time.

As the battle went on, the Luftwaffe shifted its focus from shipping in the English Channel to RAF Fighter Command and its airfields through, latterly, to the bombing of London. The scale of the losses on both sides, however, remains staggering. The British lost 1,744 aircraft and the Germans 1,977. The human costs were similarly horrendous: 3,320 Luftwaffe airmen were killed, captured or simply disappeared while the RAF lost 1,542 of its aircrew. At the same time, 40,000 civilians were killed by aerial bombing.

The victory, though costly, was a remarkable one on which Churchill capitalised to maximum effect. He used it to rally and reassure public opinion in Britain that eventual victory was achievable: that Britain could hold out and continue to fight back. He also used it to convince opinion in the United States that with American assistance, Britain could defeat Nazi Germany. If the victory of Fighter Command in 1940 has been overplayed as the chief reason that German Forces did not stage an invasion, then its strategic value as a factor in quelling isolationist opinion in the United States, and ultimately helping to bring America into the war, has been significantly underplayed. A Luftwaffe victory in 1940 might not have resulted in a successful invasion of the United Kingdom, but it probably would have been enough to force President Roosevelt to reconsider his instinctive policy of aiding the British, especially as he faced the prospect of a Presidential election in November 1940. The Battle of Britain gave Churchill a victory on which he capitalised to the fullest extent.

Submitted 20 August 1941 by Air Chief Marshal Sir Hugh Dowding (24 April 1882 – 15 February 1970 – GCB, GCVQ, CMG), Air Officer Commanding-in-Chief, Fighter Command Royal Air Force
TNA: CAB 106/1193. Published as supplement 37719 to *The London Gazette*, 10 September 1946, pp.4543–4371.

WEDNESDAY, 11 SEPTEMBER, 1946
The Air Ministry,
September, 1946.
THE BATTLE OF BRITAIN.
PREAMBLE.
1. I have been instructed by the Air Council to write a Despatch on the Air Fighting of last Autumn, which has become known as the "Battle of Britain." The conditions are a little unusual – because, firstly, the Battle ended many months ago, secondly, a popular account of the fighting has already been written and published, and, thirdly, recommendations for Mention in Despatches have already been submitted.
2. I have endeavoured, therefore, to write a report which will, I hope, be of Historical interest, and which will, in any case, contain the results of more than four years' experience of the Fighter Command in peace and war.
August 20, 1941.

THE BATTLE OF BRITAIN.
PART I.—PRELIMINARY.
3. In giving an account of the Battle of Britain it is perhaps advisable to begin by a definition of my conception of the

meaning of the phrase. The Battle may be said to have started when the Germans had disposed of the French resistance in the Summer of 1940, and turned their attention to this country.

4. The essence of their Strategy was so to weaken our Fighter Defences that their Air Arm should be able to give adequate support to an attempted invasion of the British Isles. Experiences in Holland and Belgium had shown what they could do with armoured forces operating in conjunction with an Air Arm which had substantially achieved the command of the Air.

5. This air supremacy was doubly necessary to them in attacking England because the bulk of their troops and war material must necessarily be conveyed by sea, and, in order to achieve success, they must be capable of giving air protection to the passage and the landing of troops and material.

6. The destruction or paralysis of the Fighter Command was therefore an essential prerequisite to the invasion of these Islands.

7. Their immediate objectives might be Convoys, Radio-Location Stations, Fighter Aerodromes, Seaports, Aircraft Factories, or London itself. Always the underlying object was to bring the Fighter Command continuously to battle, and to weaken its material resources and Intelligence facilities.

8. Long after the policy of "crashing through" with heavy bomber formations had been abandoned owing to the shattering losses incurred, the battle went on. Large fighter formations were sent over, a proportion of the fighters being adapted to carry bombs, in order that the attacks might not be ignorable.

9. This last phase was perhaps the most difficult to deal with tactically. It will be discussed in greater detail later on.

10. Night attacks by Heavy Bombers were continuous throughout the operations, and, although they persisted and increased in intensity as Day Bombing became more and more expensive, they had an essentially different purpose, and the

"Battle of Britain" may be said to have ended when the Fighter and Fighter-Bomber raids died down.

11. It is difficult to fix the exact date on which the "Battle of Britain" can be said to have begun. Operations of various kinds merged into one another almost insensibly, and there are grounds for choosing the date of the 8th August, on which was made the first attack in force against laid objectives in this country, as the beginning of the Battle.

12. On the other hand, the heavy attacks made against our Channel convoys probably constituted, in fact, the beginning of the German offensive; because the weight and scale of the attack indicates that the primary object was rather to bring our Fighters to battle than to destroy the hulls and cargoes of the small ships engaged in the coastal trade. While we were fighting in Belgium and France, we suffered the disadvantage that even the temporary stoppage of an engine involved the loss of pilot and aircraft, whereas, in similar circumstances, the German pilot might be fighting again the same day, and his aircraft be airborne again in a matter of hours.

13. In fighting over England these considerations were reversed, and the moral and material disadvantages of fighting over enemy country may well have determined the Germans to open the attack with a phase of fighting in which the advantages were more evenly balanced. I have therefore, somewhat arbitrarily, chosen the events of the 10th July as the opening of the Battle. Although many attacks had previously been made on convoys, and even on land objectives such as Portland, the loth July saw the employment by the Germans of the first really big formation (70 aircraft) intended primarily to bring our Fighter Defence to battle on a large scale.

14. I had 59 squadrons in various stages of efficiency. A list of these units, with supplementary information, is given in Appendix A. Many of them were still suffering from the effects of the fighting in Holland and Flanders, at Dunkerque, and during the

subsequent operations in France. Others were in process of formation and training. But, if the lessons of the Battle are to be correctly appreciated, due consideration must be given to the factors leading up to the situation existing when it began. Leaving out of account peace-time preparations and training, the Battle of Britain began for me in the Autumn of 1939.

15. The first major problem arose during the discussion of the question of sending Fighter Squadrons to France. The decisive factor was that of Supply. Our output at the beginning of the war was about 2 Hurricanes and 2 Spitfires per diem; and, although there were hopes of increasing Hurricane production, there was then no hope that Spitfire production would be materially increased for about a year. It is true that certain optimistic estimates had been made, but there were reasons to believe that these could not be implemented. At that time, we in England were out of range of German Fighters, and I had good hopes that unescorted bomb raids on this country could be met and defeated with a very small loss in Fighters; but there could be no illusions concerning the wastage which would occur if we came up against the German Fighters in France.

16. I therefore regarded with some apprehension the general policy of sending Home Defence Fighter Units to France; but, as it was clear that such an attitude was politically untenable, I wrote on the 16th September, 1939, a letter to the Air Ministry. In this letter I pointed out that the Air Staff Estimate of the number of Fighter Squadrons necessary for the defence of this country was 52, and that on the outbreak of war I had the equivalent of 34 (allowing for the fact that some Auxiliary Squadrons were only partially trained and equipped).

17. I wanted 12 new squadrons, but asked that 8 should be raised immediately, and made proposals for their location and employment. In a letter dated the 21st September the Air Ministry regretted that the most they could do towards meeting my requirements was to form 2 new squadrons and

Above left: Seapower, in the form of the ships of the Royal Navy, served Britain well in 1940, from facilitating amphibious landings in Norway to the evacuation of troops from Belgium and France, safeguarding the English Channel to prevent a German invasion, and protecting the sealanes to North America.

Above right: The eight-gun Supermarine Spitfire, icon of the Battle of Britain and a superb dogfighter. It was not, however, an easy aircraft to produce or to repair.

Winston Churchill as First Lord of the Admiralty made the most of the sinking of the German pocket-battleship *Graf Spee* on 17 December 1939. Here he greets crew members from HMS *Ajax* and HMS *Exeter* after a luncheon in their honour in London.

Above: Lord Gort, who commanded the BEF in France and Belgium in 1939–40, decorating a French soldier for gallantry. During the First World War Gort was awarded the VC, the MC and the DSO with two bars.

Left: French artillerymen prepare to fire in support of the Maginot Line.

RAF ground crew re-arming an eight-gun Hawker Hurricane in France in early 1940.

Top: RAF wireless operators at a fighter station in France in 1940.

Above left: Pilot of a Fairey Battle light bomber awaiting orders in France. The underpowered Fairey Battle proved less than successful in the Battle of France, with Battle squadrons sustaining heavy losses.

Above right: A spotter examines the skies for enemy aircraft.

Sir Hugh Dowding, Commander-in-Chief, RAF Fighter Command from 1936 until after the Battle of Britain.

A Fairey Battle flies above a Hawker Hurricane at a base in France in 1940.

Above left: French Alpine troops with their St Bernard dogs on a transport vessel going to Norway.

Above right: With their kit and rifles lined up at the quayside, these French soldiers are about to embark for Norway.

Above left: Troops of the BEF carrying their anti-tank rifles and other arms during a divisional exercise at the front.

Above right: Sherwood Foresters, serving in a forward area occupied by the BEF, going over the top during training in France.

Left: British troops returning from Norway in May 1940.

Below: Hawker Hurricane Mark Is of No. 73 Squadron, based at Rouvres, France.

This page: The fighters of RAF Fighter Command were backed by a network of anti-aircraft defences including the spotters of the Royal Observer Corps, anti-aircraft guns and searchlights to visually locate and fix aircraft at night. The 3.7-inch QF, which entered service in the late 1930s, was Britain's standard heavy anti-aircraft gun and 1,140 of them were in service for the Battle of Britain. The weapon is still in service with the Nepalese Army.

British and French troops on the dunes at Dunkirk in readiness to be taken aboard ships assisting in the evacuation. In the background, troops are marching out towards the sea to the waiting vessels near the shore.

Troops wading out to a shallow draft River Clyde steamer.

Steam tug towing a motor launch, both laden with troops. Larger vessels would often tow the smaller vessels across the Channel to save wear and tear on their engines. The Dunkirk evacuation relied on ships both great and small. Off the beaches the larger ships would wait as smaller shallow draft vessels got close to the beaches to pick up the waiting troops. They would then often be transhipped to larger vessels to allow the 'little ships' to go back to the beach and rescue another group of troops.

Regularly subjected to aerial attack, the fire and smoke of Dunkirk signalled the intensity of the fighting to the vessels approaching the port and beaches.

General Georges Blanchard commanded 1st French Army. Forces under his command played a key role in allowing the escape of so many troops from the Dunkirk pocket.

While the little ships, and amateur sailors, are rightly remembered for their role in the Dunkirk evacuation, it was the Royal Navy that organised the rescue effort and its ships brought back the majority of the troops rescued from France.

Above left: Back in London, Lord Gort speaks with General Sir John Dill, Chief of the Imperial General Staff.

Above right: A member of ground staff cleans the bomb aimer's window of an RAF Armstrong Whitworth Whitley two-engined bomber.

A Handley Page Hampden bomber is readied for a bombing mission. In 1940 the RAF routinely bombed the French Channel ports to target the invasion barges being assembled there.

Following the evacuation of the European continent likely invasion sites along the coast of Britain were fortified to hinder any landing by German forces. Here Sir Anthony Eden, the Secretary of State for War, inspects some of the defences.

ME-109 Standard single-seat German fighter in 1940 after crash landing on 11 July. Images of downed German aircraft regularly featured in the British press during the Battle of Britain.

Lieutenant-General Sir Alan Brooke. Commanding the 2nd Corps of the BEF in 1940 he distinguished himself in the Dunkirk evacuation. On 19 July he was appointed Commander-in-Chief of the Home Forces.

Head of the Home Guard (Local Defence Volunteers) Lieutenant-General H. R. Pownall.

Stephenson Street, Canning Town following a raid in 1940. The premises of the Greengate and Irwell Rubber Company, established here in the 1880s are visible in the background. Between October 1940 and June 1941 eighty-five HE bombs and eight parachute mines hit North Canning Town.

The terrifying destructive capacity of high explosive bombs on brick-built homes is evident in this photo from 1940.

The remains of a Junkers 88 twin-engined bomber are guarded by a soldier to prevent souvenir hunters from taking parts of the aircraft.

Squadron Leader Douglas Bader who lost both his legs in an air accident in 1931. On 28 June 1940 he took over No. 242 Hurricane Squadron at Coltishall. Bader was shot down and captured in August 1941.

Above left: Air Marshal Sir Arthur Barratt, Air Officer Commanding, British Air Forces in France in 1940.

Above right: Stop-gap technology; a Sea Hurricane on the deck of a CAM (Catapult Aircraft Merchant) ship, an attempt to bolster convoy cover because of a lack of escort carriers. The Hurricane isn't coming back.

ME-110 fighters. Employed as daytime long-range fighters in 1940, they later found greater success as night fighters against the aircraft of RAF Bomber Command.

2 operational training units. I was invited to a meeting of the Air Council on the 26th September.

18. On the 25th September I wrote expressing my disappointment and asking for a reconsideration. As a result of this letter, the Air Council Meeting, and a further meeting under the Chairmanship of the Deputy Chief of Air Staff, the Air Ministry wrote on the 9th October sanctioning the immediate formation of 8 new squadrons, though 6 of these could be formed initially only as half-squadrons owing to shortage of resources. This correspondence is too lengthy to reproduce here, but it deals also with my apprehensions concerning Hurricane wastage in France, which were realised in the Spring of 1940. It also dealt with an estimate worked out by the Air Ministry Organisation Staff that after 3 months of fighting we might expect the Fighter strength to have been reduced to 26 squadrons.

19. In October, 1939, the Air Ministry further reconsidered their policy, and ordered the formation of 10 additional Fighter Squadrons, 4 of which were destined for the Coastal Command.

20. In January, 1940, the Northern flank of our continuous Defence organisation was on the Forth, and the South-Western flank was at Tangmere in Sussex (with the exception of an isolated station at Filton for the local defence of Bristol and the mouth of the Severn). On the 2nd and 4th February I wrote two letters pointing out these limitations, and asking for an extension of Aerodrome facilities, Intelligence cover and communications.

21. On the 9th February I was told that a paper was in preparation, and that I would be given an opportunity to remark on the proposals at a later stage.

22. On the 16th March I received the paper referred to and forwarded my comments on the 23rd March.

23. On the 8th May I received a letter saying that a reply had been delayed. The proposals were now approved, and decisions would shortly be taken.

24. This delay was presumably unavoidable, but the result was that the organisation and development of the defences of the South and West of England were very incomplete when they were called upon to withstand the attacks which the German occupation of French aerodromes made possible.

25. The fighting in Norway has only an indirect bearing on this paper. Certain useful tactical lessons were gamed, particularly with regard to deflection shooting, and I trust that the story of the epic fight of No. 263 Squadron under Squadron-Leader J. W. Donaldson, D.S.O., near Andalsnes, may not be lost to History.

26. The outcome, as it affects this account, was the virtual loss of 2 squadrons in the sinking of the Aircraft Carrier *Glorious* after the evacuation of Narvik.

27. Next came the invasion of Holland, and the call to send Fighters to the assistance of the Dutch. The distance to Rotterdam was about the extreme range of the single-seater Fighter, which therefore operated under the disadvantage of having a very, brief potential combat-time, followed by the necessity of a long sea crossing on the homeward way. The Blenheims, of course, had the necessary endurance, but they had not been designed as fighters, and their use against day fighters proved costly in comparison with the limited success which they attained.

28. The Defiants were used here for the first time, and, although they proved very effective against unescorted bombers, they, too, suffered heavy casualties when they encountered fighters in strength. As the result of this experience I formed the opinion that the Blenheims should be kept exclusively for night fighting, if possible, while I retained an open mind about the Defiants pending some experience of short-range fighting.

29. Then began the fighting in Belgium and Northern France, and at once my fears about the incidence of wastage in this type of fighting began to be realised.

30. At the beginning of April, 1940, there were 6 Fighter Squadrons in France.

31. Then 4 more complete squadrons were sent when the fighting began.

32. Then on the 13ᵗʰ May 32 pilots and aircraft were sent—say the equivalent of 2 squadrons.

33. Almost immediately afterwards 8 Half-Squadrons were sent. This was done under the impression that the loss of 8 Half-Squadrons would affect me less than that of 4 entire Squadrons, because it was supposed that I should be able to rebuild on the nuclei left behind. But this assumption was incorrect because I had neither the time nor the personnel available for purposes of reconstruction, and the remaining half-squadrons had to be amalgamated into Composite Units with a resulting disorganisation and loss of efficiency. At this time, too, I was ordered to withdraw trained pilots from squadrons and to send them overseas as reinforcements.

34. I had now lost the equivalent of 16 Squadrons, and in addition 4 Squadrons were sent to fight in France during the day and to return to English bases in the evening.

35. Other pilots were withdrawn from the Command through the system by which the Air Ministry dealt direct with Groups on questions of Personnel.

36. It must be remembered that during this period the Home Defence Squadrons were not idle, but that Hurricane Squadrons were participating in the fighting to a considerable extent, 4 Squadrons daily left S.E. England with orders to carry out an offensive patrol, to land and refuel in France or Belgium, and to carry out a second sortie before returning to England.

37. Hitherto I had succeeded generally in keeping the Spitfire Squadrons out of the Continental fighting. The reason for this, as stated above, was that the supply situation was so bad that they could not have maintained their existence in face of the Aircraft

Casualty Rate experienced in France: between the 8th May and the 18th May 250 Hurricanes were lost.

38. When the Dunkerque fighting began, however, I could no longer maintain this policy, and the Spitfires had to take their share in the fighting.

39. When the Dunkerque evacuation was complete I had only 3 Day-Fighting Squadrons which had not been engaged in Continental fighting, and 12 Squadrons were in the line for the second time after having been withdrawn to rest and re-form.

40. All this time, it must be remembered, the attack on this Country had not begun; with a few accidental exceptions no bomb had been dropped on our soil. I was responsible for the Air Defence of Great Britain, and I saw my resources slipping away like sand in an hour-glass. The pressure for more and more assistance to France was relentless and inexorable. In the latter part of May, 1940, I sought and obtained permission to appear in person before the War Cabinet and to state my case. I was accorded a courteous and sympathetic hearing, and to my inexpressible relief my arguments prevailed and it was decided to send no more Fighter Reinforcements to France except to cover the final evacuation.

41. I know what it must have cost the Cabinet to reach this decision, but I am profoundly convinced that this was one of the great turning points of the war.

42. Another decision, of perhaps equal importance, was taken at about this time. I refer to the appointment of Lord Beaverbrook to the post of Minister of Aircraft Production. The effect of this appointment can only be described as magical, and thereafter the Supply situation improved to such a degree that the heavy aircraft wastage which was later incurred during the "Battle of Britain" ceased to be the primary danger, its place being taken by the difficulty of producing trained fighter pilots in adequate numbers.

43. After the Evacuation from Dunkerque the pressure on the Fighter Command became less intense, but it by no means disappeared. Hard fighting took place along the coast from Calais to Le Havre to cover the successive evacuations from that coast. Then the centre of gravity shifted to Cherbourg and its neighbourhood, and the "Battle of Britain" followed on without any appreciable opportunity to rest and re-form the units which had borne the brunt of the fighting.

44. The above considerations should be kept in mind when Appendix A (Order of Battle on the 8th July, 1940) is being studied.

45. The Guns and Searchlights available for the Air Defence of Great Britain were arranged as shown on the map which constitutes Appendix B.

46. The fall of Belgium and France had increased the danger to the South and West of England, and had necessitated a considerable modification of the original arrangements when bombing attacks could start only from German soil.

47. The distribution of Army Units was, as a matter of fact, in a condition of perpetual change to meet new situations as they arose, and I must pay a very sincere tribute to the flexibility of the Army organisation, and to the tact, patience and loyalty of the Commander-in-Chief of the Anti-Aircraft Command, Lt.Gen. Sir Frederick A. Pile, Bart., K.C.B., D.S.O., M.C., which enabled these constant changes to be made without disorganisation.

48. In theory the Commander-in-Chief, Fighter Command, was the authority responsible for settling the dispositions of all guns allotted to the Air Defence of Great Britain; but this was little more than a convenient fiction. The number of guns available was so inadequate for the defence of all the vulnerable targets in the country, and the interests concerned were so diverse and powerful, that it was not to be supposed that an individual member of any one Service would be left to exercise such a prerogative uninterruptedly. A disproportionate

amount of my time was taken up in discussions on gun distribution, and each decision was at once greeted with a fresh agitation, until finally I had to ask that all proposals should be discussed by a small Committee on which all interests were represented, and I normally accepted the recommendations of this Committee during quiet periods. During active operations I consulted General Pile, and we acted according to our judgment.

One rather important lesson emerged from our experience, viz., that the general fire-control of all guns in the Air Defence System should be vested in the Air Defence authorities. I do not, of course, mean that, if an invasion had taken place, the guns co-operating with the troops in the Field should have been subordinated to any A.A. Defence Commander, but the existence of "free-lance" guns[45]), the positions and even the existence of which were unknown to me, was an appreciable handicap, especially at night. It was impossible to acquaint them with the approach I of enemy raiders, or of the fact that our own aircraft were working in the vicinity.

49. When the night attacks on London began to be really serious, General Pile, in consultation with myself, decided to send heavy reinforcements. Within 24 hours the defences to the South and South-East of London were approximately doubled, and the great increase in the volume of fire was immediately noticed and had a very good effect on public morale. The physical effect in the shape of raiders destroyed was by no means negligible, but the main effect was never generally known. The track of every raid was, of course, shown on various operations tables, and on some nights as many as 60 per cent, of the raiders approaching

---

45 These guns belonged to Field Force Units. As such units were, of necessity, highly mobile, their exact location was not always known to Fighter Command. Nor, after a recent move, were they always included in the telephone system.

London from the South turned back after dropping their bombs in the open country or on the fringe of the Barrage.

50. The A.A. Guns at Dover enjoyed unusual opportunities for practice, with the result that their crews became acknowledged experts in the art of Anti-Aircraft Gunnery. Their skill, however, was attained through the circumstance that they and the Dover Balloon Barrage were continuously the objectives of German attack; they manned their guns continuously night and day, and I must pay a high tribute to their morale, enthusiasm and efficiency.

A report from the 6th A.A. Division, which was busily and typically employed, is included at Appendices C, C.A, C.B. and C.C.

51. A short Appendix (C.D) is added showing the number of rounds fired per aircraft destroyed, for the whole Anti-Aircraft Command.

52. On the map which constitutes Appendix A.A. are shown the boundaries of Groups and Sectors, and also the positions of the Balloon Barrages, together with an indication of the front covered by Radio Location Stations and the area covered by the Observer Corps.

53. The Balloon Barrages had, at this stage, had little opportunity of justifying their existence, except perhaps at Rosyth and Scapa Flow, since bombing attacks against land objectives in Britain had not yet begun. It was thought, however, (and later experience confirmed this opinion), that the heavy cost of their installation and maintenance, and their drain on man-power, were on the whole justified. It is true that their material results, in terms of enemy aircraft destroyed, were not impressive, they suffered staggering casualties in electric storms, and had brought down a number of our own aircraft; on the other hand, they exercise a very salutary moral effect upon the Germans and to a great extent protected the vital objectives, which they surrounded, against low-altitude attacks and dive-bombing.

54. This is not the place to give an account of the romantic discovery and development of Radio Location. It may be explained, however, that the backbone of the system consisted of a series of large "chain" stations at intervals averaging about 30 miles. These gave warning, by means of reflected electrical echoes, of the presence of aircraft within the radius of their effective action, which attained to nearly 200 miles in the most favourable circumstances. The average effective radius was about 80 miles, but they had the serious limitation that they failed altogether to give indications of aircraft flying below 1,000 feet.

55. To overcome this disability, which was particularly hampering to operations against low-flying minelayers, smaller units called "C.H.L. Stations" were included in the protective line.

56. These had a restricted range (about 30 miles), and were incapable of giving heights with any degree of accuracy; they were, however, extremely accurate in azimuth, and constituted an essential feature of the Defensive and Warning Systems.

57. The Radio Location system was growing so fast and had to meet so many calls from overseas that the training of the technical personnel and the maintenance of the elaborate scientific apparatus presented great difficulties. In spite of these handicaps, however, the system operated effectively, and it is not too much to say that the warnings which it gave could have been obtained by no other means and constituted a vital factor in the Air Defence of Great Britain.

58. The functions of the Observer Corps (since granted the "Royal" prefix) are too well known to require description here. Suffice it to say that this loyal and public spirited body of men had maintained their watch with admirable efficiency since the beginning of the war and throughout a winter of exceptional s verity. It is important to note that, at this time, they constituted the sole means of tracking enemy raids once they had crossed the coast line. Later experience was to show that "sound plots," which were all that could be given for night raiders, and

aircraft flying above clouds or at extreme altitudes, were not adequate for purposes of accurate interception; but their work throughout was quite invaluable. Without it the Air Raid Warning systems could not have been operated, and Inland. Interceptions would rarely have been made.

59. The credit for building up and developing the Observer Corps in recent years is due largely to its Commandant, Air Commodore A. D. Warrington Morris; CM.G., O.B.E.

60. The Air Raid Warning System was operated centrally from Fighter Command Headquarters (with a small exception in the Orkneys and Shetlands).

61. The country was divided into about 130 "Warning Districts," the boundaries of which were determined by the lay-out of the public telephone system. These districts were shown on a map in my Operations Room, and the tracks of all enemy raids, whether over the land or sea, were plotted by means of counters deposited and removed as necessary by a number of "Plotters."

62. The counters were of three colours, according to the 5-minute period in which they were placed on the table: This was necessary to facilitate their removal at the end of 15 minutes, and so to obviate the confusion caused by "stale plots."

63. Three telephone operators were in continuous communication with the Trunk Exchanges in London, Liverpool and Glasgow, and when a raid was within 20 minutes' flying distance of a warning district the Air Raid Warning officer would send a message, as, for instance: "10. Norwich. Yellow." The London operator would transmit this to the London Trunk Exchange, and the London operator would immediately retransmit it to Norwich, where other operators would pass it on to approved recipients in the Warning District. This was a preliminary caution for the information of Police, Fire Stations, & c., and involved no public warning.

64. About 5 minutes later, if the said District were still threatened, a "Red Warning" would be given. This was the signal for the Sirens to sound. A "Green" signal indicated "Raiders Passed," and the Sirens sounded the "All Clear."

65. At night, when it became essential to maintain exposed lights in Dockyards, Railway Sidings and Factories up to the last minute, so as to obviate unnecessary loss of working time, a "Purple" warning was introduced. This was a signal for the extinction of exposed lights, but it did not connote a public warning.

66. There were also subsidiary warnings, transmitted by a fourth operator, to close down Radio Stations which might assist the enemy's navigation by enabling him to use wireless Direction Finding.

67. The credit for working out this system in conjunction with the Home Office is due largely to Air Vice-Marshal A. D. Cunningham, C.B.E.

68. The Fighter Command was divided into Groups and Sectors in accordance with the arrangement shown in Appendix A A. Only Nos. 11, 12 and 13 Groups were fully organised at the beginning of the Battle. Each Group and Sector Headquarters had an Operations Table generally similar to that already described at Command Headquarters, but covering an appropriately smaller area. The British Isles and neighbouring seas were covered by an imaginary "grid " which was used by all concerned for plotting purposes. An expression consisting of one letter and four digits gave the position of a point with an accuracy of 1 square kilometre.

69. Plots from which tracks could be built up were received first from the Radio Location Station, and later from the Observer Corps (and to a small extent from Searchlight Detachments) after a raid had crossed the coast.

70. All Radio Location plots came to a "Filter Room" table at Command Headquarters (next door to the room in which the

Operations Table was situated), and, after surplus information had been eliminated, tracks were passed by direct telephone line simultaneously to my Operations Table and to those of Groups and Sectors concerned.

71. Observer Corps plots, on the other hand, went first to Observer Group Centres (where plotting tables were also installed) and thence to Sector and Fighter Group Operations tables. The tracks were then "told" to my Operations Room from the Group Tables.

72. In order to avoid waste of flying effort and false Air Raid Warnings it was obviously very necessary to differentiate between friendly and enemy formations, and this was the most difficult as well as the most important task of my Filter Room. Liaison Officers from Bomber and Coastal Commands were permanently on duty, and they were in possession of all available information concerning the operations of our own Bombers and Coastal patrols. During 1940 an electrical device became generally available which modified the echo received by the Radio Location System from our own aircraft in a characteristic manner. This was of the greatest value.

73. The credit for working out the complicated details of the Filter Room 'belongs largely to Wing Commander (now Group Captain) R. G. Hart, C.B.E.

74. It appeared to me quite impossible to centralise Tactical control at Command Headquarters, and even Group Commanders would be too busy during, heavy fighting to concern themselves, with details of Interception.

75. The system was that the Command should be responsible for the identification of approaching formations and for the allotment of enemy raids to Groups where any doubt existed. Group Commanders decided which Sector should meet any specified raid and the strength of the Fighter force which should be employed. Sector Commanders detailed the Fighter Units to be employed, and operated the machinery of Interception.

76. Various states of preparedness were laid down, *e.g.*, Released, Available (20 minutes), Readiness (5 minutes), and stand-by (2 minutes), and Sectors reported all changes to Group Headquarters, where an up-to-date picture of the state of affairs was recorded by lights on the walls of the Operations Room. Various liaison officers from the Observer Corps, guns and searchlights were maintained in Group and Sector Operations Rooms.

77. It will be seen that the Sector Commander had on his table the best available information as to the position and track of an enemy formation; but, in order to effect an accurate interception, it was necessary that he should also know the position and track of his own Fighters.

78. This was recorded by means of R/T D/F (Radio Telephony Direction Finding). R/T signals were transmitted automatically for 15 seconds out of each minute by selected Fighter aircraft and were picked up by two or three D/F stations installed in Sectors for the purpose. The readings were passed by direct telephone lines to Sector Headquarters, and a mechanical plotting device gave an almost instantaneous plot of the Fighter's position.

79. In the more recently organised Sectors these D/F stations had not been installed, and it was necessary to keep track of the Fighters by giving them precise orders as to speed and direction, and plotting their tracks by Dead Reckoning. This method was adequate only if the force and direction of the wind at various altitudes could be correctly estimated.

80. The Sector Commander could thus see on his operations tables the positions and courses of enemy formations and of his own Fighters, and was enabled so to direct the latter as to make interceptions with the former in a good percentage of occasions by day. Interception depended, of course, on the Fighters being able to see the enemy, and, although the system worked adequately against enemy formations in daylight, the degree of

accuracy obtainable was insufficient to effect interception against night raiders not illuminated by Searchlights, or against individual aircraft using cloud cover by day.

81. Orders were given to pilots in their aircraft by means of a very simple code which could be easily memorised. For instance "Scramble" meant Take off. "Orbit" meant Circle. "Vector 230" meant Fly on a course of 230 Degrees.

82. I realised that the enemy might pick up the signals and interpret them, but any elaborate code was out of the question if it included reference to some written list in the air.

83. As a matter of fact the enemy did pick up and interpret the signals in some cases, but not much harm was done, except when they were able to discover the height at which a formation was ordered to operate, and the time when it was ordered to leave its patrol line and land.

84. "Pancake" was the signal for the latter operation, and I therefore introduced several synonyms, the significance of which was not obvious to the enemy.

85. The code word for height was "Angels," followed by the number of thousands of feet; when it appeared probable that the enemy were taking advantage of this information I introduced a false quantity into the code signal. Thus "Angels 18" really meant Fly at 21,000 and not 18,000. On more than one occasion German Fighter formations arriving to dive on one of our patrols were themselves attacked from above.

86. The system as a whole had been built up by successive steps over a period of about four years, and I was not dissatisfied with the way in which it stood the test of war.

87. The steps taken to devise a system of night Interception are described later in this Despatch.

88. I must now give a brief account of the characteristics of the aircraft commonly employed on both sides. As regards the Fighter types available in the Command, the bulk of the force consisted of Hurricanes and Spitfires; the former were beginning

to be outmoded by their German counterparts. They were comparatively slow and their performance and manoeuvrability were somewhat inadequate at altitudes above 20,000ft. The Spitfires were equal or superior to anything which the Germans possessed at the beginning of the Battle.

89. The Hurricanes and Spitfires had bulletproof windscreens and front armour between the top of the engine and the windscreen. They also had rear armour directly behind the pilot, which was previously prepared and fitted as soon as we began to meet the German Fighters. The early adoption of armour gave us an initial advantage over the Germans, but they were quick to imitate our methods. While German aircraft remained unarmoured, I think it is now generally agreed that the single-seater multi-gun fighter with fixed guns was the most efficient type which could have been produced for day fighting. With the advent of armour some change in armament and/or tactics became necessary, and the subject is discussed in more detail in Appendix F.

90. The Defiant, after some striking initial successes, proved to be too expensive in use against Fighters and was relegated to night work and to the attack of unescorted Bombers.

91. The Blenheim was also unsuitable for day-time combat with Fighters, owing to its low speed and lack of manoeuvrability. It had been relegated to night duties for these reasons, and because adequate space was available in its fuselage for an extra operator and the scientific apparatus which was necessary for the development of a new night-interception technique. The cockpit had not been designed for night flying and the night view was extremely bad. Its already low performance had been further reduced by certain external fittings which were essential for the operation of the Radio Detecting apparatus.

92. The Beaufighter was looked on as a Blenheim replacement in which most of the above disadvantages would be overcome.

Its speed promised to be adequate and its armament consisted of 4 20-mm. Cannons instead of the 5 .303-inch Brownings of the Blenheim. There was thus hope that decisive fire could be brought to bear in the short period during which visual contact could be expected to be maintained at night.

93. Like the Blenheim, it had not been designed as a Night Fighter (it was an adaptation of the Beaufort Torpedo Bomber), and the night view from the cockpit was bad; but Air Vice-Marshal Sir Q. Brand, K.B.E., D.S.O., M.C., D.F.C., a veteran night fighter of the previous war, had designed a new cockpit lay-out, which did not, unfortunately, materialise during my tenure of the Fighter Command. The output of Beaufighters was also very low.

94. Another type which was pressed, into service as a Night Fighter was the Douglas D.B.-7 (now the Havoc). It had low fire power and comparatively poor performance with its original engines. Its chief advantage lay in its tricycle undercarriage, which proved very popular for landings in bad visibility. Only one Squadron of these was in being when I left the Command.

95. One Squadron of Gladiators was still in use in the Command. As explained above, the organisation of No. 10 Group was not complete, and there was no large aerodrome close enough to Plymouth to allow of direct protection being given to that town and to the Dockyard at Devonport. A squadron of Gladiators was therefore located at a small aerodrome called Roborough in the immediate vicinity. The Gladiators, though slow by modern standards, were very manoeuvrable, and had given good results in Norway by deflection shooting in the defence of fixed objectives, where the Bombers could not avoid the Gladiators if they were to reach their targets.

96. Some American single-seater aircraft were in Great Britain, but the types then available were deficient in performance and fire power and were not employed to any material extent.

97. The Whirlwind raised high hopes in some quarters. It claimed a very high top speed and carried 4 Cannon Guns. It had,

however, a totally inadequate service ceiling (about 25,000 ft.) and a poor performance at that altitude. It also suffered from a continuous series of teething troubles, and the single Squadron equipped with this type was never fit for operations in my time.

98. It is very difficult to give any kind of concise description, of the types of Enemy Aircraft used during the Battle. The Germans, while adhering to broad standard types, were continually modifying and improving them by fitting more powerful engines and altering the armament. The original Messerschmitt 109, for instance, had a performance comparable with that of the Hurricane, but the latest type could compete with the Spitfire, and had a better ceiling. Some of them had 4 machine guns and others had 2 machine guns and 2 cannons. Some of them were fitted to carry bombs and some were not.

99. The Messerschmitt 110 was a twin-engined fighter designed primarily for escorting Bombers and used also as a Fighter-Bomber. It was somewhat faster than the Hurricane, but naturally much less manoeuvrable than the single-engined types. Its usual armament was 2 fixed cannons and 4 machine guns firing forward, and one free machine gun firing to the rear. Our pilots regarded it as a less formidable opponent than the later types of M.E.109.

100. The Heinkel 113 Fighter made its appearance in limited numbers during the Battle. It was a single seater, generally resembling the M.E. 109. Its main attributes were high performance and ceiling, so that it was generally used in the highest of the several layers in which attacking formations were usually built up.

101. The Junkers 87 was a single-engined Dive-Bomber. It had a low performance (top speed well under 250 m.p.h.). It had 2 fixed machine guns firing forward and one free gun firing to the rear. When it was able to operate undisturbed by Fighters it was the Germans' most efficient Bomber against land or sea targets owing to the great accuracy with which it dropped its

bombs; but when it was caught by fighters it was nothing short of a death-trap, and formations, of J.U. 87's were practically annihilated on several occasions.

102. The Heinkel in and the various types of Dornier (17, 17Z and 215) constituted the main element of the German striking force. They were twin-engined aircraft and were generally similar, although the former was slightly the larger. Their speed was something over 250 m.p.h., and then armament consisted normally (but not always) of 4 free machine guns firing backwards and one firing forwards. Their radius of action varied with tankage and bomb load, but, if necessary, all objectives in England and Northern Ireland could be reached from aerodromes in France.

103. The Junkers 88 was the most modern of the German (Bombers. It also was a twin-engined type with a performance of about 290 m.p.h. Its armament was generally similar to that of the H.E. in and the Dorniers and it had a slightly longer range. It could be used on occasions as a Dive-Bomber and, though probably somewhat less accurate than the J.U.87, was much less vulnerable owing to its superior performance and armament.

104. Before beginning an account of the Battle, I must refer briefly to the publication entitled *The Battle of Britain,* issued by the Air Ministry. This, if I may say so, is an admirable account of the Battle for public consumption, and I am indebted to it, as well as to the book *Fighter Command,* by Wing Commander A. B. Austin, for help in the compilation of this Despatch. There is very little which I should have wished to alter, even if circumstances had permitted my seeing it before publication (I was absent in America at the time), but there are two points to which I should like to draw attention:-

105. In the diagram on page 7 the speed of the Hurricane is seriously over-rated at 335 m.p.h. I carried out a series of trials to obtain the absolute and comparative speeds of Hurricanes

and Spitfires at optimum heights. Naturally the speeds of individual aircraft varied slightly, but the average speed of six Hurricanes came out at about 305 m.p.h.

106. The second point is of greater importance. I quote from page 33: "What the Luftwaffe failed to do was to destroy the Fighter Squadrons of the Royal Air Force, *which were, indeed, stronger at the end of the Battle than at the beginning.*" (The italics are mine.)

107. This statement, even if intended only for popular consumption, tends to lead to an attitude of complacency which may be very dangerous in the future. Whatever the study of paper returns may have shown, the fact is that the situation was critical in the extreme. Pilots had to be withdrawn from the Bomber and Coastal Commands and from the Fleet Air Arm and flung into the Battle after hasty preparation. The majority of the squadrons had been reduced to the status of training units, and were fit only for operations against unescorted bombers. The remainder were battling daily against heavy odds.

108. The indomitable courage of the Fighter Pilots and the skill of their Leaders brought us through the crises, and the morale of the Germans eventually cracked because of the stupendous losses which they sustained.

109. Any attempt to describe the events of the Battle day by day would make this Despatch unduly long and would prevent the reader from obtaining a comprehensive picture of the events. I have therefore decided to show the main features of each day's fighting in an Appendix on which our own and the Germans' aircraft casualties will be shown graphically. I shall then be able to deal with the progress of the Battle by phases, thus avoiding the tedious and confusing method of day-to-day description. The information is given in Appendix D.

110. As regards our casualties, we generally issued statements to the effect that we lost "x" aircraft from Which "y" pilots were saved. This did not of course mean that "y" pilots were ready

immediately to continue the Battle. Many of them were suffering from wounds, burns or other injuries which precluded their return to active flying temporarily or permanently.

111. It might also be assumed that all German crews who were in aircraft brought down during the Battle, were permanently lost to the Luftwaffe because the fighting took place on our side of the Channel. Such an assumption would not be literally true, because the Germans succeeded in rescuing a proportion of their crews from the sea by means of rescue boats, floats and aircraft which will be later described.

112. The decisive features of the Battle were the Ratio of Casualties incurred by ourselves and the Germans, and the Ratio of Casualties to the numbers actively employed on both sides. Appendix D has been drawn up with these points in mind.

113. I must disclaim any exact accuracy in the estimates of Enemy losses. All that I can say is that the utmost care was taken to arrive at the closest possible approximation. Special intelligence officers examined pilots individually after their combats, and the figures claimed are only those recorded as "Certain." If we allow for a percentage of over-statement, and the fact that two or more Fighters were sometimes firing at the same enemy aircraft without being aware of the fact, this can fairly be balanced by the certainty that a proportion of aircraft reported as "Probably Destroyed" or "Damaged" failed to return to their bases. The figures, then, are put forward as an honest approximation. Judging by results, they are perhaps not far out.

114. The German claims were, of course, ludicrous; they may have been deceived about our casualties, but they know they were lying about their own.

115. I remember being cross-examined in August by the Secretary of State for Air about the discrepancy. He was anxious about the effect on the American people of the wide divergence between the claims of the two sides. I replied that the Americans

would soon find out the truth; if the Germans' figures were accurate they would be in London in a week, otherwise they would not.

116. Our estimate of German casualties, then, may be taken as reasonably accurate for practical purposes; but our estimates of the strength in which attacks were made is based on much less reliable evidence. The Radio-Location system could give only a very approximate estimate of numbers and was sometimes in error by three or four hundred per cent. This is no reflection on the System, which was not designed or intended to be accurate in the estimation of considerable numbers; moreover, several stations were suffering from the effects of severe bombing attacks. As the average height of operations increased, the Observer Corps became less and less able to make accurate estimates of numbers, and, in fact, formations were often quite invisible from the ground.

117. Even the numerical estimates made by pilots who encountered large formations in the air are likely to be guesswork in many instances. Opportunities for deliberate counting of enemy aircraft were the exception rather than the rule.

118. Although Secret Intelligence sources supplemented the information available, it is possible that on days of heavy fighting complete formations may have escaped recorded observation altogether.

119. This is unfortunate, because it is obviously of the greatest importance to determine the relative strengths of the Attack and the Defence, and to know the ratio of losses to aircraft employed which may be expected to bring an attack to a standstill in a given time. History will doubtless elucidate the uncertainty, but perhaps not in tune for the information to be of use in the present war.

120. My personal opinion is that, on days of slight activity, our estimates are reasonably accurate, but that they probably err

on the low side on days of heavy fighting when many and large formations were employed.

121. As has been explained above, few squadrons were fresh and intact when the Battle began. No sufficient respite has been granted since the conclusion of the Dunkerque fighting to rest the Squadrons which had not left the Fighter Command, and to rebuild those which had undergone the ordeal of fighting from aerodromes in Northern France. These last had been driven from aerodrome to aerodrome, able only to aim at self-preservation from almost continuous attack by Bombers and Fighters; they were desperately weary and had lost the greater part of their equipment, since aircraft which were unserviceable only from slight defects had to be abandoned.

122. The Battle may be said to have divided itself broadly into 4 Phases: First, the attack on convoys and Coastal objectives, such as Ports, Coastal Aerodromes and Radio Location Stations. Second, the attack of Inland Fighter Aerodromes. Third, the attack on London. And fourth, the Fighter-Bomber stage, where the target was of importance quite subsidiary to the main object of drawing our Fighters into the air and engaging them in circumstances as disadvantageous to us as possible. These phases indicated only general tendencies; they overlapped and were not mutually exclusive.

123. It has been estimated that the Germans sent over, on an average throughout the Battle, four Fighters to each Bomber or Fighter-Bomber, but any such estimate must be very rough.

124. I must emphasise, throughout, the extreme versatility of the German methods both in the timing and direction of their attacks, and in the tactical formations and methods employed.

125. They enjoyed the great advantage of having a wide front from which attacks could be delivered. First a blow would be delivered from Calais, perhaps against London; then after a carefully timed interval, when Group Fighters might be expected

to be at the end of their petrol endurance, a heavy attack would be made on Southampton and Portland. Other attacks, after being built up to formidable dimensions, would prove to be only feints, and the Bombers would turn away before reaching coast of England, only to return again in half an hour, when the Fighters, sent up to intercept them, were landing.

126. Time-honoured methods of escort were at first employed. A strong Fighter formation would fly a mile or so behind and above the Bombers. When the Germans found that our Fighters could deliver a well-timed attack on the Bombers before the Fighters could intervene, or when our Fighters attacked from ahead or below, each move was met by a counter-move on the part of the Germans, so that, in September, Fighter escorts were flying inside the Bomber formation, others were below, and a series of Fighters stretched upwards to 30,000 feet or more.

127. One Squadron Leader described his impressions of the appearance of one of these raids; he said it was like looking up the escalator at Piccadilly Circus.

128. I must pay a very sincere tribute to the Air Officer Commanding No.11 Group, Air Vice-Marshal K. R. Park, C.B., M.C., D.F.C., for the way in which he adjusted his tactics and interception methods to meet each new development as it occurred.

129. Tactical control was, as has already been stated, devolved to the Groups; but tactical methods were normally laid down by Command Headquarters. During periods of intense fighting, however, there was no time for consultation, and Air Vice-Marshal Park acted from day to day on his own initiative. We discussed matters as opportunity offered.

130. He has reported on the tactical aspects of the Battle in two very interesting documents, which are, however, too long to reproduce here.

131. A close liaison was kept between Nos.10 and 11 and 12 Groups. It sometimes happened that, in the heaviest attacks,

practically all 11 Group Fighters would be in the air. 11 Group would then ask 12 Group to send a formation from Duxford to patrol over the aerodromes immediately East of London so that these might not be attacked when defenceless.

132. Mutual help was also arranged between Nos. 10 and 11 Groups. When Portsmouth was attacked, for instance, No. 10 would help No. 11 Group, and *vice versa* when the attack was on Portland or some Convoy to the West of the Isle of Wight.

133. The amount of physical damage done to Convoys during the first phase was not excessive. About five ships (I think) were actually sunk by bombing, others were damaged, and Convoys were scattered on occasion. It was, of course, much easier to protect the Convoys if they kept as close as possible to the English Coast, but one Convoy at least was routed so as to pass close to Cherbourg, and suffered accordingly. Later, it was arranged that Convoys should traverse the most dangerous and exposed stretches by night, and Convoys steaming in daylight either had direct protection by Fighter escorts, or else had escorts at "Readiness" prepared to leave the ground directly danger threatened.

134. Three of the Radio Location Stations in the South of England suffered rather severe damage and casualties. No Station was permanently put out of action, and the worst damage was repaired in about a month, though the Station was working at reduced efficiency in about half that time. The operating personnel, and particularly the women, behaved with great courage under threat of attack and actual bombardment.

135. As regards aerodromes, Manston was the worst sufferer at this stage. It, Hawkinge and Lympne were the three advanced grounds on which we relied for filling up tanks when a maximum range was required for operations over France. They were so heavily attacked with bombs and machine guns that they were temporarily abandoned. This is not to say that they could not

have been used if the need had been urgent, but, for interception at or about our own coastline, aerodromes and satellites farther inland were quite effective.

136. Heavy damage was done to buildings, but these were mostly non-essential, because aircraft were kept dispersed in the open, and the number of men and women employed was not large in comparison with the number at a Station which was the Headquarters of a Sector.

137. Works personnel, permanent and temporary, and detachments of Royal Engineers were employed in filling up the craters on the aerodromes. Experience at this stage showed that neither the personnel nor the material provided were adequate to effect repairs with the necessary speed, and the strength and mobility of the repair parties was increased. Stocks of "hard-core" rubble had been collected at Fighter aerodromes before the war.

138. It may be convenient here to continue the subject of damage to Fighter Stations other than those attacked in the first Phase.

139. Casualties to personnel were slight, except in cases where a direct hit was made on a shelter trench. The trenches commonly in use were lined with concrete and were roofed and covered with earth; but they gave no protection against a direct hit, and, in the nature of things, they had to be within a short distance of the hangars and offices.

140. Only non-essential personnel took cover; aircraft crews and the staff of the Operations Room remained at their posts. The morale of the men and women of ground crews and staffs was high and remained so throughout.

141. At Kenley and at Biggin Hill direct hits were sustained on shelter trenches, at the latter place by a bomb of 500 kilos or more. The trench and its 40 occupants were annihilated.

142. Wooden hangars were generally set on fire by a bombing attack, and everything in them destroyed.

143. Steel, brick and concrete hangars, on the other hand, stood up well against attack, though, of course, acres of glass were broken. Hangars were generally empty or nearly so, and those aircraft which were destroyed in hangars were generally under repair or major inspection which made it necessary to work under cover.

144. It must, nevertheless, be definitely recorded that the damage done to Fighter aerodromes, and to their communications and ground organisation, was serious, and has been generally under-estimated. Luckily, the Germans did not realise the success of their efforts, and shifted their objectives before the cumulative effect of the damage had become apparent to them.

145. Damage to aerodrome surface was not a major difficulty. It was possible for the Germans to put one or two aerodromes like Manston and Hawkinge out of action for a time, but we had so many satellite aerodromes and landing grounds available that it was quite impossible for the Germans to damage seriously a number of aerodromes sufficient to cause more than temporary inconvenience.

146. This is an important point, because, in mobile warfare, Fighter aerodromes cannot be hastily improvised in broken country, and the number of aerodromes actually or potentially available is a primary factor in the "Appreciation of a Situation."

147. Sector Operations Rooms were protected by high earth embankments, so that they were immune from everything except a direct hit, and, as a matter of fact, no direct hit by a heavy bomb was obtained on any Operations Room. Communications were, however, considerably interrupted, and I must here pay a tribute to the foresight of Air Vice-Marshal E. L. Gossage, C.B., C.V.O., D.S.O., M.C., who commanded No. 11 Group during the first eight months of the war. At his suggestion "Stand-by" Operations Rooms were constructed at a distance of two or three miles from Sector Headquarters, and a move was made to these

when serious attacks on Fighter Aerodromes began. They were somewhat inconvenient make-shifts, and some loss of efficiency in Interception resulted from their use. Work was put in hand immediately on more permanent and fully-equipped Operations Rooms conveniently remote from Sector Headquarters; these though in no way bomb-proof, were outside the radius of anything aimed at the Sector Aerodrome, and owed their immunity to inconspiouousness. Most of these were finished by October 1940.

148. Aerodrome Defence against parachute troops, or threat of more serious ground attack, was an important and a difficult problem, because Home Defence troops were few and were needed on the Beaches, and the majority of troops rescued from Dunkerque were disorganised and unarmed. The Commander-in-Chief, Home Forces, did, however, make troops available in small numbers for the more important aerodromes and armoured vehicles were extemporised. The difficulty was enhanced by a comparatively recent decision of the Air Ministry to disarm the rank and file of the Royal Air Force. The decision was reversed, but it was some time before rifles could be provided and men trained in their use.

149. The slender resources of the Anti-Aircraft Command were strained to provide guns for the defence of the most important Fighter and Bomber Aerodromes. High Altitude and Bofors guns were provided up to the limit considered practicable, and the effort was reinforced by the use of Royal Air Force detachments with Lewis guns and some hundreds of 20-mm. Cannon which were not immediately required for use in Aircraft

150. A type of small Rocket was also installed at many aerodromes. These were arranged in lines along the perimeter, and could be fired up to a height of something under 1,000 feet in the face of low-flying attack. They carried a small bomb on the end of a wire. Some limited success was claimed during a lowflying attack at Kenley, and they probably had some moral

effect when their existence became known to the Enemy. They were, of course, capable of physical effect only against very low horizontal attacks.

151. The main safeguard for Aircraft against air attack was Dispersal. Some experiments on Salisbury Plain in the Summer of 1938 had shown that dispersal alone, without any form of splinter-proof protection, afforded a reasonable safeguard against the forms of attack practised by our own Bomber Command at the time. Thirty unserviceable Fighters were disposed in a rough ring of about 1,000 yards diameter, and the Bomber Command attacked them for the inside of a week with every missile between a 500-pound bomb and an incendiary bullet, and without any kind of opposition. The result was substantially:- 3 destroyed, 1 damaged beyond repair, n seriously damaged but repairable, and the rest slightly damaged or untouched.

152. I therefore asked that small splinter-proof pens for single aircraft should be provided at all Fighter Aerodromes. This was not approved, but I was offered pens for groups of three. I had to agree to this, because it was linked up with the provision of, all-weather runways which I had been insistently demanding for two years, and it was imperatively necessary that work on the runways should not be held up by further discussion about pens. I think that the 3-aircraft pens were too big. They had a large open face to the front and a concrete area, of the size of two tennis courts, which made an ideal surface for the bursting of direct-action bombs. Eventually, splinter-proof partitions were made inside the pens, and till then some aircraft were parked in the open. Losses at dispersal points were not serious; the worst in my recollection was 5 aircraft destroyed or seriously damaged in one attack. Small portable tents were provided which could be erected over the centre portion of an aeroplane, leaving the tail and wing-tips exposed. These

protected the most important parts and enabled ground crews to work in bad weather.

153. About this time an improvised Repair System was organised and worked well. With the hearty co-operation of the Ministry of Aircraft Production it was decided that Units should be relieved of all extensive repairs and overhauls, both because of their preoccupation in the Battle and because of the danger of further damage being done by enemy action to aircraft under repair. Broadly speaking, any aircraft capable of returning to its base was capable of another 15 minutes' straight flight to a Repair Depot: aircraft incapable of flight were sent by road. Small repairs, such as the patching of bullet holes, were done by the Unit. Two such Repair Depots were improvised about 30 miles to the west of London, and this undoubtedly prevented an accumulation of unserviceable aircraft at Fighter Stations.

154. It was also about this time that the final decision was made to relegate the Defiant to night operations. It had two serious disabilities; firstly, the brain flying the aeroplane was not the brain firing the guns: the guns could not fire within 16 Degrees of the line of flight of the aeroplane and the gunner was distracted from his task by having to direct the pilot through the Communication Set. Secondly, the guns could not be fired below the horizontal, and it was therefore necessary to keep below the enemy. When beset by superior numbers of Fighters the best course to pursue was to form a descending spiral, so that one or more Defiants should always be in a position to bring effective fire to bear. Such tactics were, however, essentially defensive, and the formation sometimes got broken up before they could be adopted. In practice, the Defiants suffered such heavy losses that it was necessary to relegate them to night fighting, or to the attack of unescorted Bombers.

155. The above remarks have carried me beyond the first phase of the Battle and into the second; but I find it impossible to adhere to a description of the fighting phase by phase. The Enemy's Strategical, as well as his Tactical moves had to be met

from day to day as they occurred, and I give an account of my problems and the lessons to be derived from them roughly in the order of their incidence. The detailed sequence of events is sufficiently indicated in the Diagram at Appendix "D."

156. Throughout the Battle, of course, fighting continually occurred over the sea, and German aircraft, damaged over England, had to return across the Straits of Dover or the English Channel. Far more German than British crews fell into the sea. The Germans therefore developed an elaborate system of sea-rescue. Their Bombers had inflatable rubber dinghies, and various other rescue devices were adopted. Crews were provided with bags of a chemical known as fluorescine, a small quantity of which stained a large area of water a vivid green. Floating refuges with provisions and wireless sets were anchored off the French coast. "E Boat" and rescue launches were extensively employed, and white-painted float-planes, marked with the Red Cross, were used even in the midst of battle. We had to make it known to the Germans that we could not countenance the use of the Red Cross in this manner. They were engaged in rescuing combatants and taking them back to fight again, and they were also in a position, if granted immunity, to make valuable reconnaisance reports. In spite of this, surviving crews of these aircraft appeared to be surprised and aggrieved at being shot down.

157. Our own arrangements were less elaborate. Life-saving jackets were painted a conspicuous yellow, and later the fluorescine device was copied. Patrol aircraft (not under the Red Cross) looked out for immersed crews, and a chain of rescue launches with special communications was installed round the coast. Our own shipping, too, was often on the spot, and many pilots were rescued by Naval or Merchant vessels.

158. This is perhaps a convenient opportunity to say a word about the ethics of shooting at aircraft crews who have "baled out" in parachutes.

159. Germans descending over England are prospective Prisoners of War, and, as such, should be immune. On the other hand, British pilots descending over England are still potential Combatants.

160. Much indignation was caused by the fact that German pilots sometimes fired on our descending airmen (although, in my opinion, they were perfectly entitled to do so), but I am glad to say that in many cases they refrained and sometimes greeted a helpless adversary with a cheerful wave of the hand.

161. Many of the targets attacked during the first two phases of the Battle were of little military importance, and had but slight effect on our War Effort. Exceptions to this were day-attacks carried out on the Spitfire works at Southampton and the sheds at Brooklands where some of our Hurricanes were assembled and tested. Both these attacks had some effect on output, which would have been serious but for the anticipatory measures taken by Lord Beaverbrook.

162. About this time one Canadian, two Polish and one Czech squadrons became fit for Operations.

163. A squadron of Canadian pilots of the Royal Air Force (No. 242) had been in existence for some months, and was one of the squadrons which went to France in June to cover the evacuation from the West Coast. On its return it became one of the foremost fighting Squadrons in the Command, under the leadership of the very gallant Squadron Leader (now Wing Commander) D. R. S. Bader, D.S.O., D.F.C., No.1 (Canadian) Squadron, now also came into the line and acquitted itself with great distinction.

164. I must confess that I had been a little doubtful of the effect which their experience in their own countries and in France might have had upon the Polish and Czech pilots, but my doubts were soon laid to rest, because all three Squadrons swung in the fight with a dash and enthusiasm which is beyond praise. They were inspired by a burning hatred for the Germans which

made them very deadly opponents. The first Polish Squadron. (No. 303) in No.11 Group, during the course of a month, shot down more Germans than any British unit in the same period. Other Poles and Czechs were used in small numbers in British Squadrons, and fought very gallantly, but the language was a difficulty, and they were probably most efficiently employed in their own National units. Other foreign pilots were employed in British Squadrons, but not in appreciable numbers. The American "Eagle" Squadron was in process of formation during the Battle.

165. The Auxiliary Squadrons were by this time practically indistinguishable from Regulars. It will be remembered that the Scottish Auxiliaries were responsible for the first Air success of the War in the Firth of Forth. To set off against the discontinuity of their training in peace time they had the great advantage of permanency of personnel, and the Flight Commanders at the outbreak of the War were senior and experienced. At the same time, this very permanence led to the average age of the pilots being rather high for intensive fighting, which exercises a strain which the average man of 30 cannot support indefinitely. This point has now ceased to be of importance because of fresh postings. It is mentioned only because it is a factor to be kept in mind in peace time. No praise can be too high for the Auxiliaries, both as regards their keenness and efficiency in peace time and their fighting record in war.

166. I may perhaps mention the question of the Long Range Guns which were mounted along the coast of France near Cap Grisnez. They were within range of our coastal aerodromes, which they occasionally subjected to a desultory shelling. Their main targets, however, were Dover and the Convoys passing through the Straits. So far as I am aware, neither they nor the guns which we installed as counter measures, had any great influence on the air fighting, but they did of course make it impossible for any of our warships to approach the French coast

in clear weather, and might have had an important effect if it had been possible for the Germans to launch an invading army.

167. About the end of the second phase, the problems of keeping units up to strength and of relieving them when exhausted began to assume formidable proportions. It was no new experience, because the drain of units and pilots to France, coupled with the Dunkerque fighting, had created similar problems in the Spring.

168. The comparative relaxation in the intensity of the fighting in June and July had afforded a little respite, but units had only partially recovered and were neither fresh nor up to strength when the fighting again became intense.

169. When Squadrons became exhausted, obviously the most satisfactory way of reinforcement was by means of moving complete units, and this was done when time allowed. Serviceable aircraft were transferred by air, and Operational Aircraft Crews (about 35 men per Squadron) were transferred by Civil Aircraft put at my disposal for the moves. The remainder of the personnel travelled by train or motor transport according to circumstances. Some of the distances involved were considerable, as for instance when a Squadron from Wick had to be brought down in the London Area.

170. The First-line strength of a Squadron was 16 aircraft, of which not more than 12 were intended to be operationally available at any one time. The other 4 would normally be undergoing Inspection or Overhaul. In addition to this there was a small reserve of three to five aircraft per Squadron available on the station.

171. There was a limit to the number of trained pilots which could be kept on the strength of a Squadron even in times of operational passivity, because not more than about 25 could be kept in full practice in Flying Duties.

172. A fresh squadron coming into an active Sector would generally bring with them 16 aircraft and about 20 trained pilots.

They would normally fight until they were no longer capable of putting more than 9 aircraft into the air, and then they had to be relieved. This process occupied different periods according to the luck and skill of the unit. The normal period was a month to six weeks, but some units had to be replaced after a week or 10 days.

173. Air Vice Marshal Park found that the heaviest casualties were often incurred by newly arrived Squadrons owing to their nonfamiliarity with the latest developments of air fighting.

174. It soon became impossible to maintain the to-and-fro progress of complete unit personnel from end to end of the country, and the first limitation to efficiency which had to be accepted was the retention of the majority of personnel at Sector Stations and the transfer only of flying personnel and aircraft crews. This limitation was regrettable because it meant that officers and men were strange to one another, but worse was to come.

175. By the beginning of September the incidence of casualties became so serious that a fresh squadron would become depleted and exhausted before any of the resting and reforming squadrons was ready to take its place. Fighter pilots were no longer being produced in numbers sufficient to fill the gaps in the fighting ranks. Transfers were made from the Fleet Air Arm and from the Bomber and Coastal Commands, but these pilots naturally required a short flying course on Hurricanes or Spitfires and some instruction in Formation Flying, Fighter Tactics and Interception procedure.

176. I considered, but discarded, the advisability of combining pairs of weak units into single Squadrons at full strength, for several reasons, one of which was the difficulty of recovery when a lull should come. Another was that ground personnel would be wasted, and a third was that the rate at which the strength of the Command was decreasing would be obvious.

177. I decided to form 3 Categories of Squadron:-

(a) The units of n Group and on its immediate flanks, which were bearing the brunt of the fighting.

(b) A few outside units to be maintained at operational strength and to be available as Unit Reliefs in cases where this was unavoidable.

(c) The remaining Squadrons of the Command, which would be stripped of their operational pilots, for the benefit of the A Squadrons, down to a level of 5 or 6. These C Squadrons could devote their main energies to the training of new pilots, and, although they would not be fit to meet German Fighters, they would be quite capable of defending their Sectors against unescorted Bombers, which would be all that they would be likely to encounter.

178. The necessity for resorting to such measures as this indicates the strain which had been put on the Fighter Command and the Pilot Training organisations by the casualties which the Command had suffered in this decisive Battle.

179. In the early stages of the fight Mr. Winston Churchill spoke with affectionate raillery of me and my "Chicks." He could have said nothing to make me more proud; every Chick was needed before the end.

180. I trust that I may be permitted to record my appreciation of the help given me by the support and confidence of the Prime Minister at a difficult and critical time.

181. In the early days of the War the question of the provision of Operational Training Units (or Group Pools, as they were called at that time) was under discussion. It was referred to in the correspondence which I have mentioned in paragraph 17 of this Despatch. At that time I was so gravely in need of additional Fighter Squadrons that I was willing to do without Group Pools altogether while we were still at long range from the German Fighters.

182. The functions of these Group Pools, or O.T.U.s., was to accept pilots direct from Flying Training Schools or non-fighter units of the Royal Air Force and train them in the handling of Fighter types, formation flying, fighting tactics, and R/T control and interception methods. I realised that the Fighters in France could not undertake this work and must have a Group Pool allotted primarily to meet their requirements, but I felt that, so long as we at Home were out of touch with German Fighters, I would prefer to put all available resources into new Squadrons and to undertake in Service Squadrons the final training of pilots coming from Flying Training Schools, provided that they had done some formation flying and night flying, and had fired their guns in the air.

183. Of course, when intensive fighting began, final training of pilots in Squadrons could no longer be given efficiently, and at the time of the Battle three O.T.U.s, were in existence. It was found that three weeks was about the minimum period which was of practical value, but that a longer course, up to six weeks, was desirable when circumstances permitted.

184. During the Battle the output from the O.T.U.s. was quite inadequate to meet the casualty rate, and it was not even possible to supply from the Flying Training Schools the necessary intake to the O.T.U.s.

185. The lack of flexibility of the Training system, therefore, proved to be the "bottleneck" and was the cause of the progressively deteriorating situation of the Fighter Command up till the end of September. This statement is in no sense a criticism of the Flying Training Command; The problem, as I state it here, can have no ideal solution and some compromise must be adopted.

186. Assuming that in periods of maximum quiescence the Fighter Squadrons of the Royal Air Force require an intake of x pilots per week, in periods of intense activity they require about ten times the number.

187. It is necessary to start the flying training of a pilot about a year before he is ready to engage Enemy Fighters, and therefore the training authorities should be warned, a year ahead, of the incidence of active periods. This is obviously impossible. If they try to be ready for all eventualities by catering for a continuous output to meet a high casualty rate the result is that, during quiet periods, pilots are turned out at such a rate that they cannot be absorbed, or even given enough flying to prevent their forgetting what they have been taught. If, on the other hand, they cater for the normal wastage rate, Fighter Squadrons are starved of reinforcements when they are most vitally needed.

188. The fundamental principle which must be realised is that Fighter needs, when they arise, are not comparative with those of other Commands, but absolute. An adequate and efficient Fighter force ensures the Security of the Base, without which continuous operations are impossible.

189. If the Fighter defence had failed in the Autumn of 1940, England would have been invaded. The paralysis of their fighters in the Spring was an important factor in the collapse of the French resistance. Later, the unavoidable withdrawal of the Fighters from Crete rendered continued resistance impossible.

190. Day Bomber and Army Co-operation aircraft can operate when their own Fighters are predominant, but are driven out of the sky when the Enemy Fighters have a free hand.

191. I submit some suggestions by which the apparently insuperable difficulties of the problem may be reduced.

(a) Start by aiming at a Fighter output well above that needed in quiescent periods.

(b) Ensure that at Flying Training Schools, pupils earmarked for other duties may be rapidly switched over to Fighter training.

(c) Organise the O.T.U.s with a "Normal " and an "Emergency" Syllabus, the latter lasting for three weeks and the former twice as long.

(d) Fill up the Service Fighter Squadrons to a strength of 25 pilots, or whatever the C.-in-C. considers to be the maximum which can be kept in flying and operational practice.

(e) Form Reservoirs, either at O.T.U.s, or in special units where surplus pilots may maintain the flying and operational standard which they have reached.

(f) When the initiative lies in our hands (as, for instance, when we are planning to deliver an offensive some time ahead), the intake of Flying Training Schools should be adjusted to cater for the additional stress which can be foreseen.

(g) (And this applies principally to overseas theatres of war where rapid reinforcement is impossible.) Let the Day Bomber and Army Co-operation Squadrons have a number of Fighters on which they can fly and train as opportunity offers. This is a revolutionary suggestion, but it is made in all seriousness. If their Fighters are overwhelmed the Day Bomber and Army Co-operation units will not be able to operate at all. No very high standard of training should be attempted, especially in Radio-controlled Interception methods: but the intervention of these units as Fighters, working in pairs or small formations, might well prove to be the decisive factor in a critical situation.

192. It will be observed that, at the end of the second Phase of the Battle, the power of reinforcing by complete units had substantially disappeared. We still possessed an effective reserve of trained pilots, but they could be made available only by stripping the Squadrons which were not engaged in the South and South-East of England.

193. The effective strength of the Command was running down, though the fact was not known to the public, nor, I hoped, to the Germans. They for their part must certainly be feeling the effect of their heavy losses, but there was very little indication of any loss of morale, so far as could be seen from a daily scrutiny

of the examinations of Prisoners of War. Our own pilots were fighting with unabated gallantry and determination.

194. The confidence of the German High Command probably received something of a shock about this time. The sustained resistance which they were meeting in South-East England probably led them to believe that Fighter Squadrons bad been withdrawn, wholly or in part, from the North in order to meet the attack. On the 15th August, therefore, two large raids were sent, one to Yorkshire and one to Newcastle. They were escorted by Fighters. The distance was too great for Me.109s, but not for Me.110s.

195. If the assumption was that our Fighters had been withdrawn from the North, the contrary was soon apparent, and the bombers received such a drubbing that the experiment was not repeated. I think that this incident probably had a very depressing influence on the outlook of the German High Command.

196. As I have said, our own pilots were fighting with the utmost gallantry and determination, but the mass raids on London, which were the main feature of the third phase of the Battle, involved a tremendous strain on units which could no longer be relieved as such. Some Squadrons were flying 50 and 60 hours per diem.

197. Many of the pilots were getting very tired. An order was in existence that all pilots should have 24 hours' leave every week, during which they should be encouraged to leave their station and get some exercise and change of atmosphere: this was issued as an order so that the pilots should be compelled to avail themselves of the opportunity to get the necessary rest and relaxation. I think it was generally obeyed, but I fear that the instinct of duty sometimes over-rode the sense of discipline.

Other measures were also taken to provide rest and relaxation at Stations, and sometimes to find billets for pilots where they could sleep away from their Aerodromes.

198. During this third phase the problem arose, in an acute form, of the strength of Fighter formations which we should employ. When time was the essence of the problem, two squadrons were generally used by A.V.M. Park in No.11 Group. He had the responsibility of meeting attacks as far to the Eastward as possible, and the building up of a four-squadron formation involved the use of a rendezvous for aircraft from two or more aerodromes. This led to delay and lack of flexibility in leadership.

199. On the other hand, when No.12 Group was asked to send down protective formations to guard the aerodromes on the Eastern fringe of London, it was often possible to build up big formations, and these had great success on some occasions, though by no means always.

200. Because a similar situation may well arise in future, I think that it is desirable to enter into some detail in this connection.

201. I may preface my remarks by stating that I am personally in favour of using Fighter formations in the greatest strength of which circumstances will permit, and, in the Dunkerque fighting, where we could choose our time and build up our formations on the outward journey, I habitually employed four-Squadron formations as a preferable alternative to using two-Squadron formations at more frequent intervals; but, during the attacks on London, the available strength of Fighters did not admit of this policy, nor was time available.

202. I quote from Air Vice-Marshal Park's report:-

"The general plan adopted was to engage the enemy high-fighter screen with pairs of Spitfire Squadrons from Hornchurch and Biggin Hill half-way between London and the coast, and so enable Hurricane Squadrons from London Sectors to attack bomber formations and their close escort before they reached the line of fighter aerodromes East and South of London. The remaining Squadrons from London Sectors that could not be despatched in time to intercept the first wave of the attack by climbing in pairs formed a third and inner screen by patrolling along the lines of aerodromes East and South of London. The fighter Squadrons from Debden, Tangmere, and sometimes Northolt, were employed in wings of three or in pairs to form a screen South-East of London to intercept the third wave of the attack coming inland, also to mop up retreating formations of the earlier waves. The Spitfire Squadrons were redisposed so as to concentrate three Squadrons at each of Hornchurch and Biggin Hill. The primary role of these Squadrons was to engage and drive back the enemy high-fighter screen, and so protect the Hurricane Squadrons, whose task was to attack close escorts and then the bomber formations, all of which flew at much lower altitude."

203. I think that, if the policy of big formations had been attempted at this time in No. 11 Group, many more Bombers would have reached their objectives without opposition.

204. Air Vice-Marshal Park also quotes the results of the ten large formations ordered from Duxford into No.11 Group in the last half of October, when the Germans were employing Fighter-types only. Nine of these sorties made no interception, and the tenth destroyed one Me.109.

205. The most critical stage of the Battle occurred in the third phase. On the 15th September the Germans delivered their maximum effort, when our Guns and Fighters together accounted for 185 aircraft. Heavy pressure was kept up till the 27th September, but, by the end of the month, it became apparent that the Germans could no longer face the Bomber wastage which they had sustained, and the operations entered upon their fourth phase, in which a proportion of enemy Fighters themselves acted as Bombers.

206. This plan, although the actual damage caused by bombs was comparatively trivial, was aimed primarily at a further whittling down of our Fighter strength, and, of all the methods adopted by the Germans, it was the most difficult

to counter. Apart from the previous difficulty of determining which formations meant business, and which were feints, we had to discover which formations carried bombs and which did not.

207. To meet this difficulty, Air Vice-Marshal Park devised the plan of using single Spitfires, flying at maximum height, to act as Reconnaissance aircraft and to report their observations immediately by R/T.

208. A special Flight was organised for this purpose, and. it was later recommended that the Spitfires should be employed in pairs, for reasons of security, and that the Flight should become a Squadron. A special R/T receiving set was erected at Group Headquarters so that reports might be obtained without any delay in transmission from the Sector receiving station. There is reason to believe that the Germans also adopted a system of using high-flying H.E. 113s as Scouts. Their information concerning our movements was transmitted to the ground and relayed to their Bombers in the air.

209. In the fourth phase, the apparent ratio of losses in our favour dropped appreciably. I say "apparent" because, in fighting at extreme altitudes, fighters often could not see their victims crash, and the percentage reported as Certainly Destroyed was unfairly depressed. Our own casualties, nevertheless, were such that the C. Category squadrons, which I was hoping to build up to operational strength again, remained in their condition of semi-effectiveness.

210. Serious as were our difficulties, however, those of the enemy were worse, and by the end of October the Germans abandoned their attempts to wear down the Fighter Command, and the country was delivered from the threat of immediate invasion.

211. The Order of Battle at the beginning of November is shown at Appendix E. Categories of Squadrons (A, B. or C, *vide* paragraph 177) are indicated.

212. Increasingly throughout the Battle had the importance of a high "ceiling" been manifested. It is by no means necessary that every Fighter shall have its best performance at stratospheric heights; any such policy would result in a loss of performance at lower altitude, and we must never lose sight of the basic principle that the Fighter exists for the purpose of shooting down Bombers, and that its encounters with other Fighters are incidental to this process.

213. There are, nevertheless, arguments for giving to a percentage of Fighters a ceiling (determinable by specific physiological tests) above which no enemy can climb without the use of Pressure Cabins. Just as the "Weather Gauge" was often the determining factor in the tactics of sailing ships, so the "Height Gauge" was often crucial in air combat. Exhaust-driver turbo-superchargers have certain advantages over gear-driven blowers at great height, and should be considered for adoption in spite of their disadvantages.

214. It must be remembered also that the initiative always rests with the Bomber, who can select at will the height at which he will make his attack. We must be prepared, therefore, for the appearance of the pressure-cabin Bomber, flying at a height unattainable by any non-pressurised Fighter. (I should perhaps explain that there is a height, about 43,000 feet, above which the administration of any quantity of oxygen at atmospheric pressure becomes ineffective because it cannot be inhaled and a pressure cabin or a pressure suit becomes essential.) Of course, a pressure-cabin Bomber is inefficient and vulnerable, because it is difficult to operate free guns from a pressure cabin, and pressure leakage from holes made in the walls of the cabin will prostrate the crew. The threat from pressurised Bombers is therefore serious only if we have no Fighters to meet them, and for this reason we should always possess a limited number of pressurised Fighters.

215. Various other lessons were learned from the experience of fighting at extreme altitudes. One very tiresome feature was that a considerable proportion of ultra-high-flying raids was missed by the Intelligence systems, or reported so late that time was not available to climb and intercept. This made it necessary to employ standing patrols just below oxygen height (about 16,000 feet). These patrols climbed to intercept at extreme height when ordered to do so. This cut at the roots of the Fighter Command system, which was designed to ensure economy of effort by keeping aircraft on the ground except when required to make an interception.

216. Another lesson was that the system of using an "Above Guard" should be retained even when an attack was initiated from extreme altitude.

217. Flying and fighting-fatigue increases with altitude, and the comfort of the pilot requires unremitting attention. Cockpit heating and the meticulous pursuit and elimination of air leaks are of great importance. Attention should also be paid to the elimination of icing on cockpit hoods (which are apt to freeze immovably) and on the inside and outside of windscreens.

218. A serious handicap, which I have not hitherto mentioned, was the fact that the change over from "High Frequency" to "Very High Frequency" Radio Telephony was still in progress. The V.H.F. was an immense improvement on the H.F., both in range and clarity of speech; but the change-over, which had started nearly a year before, was held up by the slow output of equipment. This meant that much work had to be done on aircraft Radio equipment during the Battle, and Squadrons equipped with V.H.F. could not communicate with H.F. Ground Stations, and *vice versa*.

219. Some of our worst losses occurred through defective leadership on the part of a unit commander, who might lead his pilots into a trap or be caught while climbing by an enemy formation approaching "out of the sun." During periods

of intense activity promotions to the command of Fighter squadrons should be made on the recommendation of Group Commanders from amongst Flight Commanders experienced in the methods of the moment. If and when it is necessary to post a Squadron Leader (however gallant and experienced) from outside the Command, he should humbly start as an ordinary member of the formation until he has gained experience. Only exceptionally should officers over 26 years of age be posted to command Fighter Squadrons.

220. The experience of the Battle made me a little doubtful if the organisation of a squadron into 2 Flights, each of 2 Sections of 3 aircraft, was ideal. It was, of course, undesirable to make any sweeping change during the Battle, and I relinquished my Command shortly after its termination; but the weakness lay in the Section of 3 when it became necessary to break up a formation in a "Dog Fight." The organisation should allow for a break up into pairs, in which one pilot looks after the tail of his companion. A Squadron might be divided into 3 Flights of 4 (which would limit the employment of half-Squadrons), or it might consist of 2 Flights of 8, each comprising 2 Sections of 4. This latter suggestion would upset standard arrangements for accommodation.

221. The matter is not one which can be settled without consultation with various authorities and Branches of the Air Ministry. I therefore merely raise the point without making any definite recommendation.

222. A great deal of discussion took place before and in the early stages of the war as to the best method of "harmonisation" of the guns of an 8-gun Fighter: that is to say the direction, in relation to the longitudinal axis of the aircraft, in which each gun should be pointed in order to get the best results.

223. There were three schools of thought:-

One maintained that the lines of fire should be dispersed so that the largest possible "beaten zone" might be formed and one gun (but not more than one) would always be on the target.

The second held that the guns should be left parallel and so would always cover an elongated zone corresponding with the vulnerable parts of a Bomber (Engines, Tanks and Fuselage).

The third demanded concentration of the fire of all guns at a point.

224. Arguments were produced in favour of all three methods of harmonisation, but in practice it was found that concentration of fire gave the best results. Guns were harmonised so that their lines of fire converged on a point 250 yards distant: fire was therefore effective up to about 500 yards, where the lines of fire had opened out again to their original intervals after crossing at the point of concentration.

225. It was very desirable to get data as to the actual ranges at which fire effect had been obtained. The Reflector Sight contained a rough range-finder which the range of an aircraft of known span could be determined if it was approached from astern, but, in spite of this, pilots, in the heat of action, generally underestimated the ranges at which they fired.

226. Cinema guns, invaluable for training purposes, were used in combat also; and many striking pictures were obtained, from which valuable lessons were learned.

227. The types of ammunition used in the guns varied during the course of the Battle. It was necessary to include some incendiary ammunition, but the type originally available gave a distinct smoke-tracer effect. Now tracer ammunition in fixed guns at any but very short range gives very misleading indications, and I wished pilots to use their sights properly and not to rely on tracer indications. (The above remarks do not apply at night, nor to free guns, where tracer is essential for one of the methods taught for aiming.)

228. During the Battle "de Wilde" ammunition became available in increasing quantities. This was an incendiary ammunition without any flame or smoke trace, and it was extremely popular with pilots, who attributed to it almost magical properties. 8-gun Fighters, of course, were always liable to be sent up at night, and it was therefore desirable to retain some of the older types of incendiary bullets.

These were preferred to the "tracer" proper, which gave too bright a flame at night.

229. A typical arrangement, therefore, was:-

      Old-type incendiary in the 2 outer guns,

      de Wilde in one gun while supplies were limited,

      Armour piercing in 2 guns, and ball in the other 3.

230. A discussion on the offensive and defensive equipment of aircraft will be found in Appendix F. It will be of interest to all concerned with the Design of Technical Equipment of Aircraft.

PART III. – NIGHT INTERCEPTION.

231. No story of the Battle would be complete without some account of the Night operations. It is true that they constituted only a subsidiary activity in comparison with the main German objective of fighting us to a standstill by day so that Air Superiority might be attained as a preliminary to Invasion. The night attacks did little directly to affect the efficiency of the Day Fighting Squadrons, though they had certain indirect effects. Although actual casualties were insignificant, disturbance and loss of sleep were caused; damage was done to factories where aircraft engines and accessories were produced; and the stress of continuous operations, day and night, imposed a very heavy strain on Formation Commanders and Staff officers, and upon the personnel of all Operations Rooms.

232. I had long been apprehensive of the effect of Night attacks, when they should begin, and of the efficacy of our defensive measures.

233. We relied on daytime interception methods, and on the Searchlights to illuminate and hold the Bombers. If they were capable of doing this, all would be well, since the distance at which an illuminated Bomber can be seen by night is comparable with the range of visibility by daylight.

234. The first night attack worthy of the name was made early in June and the results were encouraging. Aircraft were well picked up and held by the Searchlights and 6 were shot down. The attack was, however, made at comparatively low altitudes (8,000–12,000 ft.) and the Germans, profiting by this lesson, resorted thereafter to greater heights at which the Searchlights were practically ineffective. In close consultation with myself, General Pile tried every conceivable method of operation, but without material success.

235. About this time Radio Location instruments were fitted in Blenheims and it became necessary to develop at high pressure a system of operation which should enable Night Fighters to make interceptions even against unilluminated targets.

236. The difficulty of this task will be realised when it is considered that it became necessary to put the Fighter within one or two hundred yards of the Enemy, and on the same course, instead of the four or five miles which were adequate against an illuminated target.

237. It may be asked why the Searchlights were so comparatively impotent when they had afforded an accessory to successful defence at the end of the last war. The answer lies partly in the height factor already discussed, and partly in the greatly increased speed of the Bomber, which was about three times that obtaining in 1914. The sound locator, on which Searchlights mainly relied at this time, naturally registered the apparent position of the source of sound and lagged behind the target to the extent of the time taken by sound to travel from the target to the Sound Locator. When the speed of the target is low it is comparatively easy to allow for this lag, but at the speeds of

modern bombers the angular distance which must be allowed for in searching is so great that the Searchlights were generally defeated.

238. The first thing which appeared obvious to me was that a "sound Plot" track transmitted from the Observer Corps with a variable and unpredictable "lag" was good enough only for Air Raid Warning purposes and was much too inaccurate to be of use for controlled interception at night: height indications also were little better than guesswork. The Radio Location apparatus (known as A.I.) fitted in twin-engined fighters had a maximum range of 2 or 3 miles, but it was limited by the height at which the Fighter was flying. If, for instance, the Fighter was flying at 10,000 feet, ground echoes were reflected from all ranges greater than this, and an aircraft echo from 10,500 feet would be indistinguishable among the ground echoes.

239. The minimum range of the A.I. was also restricted at this time to about 1,000 feet. Below this distance the aircraft echo was swamped by instrumental disturbance. Continuous and intensive development work was in progress to minimise these limitations.

240. No Radio Location apparatus was available at this time for inland tracking, and I turned for help to the Army, which had developed for use with guns a Radio Location apparatus known as the G.L. Set. Within a limited range (about 40,000 feet) this set could give very accurate position plots, and, moreover, could read height to within plus or minus 1,000 feet at average ranges.

241. Although these sets were few in number and were urgently required for their original purpose of gun control, General Pile realised the urgency of our need and made available about 10 sets for an experiment in the Kenley Sector on the usual line of approach of London Raiders, which commonly made their landfall near Beachy Head.

242. The G.L. sets were installed at Searchlight Posts, and direct telephone communication was arranged with the Kenley Sector Operations Room. Here a large blackboard was installed, and the G.L. plots were shown at intervals of about 30 seconds and with a greater accuracy in height than had before been possible by any means.

243. The track of the pursuing fighter was determined by means of the R/T Direction Finding Stations.

244. Major A. B. Russell, O.B.E., T.A.R.O., co-operated in the development of this system in the Kenley Sector. His practical knowledge and tireless enthusiasm were of the greatest value.

245. Promising results were obtained almost from the first and numerous instances occurred where echoes were obtained on the A.I. sets in the aircraft. Practical results were, however, disappointing, partly because the A.I. apparatus proved to be unexpectedly capricious in azimuth, and partly because the Blenheim was slower than many of the German Bombers and was deficient in fire-power. Many Germans escaped after an initial A.I. "pickup" and even after visual contact had been effected.

246. The A.I. apparatus was then fitted into the Beaufighters, which were just beginning to appear in Service. The machines and their engines suffered from "teething trouble" to an unusual degree, and the adaption of A.I. to a new type was accompanied by certain difficulties. In addition, they were operating from a wet aerodrome at Redhill, and the development of delicate electrical apparatus, combined with a new type of aircraft and engine, with rudimentary maintenance facilities, was a matter of the greatest difficulty. In nine cases out of ten something would go wrong with the aeroplane or with the A.I. set or with the R/T Direction Finding apparatus or with the Communication system before an interception could be made. No. 219 Squadron, under Squadron Leader J. H. Little, were engaged in this work and

operated with great energy and enthusiasm under extremely adverse and difficult conditions.

247. It would, of course, have been desirable to carry out all this development work by day when faults would have been much more easily detected and remedied, but the low rate of Aircraft Serviceability precluded Day-and-Night work, and London was being bombed almost every night, so that I could not afford to neglect the chance of getting practical results. These, though disappointing, were not entirely negligible; several Bombers were shot down in this area during the experimental period, and many discovered that they were pursued and turned back before reaching their objectives. Night Fighting Development work was also going on at the same time at the Fighter Interception Unit at Tangmere in Sussex.

248. A supplementary use was found for the A.I. by the installation of A.I. "Beacons" in the vicinity of Night Flying Aerodromes. These afforded a valuable Navigational aid for "Homing" in cases where any defect occurred in the R/T D/F system.

249. Shortly before I left the Command a new piece of Radio-Location apparatus became available in the shape of the "G.C.I." set with the Plan Position Indicator. This was an Inland-Reading Set which showed the position of all aircraft within its range on a fluorescent screen as the aerial was rotated.

250. The main advantages of this set were that it had a longer range than the G.L. set and it was possible to track the Bomber and the Fighter by the same apparatus instead of following one with the G.L. and the other by R/T D/F. Moreover it was found that in some circumstances the accuracy of the R/T D/F method was inadequate for night interceptions.

251. On the other hand, the accuracy of height readings by the G.C.I. apparatus was less than that obtainable with the G.L. I understand that this has now been improved.

252. Whatever the exact technical method of plotting positions and tracks of aircraft, the object was to place the Fighter behind the Bomber, and in such a position that the echo of the latter

would show in the Fighter's A.I. set. The Fighter then tried to overtake the Bomber until it became visible to the naked eye.

253. At that time only multi-seaters could be fitted with A.I., and therefore, concurrently with the Night Interception experiments, methods were tried of using the Searchlights as pointers for Night Fighters, even if the target were out of range of the Searchlight Beam. Experiments were made with the Searchlights in "clumps" to increase their illuminating power and the visibility of their beams to Fighters at a distance.

254. A small Radio-Location set was designed to fit to the Searchlight itself, so as to get over the time-lag which was such an insuperable obstacle to the use of Sound Locators. It is probable that if Searchlights can substitute the speed of light for that of sound they may take on a new lease of useful life.

255. The disadvantage of relying entirely on Radio-controlled methods of Night Interception is that "saturation point" is quickly reached, and when mass raids are in progress only a limited number of fighters can be operated. Results obtained in the Spring of 1941 show that Day Fighters can obtain important results in conditions of good visibility, especially if attention is paid to all methods of improving the night vision of pilots.

256. During the Battle the "Intruder" system was initiated on a small scale. Night fighters without A.I. were sent across to France in an attempt to catch Bombers while taking off from, or landing at, their aerodromes; or to intercept them at points where they habitually crossed the French Coast.

257. I had to leave the Development of Night Interception at a very interesting stage; but it is perhaps not too much to say that, although much remained to be done, the back of toe problem had been broken. The experiments had, of course, been carried out in a small area, and raiders which avoided the area could be intercepted only by previously existing methods; but the possibilities had been demonstrated and could be applied on a larger scale as soon as the necessary apparatus was provided.

258. The method is, of course, also applicable to the day interception of raiders making use of cloud cover, which have hitherto proved extremely elusive; and it is not too much to hope, that the eventual development of very high-frequency A.I. may enable accurate fire to be opened against unseen targets, so that not even the darkest night nor the densest cloud will serve as a protection to the Raider.

259. The day may come when every Single-Seater Fighter is fitted with A.I., but this is not yet feasible. What can be done is to fit all Searchlights with Radio-Location apparatus so that every Searchlight Beam' is a reliable pointer towards an enemy, even if the range is too great for direct illumination.[46] If then the Fighter can be informed in addition of the height of the Raider, Day Fighters will be able to join usefully and economically in night operations on dark nights.

APPENDIX "C."
6TH A.A. DIVISION, JULY–OCTOBER 1940.
(*Note.*–This report relates only to 6th A.A. Division. It does not cover the operations of A.A. Command as a whole.)

Glossary of Abbreviations.
H.A.A. Heavy Anti-Aircraft.
L.A.A Light Anti-Aircraft.
G.O.R Gun Operations Room.
A.A.L.M.G. Anti-Aircraft Light Machine-Gun.
V.I.E Visual Indicator Equipment.
G.P.O. Gun Position Officer.
G.L Radio Location Set for Gun Laying.

---

46 As a result of the experience gained during this period, all searchlight equipments have since been fitted with Radar control. This, combined with intensified training, has made them, since 1941, extremely accurate.

V.P.Vulnerable Point.
F.A.S Forward Area Sight.
S.O.R Sector Operator's Room.
G.D.A Gun Defended Area.

1. *Layout of A.A. Defences.*
(a) The area covered by 6th A.A. Division coincided: with the R.A.F. sectors Debden, North Weald, Hornchurch, Biggin Hill and Kenley (*i.e.,* the major part of No.11. Fighter Group, R.A.F.). Thus the coastal boundary extended from Lowestoft (exclusive) in the North to Worthing (exclusive) in the South; the internal boundary marching with that of the Metropolitan area.
(b) Distribution of A.A. defences was briefly as follows:-
(i) *H.A.A. Guns.*
The Divisional area contained four main "gun defended areas" at Harwich, Thames and Medway North (guns emplaced along the North bank of the Thames Estuary), Thames and Medway South (guns emplaced along the South bank of the Thames Estuary and defending Chatham and Rochester) and Dover (including Folkestone). In addition, H.A.A. guns were deployed for the defence of certain aerodromes.

Each "gun defended area" was based on a Gun Operations Room: at Felixstowe, Vange, Chatham and Dover respectively. This G.O.R. was connected directly to 11 Fighter Group Operations Room at Uxbridge, from which it received plots of enemy raids, which were in turn passed down to all gun sites.

The armament of each H.A.A. site consisted of the following: 4 (sometimes 2) 4.5, 3.7 or 3-inch guns with predictor. Appendix "A" shows the H.A.A. defences as at the beginning of August 1940 and the end of October 1940.
(ii) *L.A.A. Guns.*
45 Vulnerable Points in the Divisional area were defended by L.A.A. guns. These V.Ps. consisted of Air Ministry Experimental Stations, Fighter Aerodromes, Dockyards, Oil Depots, Magazines,

Industrial Undertakings and Factories. Armament consisted of the following guns: 40-mm. Bofors (with Predictor No. 3 and Forward Area Sights), 3-inch, 20 cwt. (Case I), A.A.L.M.G. and 20-mm. Hispano. Appendix "B" shows the V.Ps. with their armament as in August and October 1940.

(iii) *Searchlights.*

Searchlights were deployed in single light stations at approximately 6,000 yards spacing throughout the area, but with a closer spacing in certain instances along the coast and in "gun defended areas" where the distance between lights was approximately 3,500 yards. These lights were deployed on a brigade basis following R.A.F. sectors, and each light was connected by direct telephone line and/or R.T. set No. 17 to Battery Headquarters via troop H.Q. and thence to an army telephone board at the R.A.F. Sector Operations Room.

The equipment of a Searchlight site consisted of the following:-
90-cm. Projector with, in most cases, Sound Locator Mk. III. In some instances sites were equipped with Sound Locators Mk. VIII or Mk. IX. During the late Summer and Autumn the number of Mk. VIII and Mk. IX Sound Locators gradually increased, and V.I.E. equipment and 150-cm. Projectors were introduced. Each Searchlight site was equipped with one A.A.L.M.G. for use against low-flying aircraft and for ground defence.

2. *Enemy Tactics.*

(a) *High Level Bombing Attacks.*

These took place generally between heights of 16,000/20,000 feet. Bombers approached their targets in close protective formations until running up to the line of bomb release, when formation was changed to Line Astern (if there was a definite objective to the attack). Attacks frequently occurred in waves, each wave flying at approximately the same height and on the same course. On engagement by H.A. guns, avoiding action was taken in three stages:-

Stage 1.–The bombers gained height steadily and maintained course and formation.

Stage 2.–Formations opened out widely and maintained course.

Stage 3.–Under heavy fire, formations split and bombers scattered widely on different courses. It was after this stage had been reached that the best opportunity was provided for fighters to engage.

(b) *Low Level and Dive Bombing Attacks.*

In the latter stages of the enemy air offensive numerous instances of low level and dive bombing attacks occurred, in particular against fighter aerodromes (Manston, Hawkinge, Lympne, Kenley).

L.A.A. and H.A.A. employed in dealing with these forms of attack met with varying success, but in cases where no planes were brought down the effect of fire from the A.A. defence almost invariably disconcerted the dive bomber so that few bombs were dropped with accuracy.

Considerable efforts were made by Me.109's and Ju. 87's to destroy the balloon barrage at Dover, and, though at times they partially succeeded, excellent targets were provided for the Dover H.A.A. and L.A.A. guns.

3. *Part played by H.A.A. Guns.*

Targets of all types presented themselves to H.A.A. sites, ranging from solid bomber formation to single cloud hopping or dive bombers, balloon strafers or hedge hoppers, all of which were successfully engaged by appropriate method of fire.

The action of the defence achieved success in the following ways:-

(a) The actual destruction or disablement of enemy aircraft (see Appendix "C").

(b) The breaking up of formations, thus enabling the R.A.F. to press home attacks on smaller groups of bombers.

(c) Destroying the accuracy of their bombing by forcing the enemy aircraft to take avoiding action.

(d) By pointing out to patrolling fighters the whereabouts of enemy formations by means of shell bursts.

The following methods of fire were in operation at this period:-

(a) *Seen Targets.*

(i) Each gun site was allotted a zone of priority and responsibility for opening fire on a target rested with the G.P.O.

(ii) Targets could be engaged by day if identified as hostile beyond reasonable doubt or if a hostile act was committed. By night, failure to give recognition signals was an additional proviso.

(iii) It was the responsibility of the G.P.O. to cease fire when fighters closed to the attack.

(b) *Unseen Targets.*

Unseen firing at this time was in its infancy and considerable initiative was displayed in evolving methods for engaging targets unseen by day or by night.

The following methods were employed:-

(i) *Geographic Barrages.*

Many forms of barrage were used by different G.D.As. but all were based on obtaining concentrations at a point, on a line, or over an area, through which the enemy aircraft must fly.

Suitable barrages for lines of approach and heights were worked out beforehand. Approach of enemy aircraft was observed by G.L. and, by co-ordination at G.O.Rs., the fire from each site could be controlled to bring a maximum concentration of shell bursts at the required point.

(ii) *Precision Engagements.*

Method A– Due to poor visibility or wrong speed settings searchlight intersections were often made without actual illumination of the aircraft. By obtaining slant range from G.L. and following the intersection on the Predictor, sufficient data were available to enable shells to burst at or near the intersection.

Method B– This provided for engagement without searchlight intersections. Continuous bearings and slant ranges from the G.L. were fed into the Predictor and engagement of target undertaken on the data thus provided. For sites which were not equipped with G.L. the appropriate information was passed down from G.O.R.

It will be appreciated that procedure varied with different Gun Zones, according to circumstances and the equipment available. It should be remembered that all engagements of unseen targets were subject to the express permission of the Group Controller at Uxbridge, so that danger of engaging friendly aircraft was obviated.

(c) *Anti-Dive-Bombing Barrage.*

Special barrages against dive bombers were organised round the following V.Ps.: Harwich Harbour, Thameshaven Oil Installations, Tilbury Docks, Chatham Dockyard, Sheerness Dockyard, Dover Harbour, Purfleet Oil and Ammunition Depots.

This barrage could be employed at any time at the discretion of the G.P.O. when he considered that other and more accurate methods were unlikely to be effective. The barrage was designed for a height of 3,000 feet and assumed a dive angle of 60°. It was based on a barrage circle round each gun site which was divided into 4 quadrants in which the barrages were placed.

The maximum effort from H.A.A. guns was required from the 19th August to the 5th October, during which time the crews had little rest, continuous 24 hour's manning being required at Dover, a "duty gun station" system being worked in all areas.

Evidence is available to show how time and time again enemy bombers would not face up to the heavy and accurate fire put up by gun stations. Particularly worthy of mention are two attacks on Hornchurch aerodrome when on both occasions fighters were on the ground for refuelling. A.A. fire broke up the formation and prevented any damage to the station buildings and aircraft on the ground.

4. *Part played by L.A.A. Guns.*

The targets which offered themselves to L.A.A. guns were in the main small numbers engaged in dive bombing or low level attacks on V.Ps. Opportunity usually only offered fleeting targets, and quickness of thought and action was essential to make fullest use of the targets which presented themselves. Success against targets by L.A.A. guns was achieved in the following ways:-

  (a) The destruction or disablement of enemy aircraft (See Appendix "C").
  (b) The prevention of accurate bombing causing the bombers to pull out of their dive earlier than they intended. Methods of firing employed by L.A.A. guns as follows:-

(i) *Bofors.*

Fire was directed either by No.3 Predictor or by Forward area Sights; some Bofors were not equipped with the Predictor when the latter method only could be used.

  The Predictor equipped guns require a 130 Volt A.C. electric supply which was provided either from engine-driven generators or from the mains. Shooting with the Predictor achieved very great accuracy and the results and destruction of aircraft and the average ammunition expenditure proved the efficiency of this equipment (see Appendix "C"). The F.A.S. method permitted quick engagements of targets although without the accuracy afforded by the Predictor.

(ii) *3-inch 20-cwt. Guns (Case I).*

Some V.Ps. were equipped with the 3-inch 20-cwt. gun without Predictor which was fired from deflection sights; shrapnel was normally used. H.E., however, was used for targets at greater height.

(iii) *A.A.L.M.G.*
Lewis Guns on A.A. mountings proved extremely effective in attacking low-flying enemy aircraft. These guns were mounted in single, double or quadruple mountings and were fired by the Hosepipe method using tracer ammunition.
(iv) *Hispano 20-mm. Equipment.*
A few of these weapons only were deployed and, owing to shortage of ammunition and lack of tracer, were not found very effective.

5. *Part Played by Searchlights.*
(a) *Day.*
Owing to the close spacing of Searchlight sites they formed a valuable source of intelligence and rapid reports were able to be made upwards of casualties to friendly and enemy aircraft, pilots descending by parachute and other incidents of importance. In addition, they have been able to provide valuable reports of isolated enemy aircraft, trace of which had been lost by the Observer Corps.

The value of the A.A.L.M.G. with which each site was equipped cannot be too highly stressed, and during the 4 months under review no less than 23 enemy aircraft were destroyed, confirmed, by A.A.L.M.G. at Searchlight sites (this includes a few in which A.A.L.M.G. at H.A.A. sites also shared). Prisoner of War reports showed that it was not generally known by the German Air Force pilots that Searchlight sites were equipped with A.A. defence.
(b) *Night.*
Tactical employment of Searchlights at night was by either-

(i) 3-beam rule, in which 3 sites only engaged the target; or
(ii) by the Master-beam system, in which one Master beam per three sites exposed and was followed by the remaining two beams acting under the orders of the Master beam.

The decision to engage was the responsibility of the Detachment Commander, and no direct tactical control was exercised from Battery Headquarters.

In the early stages of the Battle of Britain night activity was on a small scale and Searchlights had few raids to engage. Some illuminations were effected, but throughout it was difficult, by ground observations, to assess the actual numbers. Frequently illuminations were reported by sites not engaging the targets. The difficulty of illumination was increased as the number of night raids increased, owing to the difficulty of sites selecting the same target.

There is evidence to show that Searchlight activity, whilst being difficult to measure, forced enemy aircraft to fly at a greater height than they would otherwise have done. Bombs were frequently dropped when enemy aircraft were illuminated, which were possibly intended to discourage Searchlights from exposing. Evasive tactics by the enemy consisted of changing height and speed continuously to avoid being illuminated rather than a violent evasive action upon illumination.

6. G.L. Equipment.

At the beginning of August experiments had just been completed to determine whether G.L. equipment could satisfactorily be used as a Ships detector. Apart from the results of this experiment three other facts emerged:-

(a) The G.L. principle was of considerable value when used in conjunction with Searchlights.

(b) That G.L. sets sited in an anti-ship role, *i.e.,* on the top of a cliff, were of considerable value in detecting low-flying aircraft.

(c) It showed the value of small R.D.F. detectors within the main R.A.F. chain, in plotting enemy aircraft direct to sectors. At the beginning of the Battle of Britain, 21 G.L. sets were in use by 6th A.A. Division, and by October this number had been increased by another 14.

(i) *G.L. at Gun Stations.*

The main function of these equipments was to provide data for Unseen target engagements as described above. One other function of these sets is worth special mention.

Two sets were specially sited on the cliffs at Dover to pick up targets at low level. These sets were able to register aircraft taking off from the aerodromes immediately behind Calais, thereby obtaining information considerably earlier than could be provided by the main R.D.F. station on the coast. This information was reported back to Uxbridge Operations Room by a priority code message which indicated the approximate number of aircraft which had taken off and their position. This report was received some 5/6 minutes before it could be received through the usual R.D.F. channels, and therefore enabled the Controller to order his Fighters off the ground correspondingly earlier than would otherwise have been the case.

This system, which was also adopted somewhat further along the coast in the neighbourhood of Beachy Head, was of all the more value as the enemy were heavily bombing the R.D.F. stations, which were consequently sometimes out of action.

(ii) *G.L. Stations with Searchlights.*

During the latter stages of the offensive, when the night raids on London commenced, it was realised that the G.L. would be of considerable assistance to Night Fighters. An "elevation" attachment to the equipment was produced and this enabled height to be obtained, which in conjunction with a plotting scheme at S.O.R., enabled Searchlight beams to be directed more accurately on a target to assist night fighters. The results obtained from this were not completely satisfactory, but they showed the way to the development of the present system.

(iii) *Mine-Laying Aircraft.*

It was found that the experiments conducted in the ship-detector role could be very satisfactorily applied to detecting mine-laying aircraft which flew in at a height too low to be picked up by the C.H. Stations. It enabled accurate tracks of these aircraft to be kept which were afterwards passed to the Naval Authorities, who were then able to sweep up the mines which had been laid by these aircraft.

7. *Statistics.*

Careful records have been kept of ammunition expenditure and enemy aircraft shot down, and details are shown in Appendix "C." The following points are worthy of note:-

(a) The total enemy aircraft Destroyed, Confirmed Category I by 6th A.A. Division during the months July–October 1940, inclusive, was 221; of this total 104 were destroyed on seven days, thus:-

15	August	1940	15
18	"	"	22
24	"	"	10
31	"	"	20
2	September	1940	13
7	"	"	14
15	"	"	10
			104

(b) A considerable number of enemy aircraft were claimed as Probably Destroyed and Damaged.

(c) The total amount of H.A.A. expended was 75,000 rounds.

(d) The total amount of Bofors ammunition expended was 9,417 rounds.

8. *Ground Defence*

Preparations were made by all A.A. defences to assume a secondary ground defence ro l e; Bofors were provided with A/T ammunition, and sited to cover approaches to aerodromes, V.Ps., & c. Certain 3.7 inch guns suitably sited were given an anti-ship role, and preparations were made for barrages to be put on certain beaches. Under the immediate threat of invasion in May 1940, mobile columns of A.A. troops were formed, but these troops reverted to their A.A. role before the Battle of Britain began.

9. *Lessons Learnt.*

(a) The outstanding lesson learnt from this intensive air attack was undoubtedly the soundness and suitability of the organisation and arrangements of the control and direction of the anti-aircraft defences. These measures devised in peace time and perfected during the earlier arid quieter period of hostilities, stood the severe test with amazing resilience and adaptability. No major alterations in the system were indicated or, indeed, were made subsequent to these operations.[47] The way in which the activities of the anti-aircraft linked in and were capable of co-ordination with the major partners in the venture—R.A.F. Fighter Command, No.11 Fighter Group, and sector commands—is perhaps worthy of special note.

(b) Other lessons learnt are by comparison of minor import. Chief among them was the great vulnerability of aircraft if caught by accurate H.A.A. fire when in close formation. A good instance of this occurred in an action on the 8th September, when a geschwader of 15 Do.17s, flying in formation at 15,000 feet, approached a gun site South of River Thames. The opening salvo from the four 3.7-inch guns brought down the three leading aircraft, the remaining machines turning back in

---

47 This statement applies only to the higher organisation, and must not be taken to mean that no improvements were made in the control and direction of A.A. gunnery.

disorder, scattering their bombs on the countryside in their night to the coast.

The value of H.A.A. fire as a means of breaking up bomber squadrons to enable them to be more easily dealt with by our fighters was demonstrated on numerous occasions in the Thames Estuary.

The importance of A.A. shell bursts as a "pointer" to fighters, even though the guns cannot themselves effectively engage the enemy, was also frequently demonstrated.

(c) A somewhat negative lesson was the inability of A.A. guns, however well served, to completely deny an area to penetration by determined air attack. Evidence, however, was overwhelming that accurate fire, apart from causing casualties, did impair the enemy's aim, and thus avoid, or at least mitigate, the damage to precise targets.

(d) A rather unexpected result was the high proportion (about 10 per cent.) of planes brought down by A.A.L.M.G. fire. It is doubtful, however, whether with the increased armour now carried by enemy aircraft this lesson still obtains.

(e) The value of training in recognition was repeatedly emphasised throughout these operations. Fortunately, very few instances of friendly aircraft being engaged occurred. Apart from the accuracy of the information as to movement of aircraft furnished to gun sites, this was no doubt due to a reasonable standard in recognition having been attained.

It was, and still is, continually brought home to the A.A. gunner that, before all else, he must not engage a friendly aircraft. With this thought firmly impressed on the G.P.O., some instances of late engagement or failure to engage perforce occurred. In some cases, had the standard of training been higher, to enable the earlier recognition of a machine as hostile beyond reasonable doubt, the number of machines destroyed would have been increased.

Chelmsford, August 2, 1941.

APPENDIX "C.A."

H.A.A. GUN DEFENDED AREAS AND ARMAMENT.
[SEE SEPARATE TABLE ON PAGE 267]

APPENDIX "C.B."
L.A.A., V.P.'s AND ARMAMENT.
[SEE SEPARATE TABLE ON PAGE 267]

APPENDIX "C.C."
I.—AMMUNITION EXPENDITURE AND CLAIMS, CATEGORY I.
[SEE SEPARATE TABLE ON PAGE 269]

APPENDIX "C.D."
AMMUNITION EXPENDITURE AND ENEMY AIRCRAFT DESTROYED THROUGHOUT ANTI-AIRCRAFT COMMAND FOR JULY, AUGUST .AND SEPTEMBER 1940.
[SEE SEPARATE TABLE ON PAGE 271]

APPENDIX "E."
FIGHTER COMMAND.
Order of Battle, November 3, 1940.
[SEE SEPARATE TABLE ON PAGE 271]

APPENDIX "F."
NOTE ON THE OFFENSIVE AND DEFENSIVE EQUIPMENT OF AIRCRAFT.
I. The general principle of. developing the maximum possible fire power, which is accepted in all Armies and Navies, must presumably be applicable to Fighter Aircraft, provided that this can be done without unduly sacrificing Performance and Endurance.

2. The 8-gun fighter may be said to exemplify this principle, and at the beginning of the war its results were decisive against German Bombers, which were unarmoured at that time.

3. Our Fighter pilots were protected against the return fire of Bombers by their engines, and by bullet-proof glass and armour, for their heads and chests respectively.

4. Furthermore, at this time the return fire from German Bombers was negligible. They had concentrated on Performance as the principle means of evasion (a false lesson drawn from the low speed of the Fighters used in the Spanish War) and the few guns which they carried were manually controlled, and so badly mounted that they were practically useless. These facts, in combination with the fire power and armour protection of our own Fighters, made the latter virtually immune to the fire of unescorted Bombers, and their casualties in Home Defence fighting up to the Spring of 1940. were quite negligible.

5. The German Bombers had good self-sealing tanks, and this was perhaps the only important particular in which they were ahead of us. In our development work we had demanded that tanks should be "Crash Proof " as well as self-sealing, and the drastic conditions, which our experimental tanks had to meet had made them unduly heavy and cumbrous.

6. So far as our Fighters were concerned, the wing tanks in the Hurricane were removed and covered with a fabric known as "Linatex" which had fairly good self-sealing characteristics. The reserve tank in the fuselage was left uncovered, as it was difficult of access and it was thought that it would be substantially protected by the armour which had been fitted. During the Battle, however, a great number of Hurricanes were set on fire by incendiary bullets or cannon shells, and their pilots were badly burned by a sheet of flame which filled the cockpit before they could escape by parachute.

7. The reserve tanks were therefore covered with Linatex as a matter of the highest priority, and a metal bulkhead was fitted in front of the pilot to exclude the rash of flame from the cockpit.

8. The Germans soon began to fit fuselage armour to protect their pilots and crews, but for some unexplained reason neither side had fitted armour behind the engines of their Bombers. The back of the engine is much more vulnerable to rifle-calibre bullets than the front, owing to the mass of ancillary equipment which is there installed. While the back of the engine lies open to attack, the rifle-calibre machine gun remains a useful weapon, and the fact is a fortunate one for us.

9. The application of armour to Bombers did not, of course, come as a surprise to us, and its implications had long been discussed.

10. Excluding devices such as hanging wires, exploding pilotless aircraft, etc., I have always thought that the courses open to the Fighter, when rifle-calibre machine-gun fire from astern becomes ineffective, may be summarised as follows:-

(A) Deliver fire from ahead or from a flank.
(B) Pierce the armour.
(C) Attack the fuel tanks with incendiary ammunition.
(D) Destroy the structure of the aircraft by means of direct hits from explosive shells.
(E) Use large shells with Time and Percussion fuzes.

Discussing these in order:-

11. (A) Fire from ahead or from a flank is effective but difficult to deliver accurately at modern speeds. Fire from ahead proved very effective on occasions during the Battle, but relative speeds are so high that the time available for shooting is very short, and Fighters generally find themselves in a position to deliver such an attack more by accident than by design.

12. Beam attack is very difficult to deliver accurately, owing to the amount of deflection which had to be allowed. The deflection ring on a Fighter's sight allows for an enemy speed of 100m.p.h., and therefore a full diameter outside the ring must sometimes be allowed.

13. The method is effective against formations, when the aircraft hit is not always the one aimed at, and certainly the Gladiators in Norway developed this technique with great success. On the whole, however, Fighters which were constrained to this method of attack would have a very limited usefulness.

14.(B) The simplest reaction for the Fighter is to pierce the armour, but it entails the use of bigger calibres. It must be remembered also that it is not sufficient merely to pierce the armour, but the bullet must have sufficient remaining velocity to do lethal damage thereafter. High velocities, in addition to bigger calibres, are therefore necessary.

15. The .5-inch gun appeared, at first sight, to be the natural successor to the .303 inch, but experiments showed that the type available to us in the Autumn of 1940 was practically defeated by the 8-mm. armour carried in the M.E.109. It was true that the bullet would pierce 20-mm. or more of armour in the open, but it was found that the minute deceleration and deflection of the axis of the bullet, caused by its passage through the structure of the fuselage, exercised a very important diminution on its subsequent penetrative powers.

16. Experiments carried out with .5-inch guns of higher velocity in America have given encouraging results, and it is not at present possible to dogmatise on the subject. It would, however, be foolish to adopt a gun which could be defeated by a slight thickening of the armour carried by the Bomber and the aim should be to defeat the thickest armour which it is practically possible for the enemy to carry.

17. We have at present no gun of a calibre between .5-inch and 20-mm. (.8 inch). The latter was originally adopted by the French

because it was of about the right size to fire an explosive shell through an airscrew of a Hispano Suiza engine, and was adopted by us from them. If, therefore, it proves to be of the best weight and calibre for an armour piercing, that is due to accident rather than design.

18. A study of available data might lead one to suppose that a calibre of about 15-mm. would be the ideal, and I understand that this size has recently been adopted by the Germans; but we cannot now start designing a new gun for this war, and we must choose between the .5-inch and the 20-mm. We shall soon get reliable data from American Fighter types in action. They have faith in the .5-inch gun.

19. The Armament of the Royal Air Force is not its strongest point, and in my opinion we should do our own Design and Experimental work, and satisfy our requirements without being dependent on Woolwich and Shoeburyness.

20. (C) Incendiary ammunition may be fired from guns of any calibre and Bomber tanks have been set on fire by .303 inch ammunition. The bigger the bullet, however, the bigger the hole, and a small bullet stands a good chance of being quenched before it can take effect. In any case, the fuel tanks of a Bomber constitute so small a proportion of the whole target that they cannot be made the sole objective of attack; and it seems that the adoption of a large-calibre gun and the use of a proportion of incendiary ammunition therein will afford a satisfactory compromise.

21. (D) It was assumed by the French that the 20-mm. shell would be effective against the structure of modern aircraft. I do not know what trials they carried out, but the tests done by us at Shoeburyness and Orfordness indicate that the effect of a 20-mm. shell exploring instantaneously on the surface of an aircraft is almost negligible, except in a small percentage of lucky strikes. The normal effect is that a hole of about 6-inch diameter is blown in the surface, and that the effect at any distance

is nil, since the shell is blown almost into dust. Occasionally the fuze penetrates and does some damage, but this is slight in comparison with the total weight of the shell. Even the big 37-mm. shell, though it may be spectacular damage, will not often bring a Bomber down with a single hit. Greater damage is done if the fuze is given a slight delay action, so that it bursts inside the covering of the aircraft, but small delay action fuzes are unreliable in operation and difficult to manufacture, and, on the whole, it seems doubtful if explosive shells are as efficient as armour-piercing and incendiary projectiles, especially as they will not penetrate armour. Another point must be remembered, viz., that a drum of explosive shells is a very dangerous item of cargo: if one is struck and detonated by a bullet it is not unlikely that they will all go off and blow the aeroplane to pieces.

22. (E) The use of large shells (comparable to Anti-Aircraft types) from Fighter aircraft is practically prohibited by considerations of weight if a gun is used. The gun itself must be heavy and the structure must be strengthened to withstand the shock of recoil. The walls and base of the shell allhave to be made uneconomically heavy to withstand the discharge. All these difficulties, however, can be overcome if the Rocket principle is used. It is true that a Rocket can be discharged only in the direct line of flight, but that is no particular handicap to a Fighter. It can have a light firing tube, there is no recoil, and the shell can be designed for optimum fragmentation effect. (I have been told that a 3-inch Rocket shell develops the same explosive and fragmentation effect as a 4.5-inch Anti-Aircraft gun shell). It also starts with an advantage over the terrestrial rocket in that it has an initial velocity of about 300 m.p.h. through the air, which gives it enhanced accuracy. For this weapon a "Proximity Fuze" would be ideal, but, pending the development of this, there is no reason why the Rocket should not be used with a Time and Percussion Fuze used in conjunction with a range-finder in the Aircraft.

23. This item was put on the programme about 7 years ago, and I think it a great pity that it was allowed to drop. True, unexpected difficulties may be encountered, and nothing may come of the project, but it is an important experiment, and our knowledge of what is and is not possible will not be complete until it has been tried.

24. I think that our decision to adopt the 20-mm. gun is probably the wisest which we could have taken, but to carry increased load efficiently something bigger than the Hurricane or Spitfire is needed. The Typhoon with 2,000 h.p. should be ideal when it has been given an adequate ceiling.

25. In the meantime the Hurricane must be somewhat overloaded with 4 Cannons, and mixed armament (2 Cannons and 4 Brownings) in the Spitfire is merely a compromise necessitated by loading conditions. Might not the high-velocity American .5-inch gun prove a suitable armament for the small fighter?

26. As regards ammunition for the 20-mm. gun, the so-called "solid" bullet was merely a cheap steel bullet produced by the French for practice purposes. Its mass and velocity have enabled it hitherto to smash through armour to which it has been opposed, but an improved design will probably be needed before long; doubtless the matter is receiving attention. I understand that the incendiary bullet – the equivalent of the de Wilde – 303-inch – has been giving good results.

27. One other attribute of a naked steel bullet must not be overlooked, viz., its incendiary effect when it strikes a ferrous structure. During ground trials a Blenheim was set on fire by the second hit from a "solid" bullet. Unfortunately, German aircraft do not normally contain much iron or steel.

28. If we look into the not too distant future, I think we shall find that an additional and quite different reason may arise for the adoption of the high-velocity gun with a comparatively heavy projectile. I refer to the increasing intensity and effect of return fire from Bombers.

29. Our Fighters are protected to a very large degree from the return fire of Bombers which they attack from astern, so long as they have to sustain the impact only of rifle-calibre bullets.

30. The situation will be quite different, however, if turrets with .5-inch guns are commonly used in Bombers. The Bomber has the comparative advantage over the pursuing Fighter of firing "down-wind" (one may get a clear idea of the situation by imagining both aircraft to be anchored in space, with a 300-m.p.h. wind blowing from the Bomber to the Fighter). The result is likely to be that effective armouring of Fighters against return fire will be impossible, and fighting ranges in good visibility may be considerably lengthened. In such circumstances high velocity, flat trajectory and a heavy projectile will attain increasing importance; attention will also have to be paid to accurate methods of sighting, and allowance for gravity drop.

Appendix A

FIGHTER COMMAND.
Order of Battle, 8th July, 1940.

No. 10 GROUP.

Squadron.	War Station.	Type of Aircraft.
87	Exeter	Hurricane.
213	Exeter	Hurricane.
92	Pembrey	Spitfire.
234	St. Eval	Spitfire.

No. 11 GROUP.

| 43 | Tangmere | Hurricane. |
| 145 | Tangmere | Hurricane. |

601	Tangmere	Hurricane.
FIU Unit	Tangmere	Blenheim.
64	Kenley	Spitfire.
615	Kenley	Hurricane.
245	Hawkinge	Hurricane.
111	Croydon	Hurricane.
501	Croydon	Hurricane.
600	Manston	Blenheim.
79	Biggin Hill	Hurricane.
610	Gravesend	Spitfire.
32	Biggin Hill	Hurricane.
54	Rochford	Spitfire.
65	Hornchurch	Spitfire.
74	Hornchurch	Spitfire.
56	North Weald	Hurricane.
25	Martlesham	Blenheim.
151	North Weald	Hurricane.
1	Northolt	Hurricane.
604	Northolt	Blenheim.
609	Northolt	Spitfire.
236	Middle Wallop	Blenheim.

No. 12 GROUP.

19	Duxford	Spitfire.
264	Duxford	Defiant.
85	Debden	Hurricane.
17	Debden	Hurricane.
29	Digby	Blenheim.
611	Digby	Spitfire.
46	Digby	Hurricane.
23	Wittering	Blenheim.
266	Wittering	Spitfire.

229	Wittering	Hurricane.
66	Coltishall	Spitfire.
253	Kirton-in-Lindsey	Hurricane.
222	Kirton-in-Lindsey	Spitfire.

No. 13 GROUP.

Squadron.	War Station.	Type of Aircraft.
41	Catterick	Spitfire.
219	Catterick	Blenheim.
152	Acklington	Spitfire.
72	Acklington	Spitfire.
249	Leconfield	Hurricane.
616	Leconfield	Spitfire.
603 "A"	Turnhouse	Spitfire.
141	Turnhouse	Defiant.
602	Drem	Spitfire.
603 "B"	Montrose	Spitfire.
3	Wick	Hurricane.
504	Wick	Hurricane.

NON-OPERATIONAL SQUADRONS.
(Forming or reforming.)

Group.	Squadron.	Aerodrome.	Type of Aircraft.
10 Group	238	Middle Wallop	Hurricane.
	1 (Canadian)	Middle Wallop	Hurricane.
11 Group	257	Hendon	Hurricane.
12 Group	242	Coltishall	Hurricane.
13 Group	73	Church Fenton	Hurricane.
	605	Drem	Hurricane.
	607	Usworth	Hurricane.
	263	Grangemouth	Hurricane.

Appendix B

APPENDIX "C.A."
H.A.A. GUN DEFENDED AREAS AND ARMAMENT.

	August 1940.			October 1940.		
	4.5in	3.7in	3in	4.5in	3.7in	3in
G.D.A.						
Harwich	-	15	8	-	8	7
T and M North	32	8	12	24	4	12
T and M. South	32	32	14	28	20	10
Dover and Manston	-	12	16	-	12	16
Wattisham	-	-	4	-	-	4
Biggin Hill	-	-	4	-	-	4
Kenley	-	-	-	-	-	2
North Weald	-	+4	4+2	-	-	4

APPENDIX "C.B."
L.A.A., V.P.'s AND ARMAMENT.

	August 1940					October 1940				
V.P.	40mm (No. of Barrels)	AALMG	HISP ANO	3in Case I	Misc	40mm (No. of Barrels)	AALMG	HISP ANO	3in Case I.	Misc
Aerodromes.										
Debden	4	3	-	-	-	4	17	-	-	-
Wattisham	-	12	-	-	-	4	8	-	-	-
Biggin Hill	3	2	-	-	-	6	3	-	-	-
Manston	4	4	-	-	-	4	4	-	-	-
West Mailing	2	10	-	-	-	4	10	-	-	-
Croydon	-	12	-	-	-	4	8	-	-	-
Kenley	4	8	-	2	-	4	10	-	3	-

Redhill	-	-	-	-	-	3	-	-	-	-
Gravesend	4	4	-	-	-	4	-	-	-	-
Shorts (Rochester)	-	-	-	-	4	8	3	-	-	
Detling	-	-	-	-	-	2	12	2	-	-
Eastchurch	-	-	-	-	-	2	10	-	-	-
Hawkinge	4	4	-	-	-	4	4	-	-	-
Lympne	-	-	-	-	-	-	2	-	-	-
North Weald	3	12	-	-	-	5	8	-	-	-
Martlesham	4	10	-	-	-	4	11	-	-	-
Rochford	2	8	-	-	-	4	12	-	-	-
Hornchurch	3	7	-	-	-	5	7	-	-	-
Stapleford Abbots	-	-	-	-	-	2	-	-	-	-

A.M.E. Stations.

Darsham	2	7	-	-	-	2	8	-	-	-
Dunkirk	3	6	-	-	-	3	7	-	-	-
Rye	3	6	-	-	-	3	11	-	-	-
Pevensey	3	6	-	-	-	3	21	-	-	-
Bawdsey	-	-	-	-	-	3	3	-	-	-
Great Bromley	-	-	-	-	-	3	11	-	-	-
Canewdon	3	4	-	-	-	3	12	-	-	-

Industrial and Oil

Crayford	-	8	-	-	-	3	30	3	1	-
Dartford	-	-	-	-	-	1	20	4	-	-
Northfleet	-	-	-	-	-	-	16	-	-	-
Grain (Barges)	2	4	-	-	-	2	34	2	1	-
Chelmsford	-	8	-	-	-	2	21	-	-	-
Murex (Rainham)-	20	-	-	-	-	20	-	-	-	
Purfleet	-	14	-	2	-	-	16	-	2	-
Canvey	-	12	-	2	-	-	12	-	1	-
Thameshaven	-	4	-	4	-	-	-	-	3	-
Shellhaven	-	8	-	3	-	-	8	-	1	-

Naval.

Chatham	-	-	-	-	-	-	24	4	3	-
Chattenden	-	-	-	-	-	-	28	-	-	-
Sheerness	-	-	-	-	-	4	22	5	-	-
Landguard	-	-	-	-	-	-	15	-	1	-
Wrabness	-	-	-	-	-	-	23	-	-	-
Parkeston Quay	-	-	-	-	-	-	10	-	-	-
Dover	5	9	-	4	-	9	16	4	-	4AT
Tilbury	-	14	-	-	-	-	12	-	-	-
Southend Pier	-	-	-	-	-	-	-	-		
				1-2pdr				1-2pdr		

APPENDIX "C.C."
I.—AMMUNITION EXPENDITURE AND CLAIMS, CATEGORY I.

	Total Ammunition Expended	Enemy Aircraft Destroyed	Average Rounds per E/A
H.A.A. (seen targets)	48,155	161	298
H.A.A. (barrage and unseen fire)	26,869	11	2,444
L.A.A. Bofors only	9,417	47	200
A.A.L.M.G. (at S.L. and H.A.F. sites)	Not recorded	23	----

NOTES:-

(i) The above table gives records from September 3, 1939 to November 3, 1940.

(ii) The total enemy aircraft destroyed during the months inclusive July-October was 221.

(iii) The following ammunition was expended from September 3, 1939 to June 30, 1940:-

H.A.A.	2,995
L.A.A. (Bofors)	1,919

(iv) All the enemy aircraft destroyed by L.A.A. (47) have been credited to Bofors for the purpose of the average; in practice, Lewis guns had a considerable share in several of these as well as in two cases Hispano (2,941 rounds) and 3-in. Case I (194 rounds),

(v) Bofors average may be still further sub-divided thus:-

With Predictor	179 (3,187 rounds)
With F.A.S.	232 (6,230 rounds)

II.—TABLE SHOWING TYPES OF AIRCRAFT DESTROYED JULY-OCTOBER 1940.

Type.	No.
HE. IIII	30
Do. 17	39
Do. 215	14
Ju. 87	15
Ju. 88	19
Me. 109	80
ME. 110	15
Unidentified	9
221	

III.

Destroyed by day	203
Destroyed by night	18
	221

APPENDIX "C.D."
AMMUNITION EXPENDITURE AND ENEMY AIRCRAFT
DESTROYED THROUGHOUT - ANTI-AIRCRAFT COMMAND
FOR JULY, AUGUST AND SEPTEMBER 1940.

July 1940—

Day* and Night   344rds. per aircraft. (26 a/c. = 8,935rds.)

August 1940—

Day*   232 rds. per aircraft. (167 a/c = 38,764 rds.)

Night

September 1940—

Day~   1,798 rds. per aircraft. (144 a/c = 258,808 rds.)

Night

* Mainly by day, little night activity.

~ Including considerable night activity and large expenditure of ammunition by night

APPENDIX "E."
FIGHTER COMMAND.
Order of Battle, November 3, 1940.
No. 9 GROUP.

Squadron.	War Station.	Type of Aircraft.	Category.
312 (Czech)	Speke	Hurricane	C
611	Ternhill	Spitfire	C
29 (half)	Ternhill	Blenheim	Night-Flying

No. 10 GROUP.

79	Pembrey	Hurricane	C
87 (half)	Bibury	Hurricane	B
504	Filton	Hurricane	C
609	Middle Wallop	Spitfire	A

604	Middle Wallop	Blenheim	Night-Flying
238	Middle Wallop	Hurricane	A
56	Boscombe Down	Hurricane	A
152	Warmwell	Spitfire	A
601	Exeter	Hurricane	C
87 (half)	Exeter	Hurricane	B
234	St. Eval	Spitfire	C
247 (half)	Roborough	Gladiator	C

No. 11 GROUP.

25	Debden	Blenheim and Beaufighter	Night-Flying
73	Castle Camp	Hurricane	Night-Flying
17	Martlesham	Hurricane	A
229	Northolt	Hurricane	A
615	Northolt	Hurricane	A
302 (Polish)	Northolt	Hurricane	A
257	North Weald	Hurricane	A
249	North Weald	Hurricane	A
46	Stapleford	Hurricane	A
264	Hornchurch	Defiant	Night-Flying
41	Hornchurch	Spitfire	A
603	Hornchurch	Spitfire	A
222	Rochford	Spitfire	A
141	Gravesend	Defiant	Night-Flying
74	Biggin Hill	Spitfire	A
92	Biggin Hill	Spitfire	A
66	West Malling	Spitfire	A
421 (half)	West Malling	Hurricane	Reconaissance
605	Croydon	Hurricane	A
253	Kenley	Hurricane	A
501	Kenley	Hurricane	A
219	Redhill	Blenheim and Beaufighter	Night-Flying

145	Tangmere	Hurricane	A
213	Tangmere	Hurricane	Night-Flying
422 (half)	Tangmere	Hurricane	Night-Flying
602	West Hampnett	Spitfire	A
23	Ford	Blenheim	Night-Flying

No. 12 GROUP.

Squadron.	War Station.	Type of Aircraft.	Category.
303 (Polish)	Leconfield	Hurricane	C
616	Kirton-in-Lindsey	Spitfire	C
85	Kirton-in-Lindsey	Hurricane	C
151	Digby	Hurricane	C
1	Wittering	Hurricane	C
266	Wittering	Spitfire	C
29 (half)	Wittering	Spitfire	C
72	Coltishall	Blenheim	Night-Flying
64	Coltishall	Spitfire	C
242	Duxford	Hurricane	C
310 (Czech)	Duxford	Hurricane	A
19	Duxford	Spitfire	A

No. 13 GROUP.

607	Turnhouse	Hurricane	C
65	Turnhouse	Spitfire	B
232 (half)	Drem	Hurricane	C
263 (half)	Drem	Hurricane	C
1 (Canadian)	Prestwick	Hurricane	C
32	Acklington	Hurricane	C
610	Acklington	Spitfire	C
600 (half)	Acklington	Blenheim	Night-Flying
43	Usworth	Hurricane	C
54	Catterick	Spitfire	C
600 (half)	Catterick	Blenheim	Night-Flying
245	Aldergrove	Hurricane	C

No. 14 GROUP.

3	Castletown	Hurricane	C
III (half)	Dyce	Hurricane	C
III (half)	Montrose	Hurricane	C

NON-OPERATIONAL SQUADRONS.

Group.	*Squadron.*	*Station.*	*Type of Aircraft.*
9 Group	308 (Polish)	Baginton	Hurricane
12 Group	306 (Polish)	Church Fenton	Hurricane
	307 (Polish)	Kirton-in-Lindsey	Defiant
	71 (Eagle)	Church Fenton	Buffalo
13 Group	263 (half)	Drem	Whirlwind

NOTE- Two " B " Squadrons, Nos. 74 and 145, had already been thrown into the battle, leaving only two available at the end.

BIBLIOGRAPHY

A

Addison, Paul and Jeremy Crang, *The Burning Blue: A New History of the Battle of Britain*, (London: Pimlico, 2000)

Allen, H. R., *Who Won the Battle of Britain,* (London: Granada Publishing, 1976)

Atkin, Ronald, *Pillar of Fire: Dunkirk 1940*, (London: Sidgwick & Jackson, 1990)

B

Blaxland, Gregory, *Destination Dunkirk: The Story of Gort's Army*, (London: William Kimber, 1973)

Bishop, Patrick, *Fighter Boys: The Battle of Britain, 1940*, (New York: Viking, 2003)

Bond, Brian, *Britain, France and Belgium 1939–1940,* (London: Brassey's Publishing, 1990)

C

Campion, Garry, *The Good Fight: Battle of Britain Wartime Propaganda and The Few*, (Basingstoke: Palgrave Macmillan, 2010);

Churchill, Winston, *Parliamentary Debates [Commons]*, 18 June 1940, vol. 326,

Churchill, Winston S., *The Second World War*, vol.II, (New York: Houghton Mifflin, 1949)

Connelly, Mark, *We Can Take It: Britain and the Memory of the Second World War* (London: Routledge, 2014)

Cooper, Matthew, *The German Air Force 1933–1945: An Anatomy of Failure*, (New York: Jane's Publishing Incorporated, 1981)

Costello John, *Ten Days That Saved the West,* (London: New York: Bantam, 1991)

Craig, Phil and Tim Clayton, *Finest Hour: The Battle of Britain*, (New York: Simon & Schuster, 2000)

Cumming, Anthony J., *The Royal Navy and the Battle of Britain*, (Annapolis [MD]: United States Naval Academy, 2010)

D

Dildy, Douglas C., *Dunkirk 1940: Operation Dynamo,* (Oxford: Osprey, 2010)

Dix, Anthony, *The Norway Campaign and the Rise of Churchill, 1940,* (Barnsley: Pen & Sword, 2014)

E

Evans, Martin, *The Fall of France: Act with Daring,* (Oxford: Osprey, 2000)

F

Fenby, Jonathan, *The Sinking of the Lancastria: Britain's Greatest Maritime Disaster and Churchill's Cover Up,* (London: Simon and Schuster, 2005)

Fiedler, Arkady, *303 Squadron: The Legendary Battle of Britain Fighter Squadron,* (Los Angeles: Aquila Polonica, 2010)

Fisher, David, *Summer Bright and Terrible: Winston Churchill, Lord Dowding, Radar and the Impossible Triumph of the Battle of Britain,* (Emeryville[CA]: Shoemaker & Hoard, 2005)

Foreman, John, *Battle of Britain: The Forgotten Months, November And December 1940,* (Wythenshawe [Lancashire]: Crécy Publishing, 1989;

G

Gardner, W. J. R., *The Evacuation from Dunkirk: 'Operation Dynamo' 26 May–4 June 1940*, (London: Routledge, 1949)

Gelb, Norman, *Dunkirk: The Incredible Escape*, (London: Michael Joseph, 1990)

Grinnell-Milne, Duncan, *The Silent Victory: September 1940*, (London: Bodley Head, 1958)

H

Haining, Peter, *The Chianti Raiders: The Extraordinary Story of the Italian Air Force in the Battle of Britain*, (London: Robson Books, 2005); *Where the Eagle Landed: The Mystery of the German Invasion of Britain, 1940*, (London: Robson Books, 2004)

Harman, Nicholas, *Dunkirk; The Necessary Myth*, (London: Hodder and Stoughton, 1980)

Horne, Alistair, *To Lose a Battle: France 1940*, (London: Macmillan. 1969)

Hough, Richard, *The Battle of Britain: The Greatest Air Battle of World War II*, (New York: W.W. Norton, 1989)

J

Jackson, Julian, *The Fall of France: The Nazi Invasion of 1940*, (Oxford: Oxford University Press, 2003

James, T. C. G., *The Battle of Britain* (Air Defence of Great Britain; vol. 2), (London: Frank Cass Publishers, 2000); *Growth of Fighter Command, 1936–1940* (Air Defence of Great Britain; vol. 1), (London: Frank Cass Publishers, 2000); *Night Air Defence During the Blitz*, (London: Frank Cass Publishers, 2003)

K

Karslake, Basil, *1940 The Last Act: The Story of the British Forces in France after Dunkirk*, (London: Leo Cooper, 1979)

Kelly, John, *Never Surrender: Winston Churchill and Britain's Decision to Fight Nazi Germany in the Fateful Summer of 1940,* (New York: Scribner, 2015)

Kreipe, Werner, 'The Battle of Britain' in Werner Kreipe [et. al.], *The Fatal Decisions,* (London, Michael Joseph, 1956)

L

Leuze, James [ed.], *The London Journal of Raymond E. Lee, 1940-41,* (Boston: Little Brown, 1971), entry for 8 December 1940

Longden, Sean, *Dunkirk: The Men They Left Behind,* (London: Constable and Robinson, 2009)

Lord, Walter, *The Miracle of Dunkirk,* (London: Allen Lane, 1983)

Lukacs, John, *The Duel: The Eighty Day Struggle between Churchill and Hitler* (Newhaven [CT], Yale University Press, 1990)

M

Mackenzie, S. P., *The Battle of Britain on Screen: 'The Few' in British Film and Television Drama,* (London: Bloomsbury, 2016)

Mitchell, Allan, *Nazi Paris: The History of an Occupation, 1940-1944,* (Oxford: Berghahn Books, 2008)

More, Charles, *The British Expeditionary Force and the Battle of the Ypres-Comines Canal, 1940,* (London: Frontline Books, 2013)

N

Newton, Scott, *Profits of Peace: The Political Economy of Anglo-German Appeasement,* (Oxford: Oxford University Press, 1996)

Noakes, Lucy and Juliette Pattinson, *British Cultural Memory and the Second World War,* (London: Bloomsbury, 2014)

O

Olson, Lynne, and Stanley Cloud, *A Question of Honor: The Kościuszko Squadron: Forgotten Heroes of World War II,* (New York: Knopf, 2003)

R

Ray, John, *Battle of Britain*, (London: The Orion Publishing Co., 2003)

Ray, John Philip, *The Battle of Britain: Dowding and the First Victory 1940*, (London: Cassel & Co., 2001); *The Battle of Britain: New Perspectives: Behind the Scenes of the Great Air War*, (London: Arms & Armour Press, 1994)

Robbins, Keith, *Churchill,* (London: Routledge, 2014)

Runyan, William McKinley [ed.], *Psychology and Historical Interpretation,* (Oxford: Oxford University Press, 1988)

S

Self, Robert C., *Neville Chamberlain: A Biography,* (Aldershot: Ashgate, 2006)

Stewart, Geoffrey, *Dunkirk and the Fall of France,* (Barnsley: Pen & Sword Military, 2008)

T

Taylor, Telford, *The Breaking Wave: The German Defeat in the Summer of 1940,* (London: Weidenfeld & Nicolson, 1967)

Thompson, Julian, *Dunkirk: Retreat to Victory*, (New York: Arcade, 2008)

W

Warner, Philip, *The Battle of France, 1940: 10 May–22 June,* (London: Simon & Schuster, 1990)

Winser, John de D., *B.E.F. Ships before, at and after Dunkirk,* (Gravesend: World Ship Society, 1999).

Wrigley, Chris, *Winston Churchill: A Biographical Companion* (Santa Barbara [CA]: ABC Clio, 2002)

INDEX

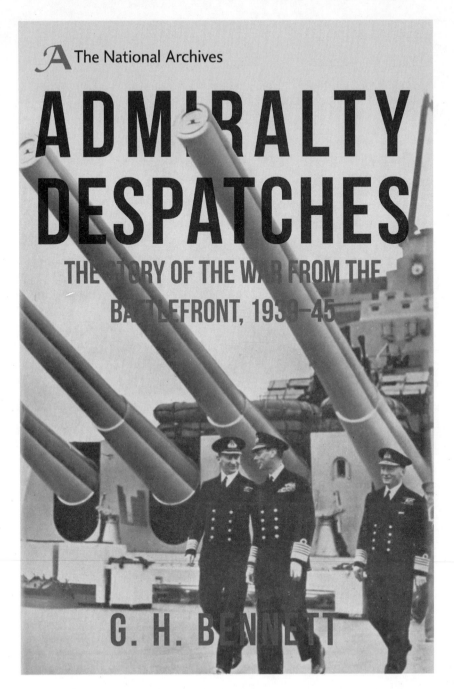